P9-DJL-968

BREAD AND CIRCUSES

BY THE SAME AUTHOR

The Spirit of Reform:
British Literature and Politics,
1832–1867

BREAD & CIRCUSES

Theories of Mass Culture as Social Decay

by Patrick Brantlinger

HM
258
.B735
1983

CORNELL UNIVERSITY PRESS · *Ithaca and London*

WITHDRAWN
Indiana
University
Library
Fort Wayne

Cornell University Press gratefully acknowledges
a grant from the Andrew W. Mellon Foundation
that aided in bringing this book to publication.

Copyright © 1983 by Cornell University Press

All rights reserved. Except for brief quotations in a review,
this book, or parts thereof, must not be reproduced in any form without
permission in writing from the publisher. For information address
Cornell University Press, 124 Roberts Place, Ithaca, New York 14850.

First published 1983 by Cornell University Press.
Published in the United Kingdom by
Cornell University Press Ltd., London.

International Standard Book Number 0-8014-1598-5
Library of Congress Catalog Card Number 83-45134
Printed in the United States of America
Librarians: Library of Congress cataloging information
appears on the last page of the book.

*The paper in this book is acid-free and meets
the guidelines for permanence and durability
of the Committee on Production Guidelines for
Book Longevity of the Council on Library Resources.*

msr 1-27-88

For Andy, Susan, and Jeremy

Contents

Preface

F OR better or worse, the most powerful, influential instruments
for the dissemination of values, knowledge, and art are today the
mass media. Among artists and intellectuals, the cultural domination
of radio, film, and television is normally viewed with apprehension.
Teachers of literature, for example, often express the fear that books
are an endangered species, that literacy is dying out, that it is giving
way to what Jerzy Kosinski calls "videocy."[1] Political theorists on both
the right and the left argue that the mass media are "totalitarian"
rather than "democratic," that they are a major—perhaps *the* major—
destroyer either of "individualism" or of "community." Often these
apprehensions are expressed in terms of a mythology that I call "negative classicism," according to which the more a society comes to depend on "mass culture," the more it falls into a pattern of "decline and
fall" once traced by Rome and perhaps by other extinct civilizations.
These apprehensions are not necessarily mistaken, but the mythology
of negative classicism tends to obscure what is new and potentially
liberating in our present situation.

1. See the interview with Jerzy Kosinski by David Sohn, "A Nation of Videots,"
Media and Methods, 11 (April 1975), 24–31, 52–57. A recent study of responses to
literacy and the forces that threaten it is Robert Pattison, *On Literacy: The Politics of
the Word from Homer to the Age of Rock* (New York: Oxford University Press, 1982).
Pattison's book unfortunately appeared too late for me to consider it here. See also my
essays "The Multiversity as a Mass Medium," *Radical Teacher*, 13 (March 1979),
28–32, and "Mass Communications and Teachers of English," *College English*, 37
(January 1976), 490–509.

The purpose of this book is to criticize negative classicism as it has been applied to mass culture not just in our electronic present but over the last two centuries. The most recent "bread and circuses" responses to television and the welfare state are hardly new; they echo the reactions of artists and intellectuals from as long ago as Juvenal's age to the entry of "the common people" into the cultural arena, or to the imposition on society of a centralized or mass-produced culture. Negative classicism is the product of several traditions of culture theory, from offshoots of Burkean conservatism to the esthetic postulates of Marxism. My hope is that a critique of the mythology of negative classicism will help to open the way for new ideas about culture and society.

I do not wish to revive or defend older forms of culture, either "high" or "mass," any more than I wish to champion the electronic mass media as they are now employed in both capitalist and socialist countries to distract, to narcotize, to sell toothpaste and beer, fascism and Soviet Marxism. The two major arguments in defense of the mass media which have developed over the last twenty years I find largely unacceptable. The first line of defense is that of Marshall McLuhan and his disciples; the second is the case for "cultural pluralism" as fully compatible with—indeed, as partly a product of—the mass media, an argument that Herbert Gans, for example, makes in *Popular Culture and High Culture*.[2] If McLuhan counters the mythology of negative classicism, it is only to substitute another mythology, equally suspect, based on the belief that the mass media are making the world over into an electronic utopia. Gans, on the other hand, represents a pragmatic liberalism whose main tenets have been directly challenged by the monopolistic, perhaps even totalitarian, tendencies of the mass media. Where others find the erosion of democracy, Gans finds an enduring vitality. His vision reconciles democracy and massification in a way that, I believe, cannot be squared with reality. A third defense of mass culture and the mass media might be expected to develop from Marxism, but the most influential versions of Marxist culture theory in Western Europe and America have treated the media in terms of reification, negation, monopoly capitalism, and therefore in

2. Raymond Rosenthal, ed., *McLuhan: Pro and Con* (Baltimore: Penguin, 1969); Herbert J. Gans, *Popular Culture and High Culture: An Analysis and Evaluation of Taste* (New York: Basic, 1974).

terms of "empire and decadence," "bread and circuses"—as in Herbert Marcuse's *One-Dimensional Man.*

In my own reading and thinking about the mass media, I have wished to find some theory that would convince me that, somehow or other, in some not too remote future, mass culture and democratic community will coincide. They promise to do so, as Raymond Williams, among other theorists, has suggested; but that promise seems to recede just as fast as the mass media achieve new levels of power, influence, and sophistication.[3] Given this disillusioning pattern, we may indeed be justified in using some version of negative classicism to understand where the mass media are leading us. But whatever liberating potential there may be in the technology of the media counts for little in an apocalyptic mythology that reads the doom of empires in what seem to be among the most constructive, original developments of the age. How can this contradiction be understood? The history of theories about mass culture—which is more often than not the history of negative classicism, Roman analogizing, "bread and circuses"—may provide at least some clues to the future toward which the mass media are propelling us, or to the future we may create for ourselves through learning to use the mass media in democratic ways.

Many people and several institutions have helped me complete this project. I am grateful to the John Simon Guggenheim Memorial Foundation; their fellowship allowed me to spend 1978-79 at the University of California, Berkeley, beginning research that must have sounded strange and unlikely at the proposal stage. I am also grateful to Kenneth Gros Louis, John Reed, Jerome Buckley, and Patrick McCarthy for their support in the early going, and to Indiana University for the "leave without pay" and Summer Faculty Fellowships that added both free time and financial support to the Guggenheim.

I went to Berkeley in part because the University of California is blessed with two scholars, Leo Löwenthal and Martin Jay, who know

3. Raymond Williams, *Culture and Society, 1780–1950* (New York: Harper and Row, 1966 [first published in 1958]); *The Long Revolution* (London: Chatto and Windus, 1961); *Television: Technology and Cultural Form* (New York: Schocken, 1975 [1974]). The influence of Williams's thinking on my own will be apparent throughout this book.

more about the history of the Frankfurt Institute than anyone else. They offered me their time, ideas, criticisms, and even their libraries with great generosity. Both read parts of this book in early and embarrassingly rough drafts, and both offered suggestions that were astute, usable, and yet also encouraging.

Others—Ellen Anderson Brantlinger, Martha Vicinus, Eugene Kintgen, and Matei Calinescu—also read and criticized parts of this book at various stages. I am grateful to all of them, but especially to Ellen and Matei. Ellen not only helped and encouraged me in numerous ways, but patiently endured a good deal of absent-mindedness, sloppy housekeeping, and plain blue funk from me while I was writing. With his criticisms and suggestions about new books and articles to read, Matei helped me to sharpen most of the chapters, focusing my attention on the paradox of progress as decadence.

Some of the ideas in this study I first tried out in a graduate course at Indiana: L680, Literary Theory. I team-taught that course with Christoph K. Lohmann, whose knowledge of American writers helped me at the start of this project. During the semester we taught together, Chris brought many of my thoughts about mass culture into better focus. I also imagine that many of the comments and questions of our L680 students are registered in this book. Other students and colleagues have helped with suggestions, information, conversation, research, translating, and typing, including Marilyn Breiter, Joan Corwin, Linda David, Joseph Donovan, John Eakin, Catherine Gallagher, Camille Garnier, Daniel Granger, Donald Gray, Raymond Hedin, Joonok Huh, Lewis Miller, James Naremore, Robert Nowell, Marsha Richmond, Sheldon Rothblatt, Scott Sanders, Michael Sheldon, Anthony Shipps, Robert Smith, Elisa Sparks, Lee Sterrenburg, Paul Strohm, Timothy Wiles, and John Woodcock. I also thank Jerzy Kosinski for coming to my aid when a journal mangled an essay of mine, the better parts of which I have revived in this book. And both David Riesman and Michael Grant generously answered my requests for information.

Whom have I left out? Perhaps our television set, but it is occupied most of the time when I want to watch it by Andy, Susan, and Jeremy (no, they have not been transmogrified into "videots," and they are not usually "barbarians" either). I suppose I have them to thank for keeping me at work those evenings when what I wanted to watch was not what they were watching. And I can be even more thankful to them for another reason: someday they may read this book and understand why I wrote it for them.

PATRICK BRANTLINGER

Bloomington, Indiana

BREAD AND CIRCUSES

CHAPTER 1

Introduction:
The Two Classicisms

*We change cures, finding none effective, none valid, because
we have faith neither in the peace we seek nor in the pleasures
we pursue. Versatile sages, we are the stoics and epicureans of
modern Romes.*

— E. M. CIORAN, *A Short History of Decay*

THIS is an examination of reactions to mass culture that interpret
it as either a symptom or a cause of social decay. Television, for
example, is sometimes treated as an instrument with great educational
potential which ought to help—if it is not already helping—in the
creation of a genuinely democratic and universal culture. But it just as
often evokes dismay, as in Jerzy Kosinski's novel and movie *Being
There;* its most severe critics treat it as an instrument of totalitarian
manipulation and social disintegration. All critical theories of mass
culture suggest that there is a superior type of culture, usually defined
in terms of some historical model: the Enlightenment, the Renaissance, the Middle Ages, Periclean Athens. I shall call looking to the
past for an ideal culture "positive classicism." But critical theories of
mass culture also often suggest that the present is a recreation or
repetition of the past in a disastrous way: the modern world is said to
have entered a stage of its history like that of the decline and fall of the
Roman Empire. Hence, "bread and circuses." Comparisons of modern society with Roman imperial decadence I shall call "negative
classicism."

Frequently what a social scientist or a literary critic or a popular journalist offers as analysis of mass culture or the mass media proves to be something else: a version of a persistent, pervasive mythology that frames its subject in the sublime context of the rise and fall of empires, the alpha and omega of human affairs. Very little has been written about mass culture, the masses, or the mass media that has not been colored by apocalyptic assumptions. It would be too easy to say that where genuine analysis ends mythologizing begins, but that is often the case. The terms of this mythology—"mass culture" itself, but also "the masses," "empire," "decadence," "barbarism," and the like—defy definition. Their meanings shift with each new analysis, or rather with each new mythologizing. Unless it is rooted in an analysis of specific artifacts or media, the phrase "mass culture" usually needs to be understood as an apocalyptic idea, behind which lies a concern for the preservation of civilization as a whole. I call negative classicism a "mythology" both because it is apocalyptic and because it pervades all levels of public consciousness today, from scholarly and intellectual writing to the mass media themselves. Of course it is a secular mythology, close to Roland Barthes's concept of "myth as depoliticized speech"; a near synonym for it might be "ideology." But negative classicism transcends the specific ideologies—conservatism, liberalism, radicalism, fascism, socialism, Marxism—and is used in different ways by them all. Its most thoughtful expositors elaborate and qualify it with great sophistication and rationality, but it still functions more like an article of faith than like a reasoned argument: in many cases, a mere passing allusion to "bread and circuses" or to such related notions as "decadence" and "barbarism" is meant to trigger a chain of associations pointing toward a secularized Judgment Day in which democracy, or capitalism, or Western civilization, or "the technological society" will strangle upon its own contradictions, chief among which is likely to be an amorphous monstrosity called "mass culture."

My chief purpose has been to provide a critique of the mythology of negative classicism as it has developed over the last two centuries in relation to "mass culture": the mass media, journalism, mass education, the cultural effects of the processes of democratization and industrialization. Since a complete history of this mythology would have to survey most writing about culture and society over the same time span, I have chosen instead to focus on major patterns and major cultural theorists. The first chapter offers an overview of some of the assumptions and theories that shape contemporary responses to mass culture, as well as a capsule history of the "bread and circuses" analogy. The second looks back to the Greek and Roman origins of modern culture theories, including the two classicisms themselves. The third returns to the modern world via an examination of some of the main contributions of the Christian tradition to contemporary theorizing about mass culture. It focuses on the idea of religion as the antithesis of classical culture, and as somehow proletarian or for the masses, and therefore as a version of mass culture—"the opium of the people." The fourth chapter then turns to the "decadent movement," primarily among nineteenth-century French and British writers, to show how it developed as a defensive response to the democratization and industrialization—that is, the "massification"—of culture. "Decadent" poets and artists were the first major group of intellectuals to develop a mythology based upon the analogy of modern society to the declining Roman Empire. The fifth chapter turns to the origins of Freud's theories of civilization in his group psychology and its forebears, such as Gustave Le Bon's "crowd psychology." Freud adopts much of the negative thinking about "the masses" present in Le Bon, Nietzsche, and other late nineteenth-century writers; the emergence of "the masses" or of "mass culture" is a sign of the beginning of the end of civilization, a return to barbarism. Chapter 6 explores the culture theories of three contrasting figures from the first half of this century: José Ortega y Gasset, T. S. Eliot, and Albert Camus. The first two offer elaborate versions of negative classicism; Camus has enough faith in ordinary human nature to believe in the prospect of a mass culture that is not decadent, but that is instead synonymous with a free, humane civilization. The seventh chapter examines the mass culture theories of the chief representatives of the Frankfurt Institute—Theodor Adorno, Max Horkheimer, Herbert Marcuse, and Walter Benjamin. The concept of the "dialectic of enlightenment" points to a regression of civilization that, according to these theorists, is largely caused by mass culture and the mass media, at least as these have developed under capitalism. The last chapter focuses on television, as reflected in the apocalyptic ideas of Harold Innis, Marshall McLuhan, and others, including the Frankfurt theorists. The mythology of negative classicism seems inevitably to point to television as the chief culprit in the alleged decline and fall of contemporary culture. Yet

television and the other mass media are historically without precedent, and the "bread and circuses" analogy may finally be no more
than a term in an eschatological fantasia that obscures the liberating
potential of the new communications technology. In the conclusion, I
suggest some of the factors that obstruct the realization of this potential, including some forms of negative classicism.

In general negative classicism has involved associating mass culture
and the mass media with other socioeconomic factors that are clearly
destructive or "decadent." In a recent essay that discusses uncon-
trolled industrial expansion, overpopulation, international conflict,
and an alleged demise of political leadership, I. Robert Sinai pays
most attention to "mass culture" or "mass civilization" as the principal
cause of the "disaster and decay" that he forecasts as the immediate
future of the world. Even something so apparently constructive as
"mass literacy" is, from Sinai's perspective, destructive: "mass literacy has, as ought to be more than apparent by now, lowered the
general level of culture and understanding."[1] A McLuhanesque addi-
tion to this idea is that, according to Sinai, "the old verbal culture is in
decline and there is everywhere a general retreat from the word." As
in McLuhan, the visual mass media, cinema and television, are the
main saboteurs of mass literacy, although mass literacy itself has been
a cause of the decay of something else—high culture or civilization,
developed only through the leadership of creative elites.

> The high culture based on privilege and hierarchical order and sus-
> tained by the great works of the past and the truths and beauties
> achieved in the tradition destroyed itself in two World Wars. We are
> now living in a cruel "late stage in Western affairs" marked by
> feelings of disarray, by a regress into violence and moral obtuseness,
> by a central failure of values in the arts and in the graces of personal
> and social behaviour. Confused and bombarded, modern man is
> suffused with fears of a new "Dark Age" in which civilisation itself as
> we have known it may disappear or be confined to . . . small islands
> of archaic conservation.   [16]

Sinai is undoubtedly speaking loosely here, because what he says in
the rest of his essay is not that high culture committed suicide, but
that mass culture has assassinated the genuine article, the elitist civi-

---

1. I. Robert Sinai, "What Ails Us and Why: On the Roots of Disaster and Decay,"
Encounter, April 1979, p. 15.

lization of the past. And, where mass culture is perceived as a destructive force or tendency, as in an example of negative classicism like Sinai's, the fall of empires is rarely far behind. "All social systems are ruled by an iron law of decadence," says Sinai, and ours is no exception. If the term "decadence" alone does not point clearly to the decline and fall of the Roman Empire, then the term "barbarism" brings the pattern into focus. Echoing Toynbee, Ortega, Spengler, Nietzsche, Tocqueville, and many other negative classicists, Sinai believes that high culture is today besieged by "the masses," bent on the "vulgarisation and proletarianisation" of "the arts and sciences." The masses represent "the new barbarism," which has "arisen within modern civilisation rather than being an invasion from without."

In a discussion of Sinai's essay published in a later issue of *Encounter*, several writers, while agreeing with much of his analysis, offer wry, thoughtful comments about his doomsaying. They point out that, if the emergence of the masses and the development of mass culture has its destructive side (and what process of social change has not?), it has also its constructive side. Elitism or aristocracy may have given rise to high culture, but on the backs of the vast majority. Furthermore, as Ronald Butt writes, "if it is the fate of all civilisations" to decline and fall, "why should it disturb us intellectually (whatever the inconvenience to us personally), particularly if it is part of a natural process of death and rebirth?"[2] Butt's question, of course, reveals an illogicality characteristic of all prophetic social criticism, including the mythology of negative classicism. If the falls of empires can be prophesied, they must be predetermined. Because the "iron law of decadence" must be inescapable to be "iron," the better part of intellectual valor would seem to entail making the best of a bad situation rather than writing Jeremiads about it. Besides, as Butt goes on to say, although Rome did indeed fall, out of its decay "came the much higher, more spiritual and humane aspirations of Christian Europe." He adds: "It is not a fashionable thing to say, but . . . I would personally have preferred to live in the humane cultural excitement of Alfred the Great's Christian court than in the bread-and-circuses atmosphere of Imperial Rome. Except, of course, for the lack of hot water and heating."

The phrase *panem et circenses*, or "bread and circuses," comes

2. "The Sinai Discussion," *Encounter*, February 1980, pp. 87–93.

from Juvenal's tenth satire. Referring to the attempted coup by Sejanus against Tiberius, Juvenal writes:

> And what does the mob of Remus say? It follows fortune, as it always
> does, and rails against the condemned [Sejanus]. That same rabble,
> if Nortia [Etruscan goddess of fortune] had smiled upon the
> Etruscan [Sejanus], if the aged Emperor had been struck down
> unawares, would in that very hour have conferred upon Sejanus the
> title of Augustus. Now that no one buys our votes, the public has
> long since cast off its cares; the people that once bestowed com-
> mands, consulships, legions and all else, now meddles no more and
> longs eagerly for just two things—Bread and Circuses![3]

Juvenal suggests that the Roman Republic has given way to the Empire because the fickle populace has abandoned its political responsibilities for doles of food and the lures of the racetrack and the arena.
In modern writing, his phrase is often cited in criticisms of mass
culture to denote a process of social decline. The modern masses (so
goes the argument) have abandoned political involvement in favor of
welfare programs and the distractions of the mass media. The result is
the betrayal of the Enlightenment ideal of democracy based on an
educated, egalitarian public and the emergence of fascist and socialist
tyranny, the final totalitarian shapes of "mass society." Analyzing the
"Caesarian democracy" established in nineteenth-century France by
Napoleon III, Sir Lewis Namier uses Juvenal's phrase in a way that
sums up what it has come to mean in contemporary discourse: "*Panem
et circenses* once more—and at the end of the road, disaster."[4] It
hardly matters that when Juvenal wrote, the Empire's star was still
rising and Roman civilization was at its height. Juvenal's is the with-
ered hand of the satirist—almost of the prophet—that seems to point
to the precipice. So Juvenal takes his place in the already well populated ranks of modern forecasters of doom.

In his survey of theories of mass society, Salvador Giner says, "Of
all the contributions made by Roman thought and imagery to what
would later become the mass society outlook, probably the most

3. Juvenal, *Satires*, x, in G. G. Ramsey, ed. and tr., *Juvenal and Persius*
(Cambridge, Mass.: The Loeb Classical Library, 1918). I have altered Ramsey's "bread
and games" to "bread and circuses."

4. Sir Lewis Namier, *Vanished Supremacies: Essays on European History,
1812–1918* (New York: Harper and Row, 1963 [1958]), p. 55.

important was the belief that the multitude must be fed bread and cheap entertainment if it was to be kept quiet, submissive and loyal to the powers that be."[5] This belief has remained powerful long after the Roman circuses and coliseums have fallen to ruins. How often it has served as a Machiavellian rule for actual policymaking cannot even be guessed. But it has frequently been asserted that "bread and circuses" underlies a supposed collusion between governments and the producers of culture and entertainment. According to David Riesman, "'conspiracy' theories of popular culture are quite old" and are "summed up . . . in the concept of 'bread and circuses.'" Riesman cites Thorstein Veblen's 1929 *Dial* editorial, "The Breadline and the Movies," for presenting "a more sophisticated concept, namely, that the modern American masses paid the ruling class for the privilege of the very entertainments that helped to keep them under laughing gas."[6]

From Veblen's perspective and more generally from that of the left, "bread and circuses" has proved a useful phrase for helping to explain and condemn the processes by which capitalism has managed to deflect "the proletariat" from its revolutionary goal. From the viewpoint of the right, the phrase has been just as useful for helping to explain and condemn the failures of egalitarian schools and mass cultural institutions such as television and the press to educate "the masses" to political responsibility. In both cases, the culture and also the political attitudes of "the masses" are criticized, as are the ways in which the ruling class or the government manipulates them. And in both cases, the shade of Rome looms up to suggest the fate of societies that fail to elevate their masses to something better than welfare checks and mass entertainments.

Those who have translated, imitated, or cited Juvenal have no doubt always interpreted "bread and circuses" as showing the political and cultural irresponsibility of the common man, though they have not always found something clearly analogous in their own eras. Thus, John Dryden drew a neoclassical moral from Juvenal about the "folly"

5. Salvador Giner, *Mass Society* (New York: Academic, 1976), p. 23.
6. David Riesman, *The Lonely Crowd* (New Haven: Yale University Press, 1961 [1950]), p. 153. Thorstein Veblen, editorial on *panem et circenses* from *The Dial*, 14 June 1919, reprinted in *Essays in Our Changing Order* (New York: Viking, 1934), pp. 450–53.

of "the Mob" or the "Rascal crowd" when it tried to play politics, but he could not think of a better translation of *panem et circenses* than this:

> But we who give our Native Rights away,
> And our Inslav'd Posterity betray,
> Are now reduc'd to beg an Alms, and go
> On Holidays to see a Puppet Show.[7]

Needless to say, "puppet show" is an inadequate rendering of the excitement of the mass "spectacles" of chariot races in the Circus or of gladiatorial combats in the Coliseum. Samuel Johnson's "imitation" of Juvenal's tenth satire, "The Vanity of Human Wishes," gets no closer:

> Through Freedom's sons no more remonstrance rings,
> Degrading nobles and controuling kings;
> Our supple tribes repress their patriot throats,
> And ask no questions but the price of votes;
> With weekly libels and septennial ale,
> Their wish is full to riot and to rail.[8]

This is not to say that Dryden and Johnson were unclear about the meaning of Juvenal's phrase; they were both good neoclassicists who knew Roman history thoroughly. But they could think of no close parallels either for *panem* or for *circenses* in their own society, Britain between the Restoration and 1749. Both Montesquieu in 1734 and Gibbon starting in 1764 gave explanations of the imperial policy of bread and circuses, but no more than Dryden and Johnson did they think of it as a contemporary problem.

The great historian of *Decline and Fall of the Roman Empire* was an ardent believer in modern enlightenment and progress, who did not think that "the triumph of barbarism and religion" which had destroyed ancient civilization would repeat itself in the modern world. Though Gibbon believed that the Roman experience offered lessons that any wise nation should learn, he saw little danger of Europe's

7. John Dryden, "The Tenth Satyr of Juvenal, Translated into English Verse," in *Poems*, ed. James Kinsley, 4 vols. (Oxford: Clarendon, 1958), II, 723–24.
8. Samuel Johnson, "The Vanity of Human Wishes, The Tenth Satire of Juvenal Imitated," in *Rasselas, Poems and Selected Prose*, ed. Bertrand H. Bronson (New York: Holt, Rinehart and Winston, 1952), p. 50.

being plunged into a new Dark Age. "The experience of four thousand years should enlarge our hopes and diminish our apprehensions: we cannot determine to what height the human species may aspire in their advances towards perfection; but it may safely be presumed that no people, unless the face of nature is changed, will relapse into their original barbarism."[9] The experience of the French Revolution, however, led more conservative thinkers to believe that Europe as a whole was threatened by a reversion to barbarism, the Dark Ages, or worse. Metaphors drawn from Roman history are always close at hand in Edmund Burke, for example, as when he worries about "barbarism with regard to science and literature" as a result of revolutionary values, or when he writes of the property confiscations in France in terms of similar confiscations under Sulla.[10]

Much modern history has involved at least a surface imitation of classical models, from the architecture of government buildings to the outward shape of events. "The tradition of all the dead generations weighs like a nightmare on the brain of the living," wrote Marx. He had in mind the way the French Revolution "draped itself alternately as the Roman Republic and the Roman Empire." So France between 1789 and 1814 had been haunted by the ghosts of "resurrected Romans—the Brutuses, Gracchi, Publicolas, the tribunes, the senators and Caesar himself," the last in the shape of Napoleon. Either history repeats itself or we make it repeat itself by imitating classical models. This happens, Marx believed, either because people cannot shape the future freely (which partly means without making the same mistakes twice) or, what amounts to the same thing, because most people are not heroes.

> Wholly absorbed in the production of wealth and in the peaceful struggle of competition, [the French bourgeoisie after 1830] no longer comprehended that ghosts from the days of Rome had watched over its cradle. But unheroic as bourgeois society is, yet it had need of heroism, of sacrifice, of terror, of civil war and of national battles

9. Edward Gibbon, *Decline and Fall of the Roman Empire*, 6 vols. (New York: Everyman's Library, 1954 [1910]), IV, 111. Montesquieu, *Considerations on the Causes of the Greatness of the Romans and Their Decline*, tr. David Lowenthal (New York: The Free Press and Collier-Macmillan, 1965).

10. Edmund Burke, *Reflections on the Revolution in France* (Baltimore: Penguin, 1969), pp. 193, 216–17.

to bring it into being. And in the classically austere traditions of the Roman Republic its gladiators found the ideas and the art forms, the self-deceptions that they needed in order to conceal from themselves the bourgeois limitations of the content of their struggles.[11]

Implicit in Marx's Roman analogizing is the question of the extent to which the past always shapes the future, and beyond this lies the further possibility—of course rejected by all orthodox Marxists—that the future may inevitably be a repetition of the past, or that, as many of the great classical writers thought, history moves in a circle.

Toward the end of the eighteenth century, partly as a reflection of revolutionary times, references to bread and circuses begin to point morals that foreshadow modern critiques of mass culture. Montaigne, Robert Burton, and Sir Richard Steele wrote about the Roman games more or less as did Montesquieu and Gibbon, without any great moral concern. But in 1782 Joseph Priestley criticized "the barbarous exhibition of gladiators," and in the early nineteenth century, Chateaubriand, Byron, Sismondi, and De Quincey all condemned the Roman games on humanitarian grounds.[12] In "Childe Harold's Pilgrimage," Byron's hero, standing in the ruins of the Coliseum, remembers the fallen gladiators and praises barbarian innocence, "butcher'd to make a Roman holiday" (stanza CXLI). Byron's full moral goes beyond humanitarian sympathy to imply a connection between bread and circuses and the downfall of ancient civilization.

> But here, where Murder breathed her bloody steam;
> And here, where buzzing nations choked the ways,
> And roar'd or murmur'd like a mountain stream
> Dashing or winding as its torrent strays;

11. Karl Marx, "The Eighteenth Brumaire of Louis Bonaparte" (1852), in Robert C. Tucker, ed., *The Marx-Engels Reader* (New York: Norton, 1972), p. 437.

12. Michel de Montaigne, *Essays*, tr. E. J. Trenchmann, 2 vols. (London: Oxford, 1927), II, 134–35; Robert Burton, *The Anatomy of Melancholy*, 2 vols. (London: Peter Parker, 1676), II, 171–72; Richard Steele, *The Spectator*, nos. 449 and 436; Joseph Priestley, *Institutes of Natural and Revealed Religion*, 2 vols. (London: Johnson, 1782), I, 219; Byron, "Childe Harold's Pilgrimage," canto IV, stanzas 128–45; Vicomte de Chateaubriand, *Etudes ou discours historiques sur la chute de l'empire Romain . . .* (Paris: Garnier, 1873 [1831]), pp. 402–3; I.C.L. de Sismondi, *A History of the Fall of the Roman Empire* (London: Longman, Brown, Green, and Longmans, n.d.), I, 24–25 and 121–22; Thomas De Quincey, *The Caesars* (Boston: Ticknor, Reed, and Fields, 1851), pp. 120–21.

> Here, where the Roman millions' blame or praise
> Was death or life, the playthings of a crowd,
> My voice sounds much, and fall the stars' faint rays
> On the arena void—seats crush'd—walls bow'd—
> And galleries, where my steps seem echoes strangely loud.

This is not a translation or imitation of Juvenal, of course, but something better: a critical interpretation of history. In this regard, romanticism seems preferable to classicism: it offers the belief that Rome fell to make way for progress, or the more general belief that it is possible to improve upon the past. In any case, only in Byron's time does the idea of bread and circuses come to be viewed with a certain horror, as a pattern that modern society is unfortunately imitating all too closely, but also one that, if understood critically, can perhaps be avoided.

"When under the Emperors, the old Romans asked for nothing but *bread* and *amusements*," wrote Giuseppe Mazzini in 1844, "they became the most abject race conceivable, and after submitting to the stupid and ferocious tyranny of the Emperors they basely fell into slavery to the invading Barbarians."[13] Here is a nemesis to avoid, if at all possible. Mazzini is concerned with the waning of moral idealism in the modern world, both on the part of rulers and on the part of the people. He still does not have an exact analogy for Juvenal's circuses in mind, but is rather thinking about the encroachments of bourgeois industry and commerce upon the life of the spirit, much as Marx does in the "resurrected Romans" passage. In 1836 Mazzini had written: "We remember that when the *material* factor began to hold the field in Rome, and duty to the people was reduced to giving them *bread* and *public shows*, Rome and its people were hastening to destruction; because we see today in France, in Spain, in every country, liberty trodden under foot, or betrayed precisely in the name of commercial interests and that servile doctrine which parts material well-being from principles."[14] So for Mazzini as for many later social critics, what may seem like progress in one sense—the ruthless advance of "commercial interests"—seems like decadence in another.

As an Italian, Mazzini inherited both a negative and a positive

---

13. Giuseppe Mazzini, *The Duties of Man, and Other Essays*, ed. Thomas Jones (New York: Everyman's Library, 1907), p. 16.
14. Ibid., p. 133.

classicism. The aim of his liberal nationalism was to resurrect Roman unity and glory in their best forms, while avoiding the problems of decadence and barbarism. Much the same aim was later adopted by a far less liberal nationalist party, the Fascists, who quite literally sought to resurrect the Roman Empire and who saw in their Duce the ghost of Caesar. Mazzini was an ardent republican and believer in national self-determination, never an imperialist. But empire was the order of the day for the Fascists, as indeed it had become for many of the other nations of Europe after the Franco-Prussian War. And modern imperialism more than ever called up Roman ghosts. "For Fascists the tendency to Empire, that is to say, to the expansion of nations, is a manifestation of vitality; its opposite, staying at home, is a sign of decadence."[15] So wrote the new Caesar, Mussolini, in his 1932 encyclopedia article, "The Doctrine of Fascism." Mussolini could also say, echoing Mazzini's call for a spiritual revival: "All belief is extinct, we have no faith in our gods, no belief in the Republic. Great principles are no more. Material interests reign supreme. The multitude demands bread and amusements."[16] Part of the sad irony is that Mussolini gave the Italian masses bread and amusements and little else except for political violence and tyranny at home and warfare abroad—in Ethiopia, in Spain, and in the rest of Europe. The Roman Empire was indeed reborn in Italy in the 1920s, but its life was brief and tragic: it rushed through the cycle of rise, decline, and fall in twenty rather than in a thousand years.

From 1870 down to World War II, meanwhile, the other countries of Europe also marched across much of the rest of the world like new legionnaires. Some Englishmen expected their empire to be the new Athens instead of the new Rome, but it is not clear that Britain was more successful at spreading civilization than at exploiting the "dark" corners of the earth. The *Pax Britannica* was at least metaphorically parallel to the *Pax Romana* (a "peace," however, which in both cases

15. Benito Mussolini, "The Doctrine of Fascism" (1932), reprinted in Adrian Lyttelton, ed., *Italian Fascisms: From Pareto to Gentile* (New York: Harper and Row, 1973), p. 56. It is clear from the same document that Mussolini thought of his movement as a "classical revival" (p. 66).

16. Mussolini quoted by Mario Palmieri, *The Philosophy of Fascism* (Chicago: The Dante Alighieri Society, 1936), p. 46.

was characterized by almost continuous warfare somewhere in the world), though there were many who believed, with Sir John R. Seeley, that the British Empire was destined to more glorious ends than Rome: "No greater experiment has ever been tried on the globe, and . . . the effects of it will be comparable to the effect of the Roman Empire upon the nations of Europe, nay probably they will be much greater."[17] German expansionists, by way of contrast, often dreamed about rekindling barbarian vigor rather than about restoring Roman imperial or classical greatness; after Herder, Fichte, and Wagner, *Kultur* meant something pristine and Germanic, rising out of the forests whence long ago had come the Cimbri and the Teutons. While their Italian allies yearned for Augustan power and glory, many Germans—perhaps more honestly—joined up for new barbarian invasions, to overwhelm and to purify the decrepit civilization first planted by Rome.[18]

Mussolini's "classical revival" was of course a fraudulent classicism and an affront to those humanists who believe that knowledge of the classical past is necessary to the defense of modern civilization, who think that learning is a keystone of freedom, and who see in fascism not a revival of an ancient heritage but a travesty of it—a revival at best of barbarism. All the same, the classicist defenders of high culture against the depredations of "the masses" have themselves frequently been fascists or fascist sympathizers: the "case" of Ezra Pound is not unique, but is to greater or lesser degree the case also of the other "reactionaries" whose politics have been analyzed by John R. Harrison: T. S. Eliot, W. B. Yeats, Wyndham Lewis, D. H. Lawrence.[19] To their number must be added many other intellectuals who managed through the first half of this century to be both classicists and

17. Sir John R. Seeley, *The Expansion of England* (Chicago: University of Chicago Press, 1971 [1883]), p. 240.

18. The idea that England should be the new Athens rather than Rome of the world was expressed, e.g., by F. Seebohm, "Imperialism and Socialism," *Nineteenth Century,* 7 (April 1880), 728. For British-Roman parallels, see Raymond F. Betts, "The Allusion to Rome in British Imperialist Thought of the Late-Nineteenth and Early-Twentieth Centuries," *Victorian Studies,* 15 (1971–72), 149–59. For German-barbarian parallels, see Peter Viereck, *Metapolitics: From the Romantics to Hitler* (New York: Knopf, 1941).

19. John R. Harrison, *The Reactionaries* (New York: Schocken, 1966).

fascists, or who otherwise put high culture into the service of totalitarian causes. The case against the reactionaries can be matched by
that against those Marxists who, in the face of Stalinism, continued to
be apologists for Soviet totalitarianism. But conscious declarations of
positive classicism—as for example those of T. S. Eliot and Ezra
Pound, Charles Maurras and T. E. Hulme, Friedrich Nietzsche and
Irving Babbitt—have usually involved reactionary rather than leftist
or even liberal political attitudes.

As defined within the framework of the two classicisms, "mass culture" emerges as an apocalyptic concept, the undoing of true culture
or civilization. Negative classicism may be a natural and perhaps even
logical response to modern political and ecological crises. It is harder
to understand why mass culture or the mass media should be included
among the major causes of crisis. From a liberal perspective, any
diffusion of culture outward or "downward" to the vast majority
should be seen as a sign of progress rather than decadence. But the
very phrase "mass culture" was first used in diagnoses of social disease
and breakdown. Closely linked to the emergence of "the masses" as a
revolutionary threat in the last century, and then also to the reactionary and fascist threat in this century, "mass culture" as a theoretical
category is viewed as the special product of "mass society," which in
turn is either totalitarian or a stage between democracy and totalitarianism, as the former collapses into the latter. The phrase "mass culture" originated in discussions of mass movements and the effects of
propaganda campaigns, film, and radio shortly before the outbreak of
World War II. The systematic study of propaganda techniques began
somewhat earlier, just after World War I, at approximately the same
time that psychoanalysis was becoming widely influential. Kindred
terms—"mass art," "mass entertainment," and "mass communications"—also crop up in the 1930s. The main reason is not hard to
discover: the convergence in that decade of concern about the effects
of radio and the movies (with television clearly on the horizon) and
concern about the rise of totalitarian parties and "mass societies" in
Italy, Germany, and the Soviet Union.[20]

Framed by the totalitarian movements of the 1930s, "mass culture"

20. *Oxford English Dictionary, Supplement* (Oxford: Clarendon, 1976), II, 849.

from the outset has carried negative connotations. The terms closest
to it in English, "popular" and "folk culture," are both older and less
pejorative, though sometimes they, too, have been linked to "barbarism" and "decadence." Unlike "the folk" or even "the people," however, "the masses" have usually been perceived as a threat to the
existence of civilization, closer to the second than to the first term in
Matthew Arnold's title, *Culture and Anarchy,* or to "ignorant armies
clashing by night" than to the "sweetness and light" of the "classics."
Hence, "mass culture" appears on the modern scene as a primarily
political and apocalyptic term, used to refer to a symptom of social
morbidity, the cancer or one of the cancers in a failing body politic.

Unlike the phrase "mass culture," the mythology of negative classicism did not originate as a response to European social breakdown
between the two world wars, but much earlier, as a response to
industrial and democratic "progress" perceived as breakdown. It first
developed and thrived upon the weaknesses and inconsistencies of
nineteenth-century liberalism. The "decadent movement" of Théophile Gautier and Charles Baudelaire arose in opposition to bourgeois notions of social advance through technological and commercial
expansion. Liberalism in both Europe and America looked forward to
the gradual extension of democracy to all social classes and eventually
to all nations. Democratization was to be made effective through universal education and an extension of industrial prosperity to all classes
and nations. But the change would occur through the elevation of "the
lower orders" or "masses" toward the standard of living of the upper
classes rather than through the "leveling" of those upper classes. The
liberal utopia of the future would stop short of egalitarianism and of
any radical tampering with the institution of private property. Social
class differences might diminish, but the hegemony of the bourgeoisie
would remain intact through the gradual incorporation of the working
class into the political system. As Raymond Williams has shown for
Britain, "culture" became a key term in nineteenth-century liberal
theory, for it was by the diffusion of culture partly through state-
supported schools that "the masses" could gradually be pacified and
brought into the fold. To cite Matthew Arnold's title again, "culture"
was to supplant "anarchy."

No matter how optimistic, most liberal theories of progress barely concealed a number of fears. One was that the working-class "masses" would not be patient enough for a gradual program of enculturation to take effect. Trade unionism, socialism, and revolution were among tbe working-class responses to social injustices that seemed unmitigated by piecemeal measures of liberal reform. A related fear, finding frequent expression toward the end of the nineteenth century in theories of "crowd psychology" such as Gustave Le Bon's, was that "the masses," rather than being transformed into some approximation of the bourgeoisie, would "invade" or "engulf" the bastions of privilege. Defenses of "elites" and "minorities," like those in Alexis de Tocqueville's *Democracy in America* and John Stuart Mill's *On Liberty*, appeared to be liberalized versions of conservative defenses of class and of "noble" values. Instead of their elevation through a wholesome absorption of "high culture," "the masses," it was often feared, would drag everything down to their level, perhaps smashing the very machinery of civilization in the process. These fears, only shadows in much liberal writing, were forthrightly expressed in conservative theories that sought to counteract democratization, as for example in Edmund Burke's *Reflections on the Revolution in France* and Joseph de Maistre's *Soirées de Saint Pétersbourg*.

The recent history of theorizing about mass culture has involved a repetition of many of the ideas first expressed by Burke and de Maistre. In the 1960s, negative classicism was partly balanced by optimistic and utopian themes like those summed up in Theodore Roszak's *The Making of a Counter Culture* (1969) and Charles Reich's *The Greening of America* (1970). Much of the optimism of that decade was generated by the activist hopes of the New Left. But, like some other hopeful movements, the New Left has followed a course of disillusionment that can be illustrated by another title, from a work by one of the disillusioned, Jim Hougan—*Decadence: Radical Nostalgia, Narcissism, and Decline in the Seventies* (1975). America has not "greened," and the counterculture, fragilely blooming in the wasteland, has proved to be easily co-optable by the mass media. Hougan's title is similar to others from the mid-seventies on, which purport to show where society has gone wrong and which suggest that it is entering a new period of "decadence" or "barbarism" or both, perhaps to be followed by a new "Dark Age." According to L. S. Stavrianos in his paradoxically hopeful essay, *The Promise of the Coming Dark Age*

(1976), "the circumstances of the fall of Rome . . . are very relevant to the present world."[21]

On the basis of the term's most frequent uses in contemporary discourse, no strict definition of "mass culture" is possible. It is everything and anything, depending on what a particular critic most wishes to anathematize. Radicals may see omens of decline and fall in the demise of the New Left and the co-optation of the counterculture by the mass media. Conservatives find evidence of social decay in the New Left and the counterculture themselves. In *The Death of Progress* (1972), Bernard James cites Arnold Toynbee's distinction between external and internal barbarians, and writes:

> Where the external barbarian pounds at the gates of civilization with battering ram and war club, the internal barbarian insinuates values and habits that degrade civilized life from within. I interpret much of the so-called counter-culture we witness about us today as evidence of such internal barbarism. It takes the form of vandals scratching obscene graffiti on the wall of a synagogue or a courthouse; it is a mass of middle-class youth milling about at rock fests, knee deep in the rubbish of spent affluence; it is the faddish imitation of primitive dress and body paint.[22]

This assessment of the "barbarism" of the counterculture contains nothing new; members of the Beat Generation of the 1950s, after all, were dubbed "holy barbarians," and they in turn were only the modern American carriers of the "barbarism" and "decadence" of nineteenth-century Bohemianism. But, as "rock fests" suggests, there is more than a hint in James's account of "the decay of meaning" of a confluence between "mass" and "counter" culture; for him, "barbarism" stands for both. James goes on to say that the significance of the new barbarians "is that they betray gross and alien values, bellowing curses from beyond the walls of civility. . . . They are evidence that something has gone out of modern Western civilization, that something is also insinuating itself through every breach in Western ideals. They bring to mind images of goatskin-clad Visigoths stumbling

21. L. S. Stavrianos, *The Promise of the Coming Dark Age* (San Francisco: Freeman, 1976), p. 6. For the transition from the more optimistic mood of the 1960s to the pessimism of the 1970s, see Daniel Yankelovich, *The New Morality: A Profile of American Youth in the 70's* (New York: McGraw-Hill, 1974).

22. Bernard James, *The Death of Progress* (New York: Knopf, 1973), p. 38.

among the ruins of ancient Rome, draping themselves with loot, grinning as they urinate at the base of empty temples in the Forum. These symbols of Classic ideals had no meaning to such men."[23]

The "symbols of Classic ideals," however, have a great deal of meaning to most radical intellectuals, even though they do not always admit it. Like Marx and like the Frankfurt Institute theorists, contemporary radicals are often at least covert classicists. Many of the creators of the counterculture of the 1960s saw themselves working in opposition to various stifling versions of mass and middle-class culture (often treated under the same rubric), as Todd Gitlin's recent assessment of the largely destructive impact of the mass media on the New Left suggests (*The Whole World Is Watching,* 1980). And if modern Bohemianism and student unrest bear more than a superficial resemblance to their nineteenth-century counterparts, then perhaps their self-consciously "decadent" and "barbaric" features have partially obscured their cultural originality and energy. The nineteenth-century artistic "decadence," far from signaling a cultural decline and fall, was a major source of artistic renewal and of modern avant-gardism, in opposition to bourgeois and academic conformity. Much that is most vigorous in contemporary culture may also delight in naming itself—and in being named by its critics—"decadent" and "barbaric."

The irony of historical cyclism lends to many expressions of negative classicism a quality of paradox: out of progress comes decline and fall. "Growing efficacy involves growing degeneration of the life instincts," writes I. Robert Sinai in *The Decadence of the Modern World* (1978), "the decline of man. Every progressive impulse must sooner or later become fatigued . . . a culture may founder on real and tangible progress."[24] As the leading edge of progress, the promise of fulfillment toward which all industrial and democratic effort at least ought to be directed, "mass culture" emerges in much contemporary discourse as the biggest of recent historical disappointments or frauds, the apocalyptic pivot upon which the rise of "the masses" or "the common man" or "mass democracy" turns back on itself. Sinai's paradox of the decadence of progress can be seen in similar assertions by many recent writers. Marya Mannes wonders whether, "in the midst of the

23. Ibid., p. 39.

24. I. Robert Sinai, *The Decadence of the Modern World* (Cambridge, Mass.: Schenkman, 1978), p. 5.

greatest technological leap known to man, the mastery of [the] universe," we may not be facing "a night of the soul, a return to a new form of barbarism?"[25] And Hans Morgenthau declares that "it is one of the great ironies of contemporary history that the moral and material decline of the West has in good measure been accomplished through the moral and material triumphs of the West."[26]

Pride goeth before a fall. Gibbon and Montesquieu had written that Rome fell because of her "immoderate greatness." In his "Discourse on the Arts and Sciences," Rousseau makes a stern Fabricius denounce the "fatal arts"—everything from rhetoric to amphitheaters—of Rome, all of which might be construed as signs of progress, but which Fabricius interprets instead as fatal to "the ancient Roman simplicity." "The Roman Empire in its turn, after having engulfed all the riches of the universe, fell a prey to peoples who knew not what riches were."[27] Luxury undermines empires, which is another way of saying that civilization leads to the death of civilization. The same paradox or perhaps tautology is central to much contemporary writing about mass culture. The mass media are the most powerful instruments ever invented for the dissemination of civilization; they are also frequently declared to be the tools of our cultural suicide. Viewed through the telescope of negative classicism, mass culture is the culture of imperialism, and the end of all empires is "barbarism" and "decadence." As Rome was both the zenith and the burying ground of ancient civilization, so modern mass society with its mass culture is both zenith and nadir of modern progress, acme and end of the line for the "dual revolutions" of industrialization and democratization. Or so negative classicists either fear or hope.

For the mythology of negative classicism, mass culture is only one factor, although often the main one, in a larger system of parallels between the Roman Empire and modern society. According to Robert Nisbet in *Twilight of Authority* (1975), "The Romanization of Western society proceeds apace."[28] From Caesar to Charlemagne to Napoleon to Napoleon III to Mussolini and Hitler and Stalin: such has been the

25. Marya Mannes, *They* (Garden City, N.Y.: Doubleday, 1968), p. 32.

26. Hans Morgenthau, "Decline of the West," *Partisan Review*, 42 (1975), 514.

27. Jean-Jacques Rousseau, "A Discourse on the Arts and Sciences," in *The Social Contract and Discourses*, tr. G. D. H. Cole (New York: Dutton, 1973), pp. 12 and 17.

28. Robert Nisbet, *Twilight of Authority* (New York: Oxford University Press, 1975), p. 174.

repetitious course of the nations of Europe, doomed apparently to call
and recall the ghost of Caesar. Even more frequently, America rather
than Europe is seen as the new Rome. In *The Crisis of Our Age*
(1941), Pitirim Sorokin writes: "Many signs suggest a possibility that
America may play, in a modified form, in regard to Europe, the role of
Rome in regard to Greece."[29] Similarly, Arnold Toynbee, that great
exponent of negative classicism, declares that America "now stands for
what Rome stood for"—that is, for the defense of imperial vested
interests against the needs of the poor and of the Third World countries.[30] More recently, casting a jaundiced glance back at the deterioration of "the American dream" in the 1970s, Malcolm Muggeridge
quotes Gibbon's statement that "it was artfully contrived by Augustus
Caesar that in the enjoyment of plenty, the Romans should lose the
memory of freedom," and comments: "In the case of the American
dream, for Augustus Caesar read the media and the advertisers who
support them."[31] "Bread and circuses" is here synonymous with mass
culture and also with the economic prosperity associated with consumerism, which from a liberal perspective might be viewed as signs
of progress rather than decadence.

Equivalent examples abound. Arthur M. Schlesinger's *The Imperial Presidency* (1973) invokes the Roman transition from Republic to
Empire, as do also the titles of Amaury de Riencourt's two books on
American politics: *The Coming Caesars* (1957) and *The American Empire* (1968). "The parallel established in *The Coming Caesars* between
the development of the Classical world and the development of the
modern Western world provides the conceptual framework for
[Riencourt's later] study of the rising American empire. In particular,
the similarity of the ancient Greeks to the modern Europeans, and of
the ancient Romans to the modern Americans, remains implicit
throughout."[32] A striking example of the persistence of negative classicism occurs in *America as a Civilization* (1957), when Max Lerner

29. Pitirim Sorokin, *The Crisis of Our Age: The Social and Cultural Outlook* (New
York: Dutton, 1941), p. 256.
30. Arnold J. Toynbee, *America and the World Revolution* (New York: Oxford
University Press, 1962), p. 92.
31. Malcolm Muggeridge, "On the Threshold of the Eighties," *The American Spectator*, May 1980, p. 15.
32. Amaury de Riencourt, *The American Empire* (New York: Dell, 1970 [1968]), p.
xi.

tries to reject Roman parallels to the American experience. His list of the possible similarities between America and Rome (including everything from "bread and circuses" and "the turning toward new religious cults" to the importance of the military and "the premonition of doom in the distant march of barbarian tribes") is so long that it finally seems difficult to think of ways in which America is not Rome: "To finish the portrait, add the cult of magnificence in public buildings and the growth of the gladiatorial arts at which the large number of the people are passive spectators but emotional participants; the increasing violence within the culture; the desensitizing and depersonalizing of life; the weakening of the sense of place; the decay of rural life; the uprooting of people in a mobile culture; the concentration of a megalopolitan urbanism." But even this does not "finish the portrait," because Lerner continues with "the greater looseness of family ties and sexual relations . . . the exploration of deviant and inverted forms of behavior; the Byzantinism of life, the refinements of luxury"—and so forth.[33] After this grand summation of all the ways in which America seems to be repeating Rome, Lerner concludes anticlimactically that "America is not Rome but itself." Well, yes, but what he really shows is how negative classicism can overshadow even the writings of the liberal believers in social progress.

That our age and culture are apocalyptic is a truism. As Frank Kermode remarks, we are always striving to satisfy "our deep need for intelligible Ends," and to do so we often resort to "myths of Empire and Decadence."[34] Doomsaying, present to greater or lesser extent in all ages, has become the chief mode of modern culture. In the early 1970s the report of the Club of Rome, *The Limits to Growth*, gave the world approximately a century to survive. Also in 1972, in *The Doomsday Syndrome*, John Maddox questioned the more extreme prophecies of the ecologists and wrote:

> It used to be commonplace for men to parade city streets with sandwich boards proclaiming "The End of the World is at Hand!" They have been replaced by a throng of sober people, scientists, philosophers, and politicians, proclaiming that there are more subtle

33. Max Lerner, *America as a Civilization*, 2 vols. (New York: Simon and Schuster, 1967 [1957]), II, 934–35.

34. Frank Kermode, *The Sense of an Ending* (New York: Oxford University Press, 1967), p. 8.

calamities just around the corner. The human race, they say, is in danger of strangling itself by overbreeding, of poisoning itself with pollution, of undermining its essential human character by tampering with heredity.[35]

For the first time in the history of America (Europe has had earlier and perhaps greater causes for pessimism), the general public's faith in progress has broken down. Images of ecological catastrophe, energy shortages, economic depression, and the neo-Malthusian "population bomb" have merged with older fears of a nuclear holocaust. According to Jeremy Rifkin in *Entropy* (1980), the second law of thermodynamics and not progress is the shape of things to come. Even the mass media now frequently convey the message of a social decline for which, according to the "bread and circuses" analogy, the mass media themselves are largely to blame. Beneath the gimcrack surface of happy gadgetry and smiling toothpaste ads which is often mistaken for the whole of American mass culture, a quite dismal, catastrophic vision of the future has been spreading. Perhaps this means that the gap between disenchanted intellectuals (whose business it has always been to express critical alienation) and the public or the masses is closing. Perhaps it means that a new wave of gloomy religious emotion is sweeping over the masses, with as yet unforeseen consequences. Neither prophecies of doom nor mass religious movements, however, are new historical phenomena. Just as an analogy for the welfare state and the modern mass media is frequently found in "bread and circuses," so an analogy for modern mass eschatology is frequently found in the rise and spread of Christianity through the Roman Empire. Mass culture is often attacked as the ultimate result of secularization; "bread and circuses" are held to be among the worst products of an age that has liquidated the sacred. But mass culture is frequently also attacked as a surrogate religion, or at least as a breach in the walls of civilization through which the religious irrationality of the masses is beginning to intrude. Ironically, the mythology of negative classicism frequently warns us against the mythologizing or the quasi-religious functions of the mass media.

The apocalyptic warnings of negative classicism have their reflections in the mass media themselves. According to W. Warren Wagar,

35. John Maddox, *The Doomsday Syndrome* (London: Macmillan, 1972), p. 1.

at least since 1914 "the serious literature of most Western countries" has been "drenched with apocalyptic imagery." Among other examples, Wagar points to "the 'cyclical' historians, Spengler, Toynbee, Sorokin, and their disciples, [who] predict the imminent going-under of modern civilization."[36] A recent, rather diluted version of Spengler and Toynbee is Roberto Vacca's *The Coming Dark Age* (1971). Despite his fears about the masses and mass culture, moreover, Vacca expresses apocalyptic themes not far removed from those in such mass circulation science fiction stories and films as *A Canticle for Liebowitz, Omega Man, Dune,* and *Star Wars.*[37] In all of these works, "the end of our time is upon us," and the barbarization—if not the total destruction—of the world is at hand. Perhaps the major difference between negative classicism in the cyclical historians and apocalyptic themes of social decay or destruction in the mass media is the degree to which the former accuse mass culture itself of subverting civilization. But often there seems little to choose between the gloomy news of "the last days" as expressed in the writings of an intellectual doomsayer like I. Robert Sinai and the mass eschatology that filters through television and newspaper headlines. In both cases, it seems appropriate to wonder if we are witnessing a rebirth of religious irrationality, and perhaps even to wonder if warnings of social disintegration may be symptoms of the disease they warn us against.

The distinction between "high" and "mass" culture, dubious at best, breaks down when it comes to such widely shared phenomena as the mythologization of history or apocalyptic doomsaying. Though it is more common to see the mass media as purveyors of shinier toothpastes than of eschatological dread, a major theme of current mass culture is that the mass media themselves are either "decadent" or "barbaric" or both, that they are instruments of our destruction, that they are leading society down the garden path to totalitarianism. The displacement of books by television in Ray Bradbury's dystopian novel and film *Fahrenheit 451* is an example, and so is Paddy Chayefsky's movie *Network.* And Jerzy Kosinski's *Being There,* with its "videot"

36. W. Warren Wagar, *The City of Man* (Baltimore: Penguin, 1968), p. 4. See also George Watson, "The Myth of Catastrophe," *The Yale Review,* 65 (Spring 1976), 359: catastrophe was "the nearly universal myth of literary intellectuals between the wars."

37. See Harold L. Berger, *Science Fiction and the New Dark Age* (Bowling Green, Ohio: Bowling Green University Popular Press, 1976).

antihero Chance, expresses in fable form the now quite widespread fear that television is rotting people's minds. Kosinski echoes older fears about the totalitarian tendencies of the mass media—the arguments of the Frankfurt Institute theorists, for example, according to which the "culture industry" operates as propaganda machinery first for capitalist exploitation of the masses, and then (capitalism inevitably breaking down) for fascism.[38]

Not only is the intellectual concept of mass culture often an eschatological one, but tbe mass media also convey apocalyptic self-reflections, including negative classicism. These eschatological self-reflections derive partly from the fact that television, for example, especially in its commercial forms, tends to destroy all boundaries between one thing and another—between toothpaste ads and Shakespeare, crime and politics, sexual reticence and sexual exploitation, soap operas and news, "children's hours" and adult programming, and so forth. It also derives from the commercially strategic antithesis between "entertainment" and everything deemed culturally "serious." As Erik Barnouw observes, "As used for decades by Hollywood and today by networks and sponsors, [entertainment] implies that there is no message—messages being for Western Union—and no purpose of any sort other than to fill leisure time and make you feel good."[39] A crude cultural judgment is thus built into television, contrasting information and entertainment. The news is supposed to be serious and important; the rest is supposed to be one form or another of distraction from the world's woes. This, too, is a kind of classicism and a faint affirmation of the political responsibility that Juvenal thought had in his day been abandoned for bread and circuses. Most watchers of the Super Bowl or of World Cup soccer do not realize that they are mimicking the spectators in Roman arenas, cheering madly and turning thumbs up or down for their favorite gladiators, but that comparison is nevertheless implicit in the very structure of televised sports "spectaculars." In *The Culture of Narcissism,* Christopher Lasch quotes a surfboard rider on how the intrusion of the networks

38. Jerzy Kosinski, "A Nation of Videots," *Media and Methods,* 11 (April 1975).

39. Erik Barnouw, *The Sponsor: Notes on a Modern Potentate* (New York: Oxford University Press, 1978), p. 101.

has affected his avocation: "Television is destroying our sport. The TV producers are turning a sport and an art form into a circus."[40]

Negative classicism, however unconsciously, has become part of the self-definition of the mass media. Those critics who believe that mass culture is only a uniform mush that wipes out all distinctions fail to see that the media produce their own negations. They know themselves to be inferior, ephemeral, throw-away, decadent, even while they are all-pervasive and seemingly all-powerful. Their empire, too, is built on sand. And they are forever implying or echoing classical ghosts, shadowy memories of high culture. Most television drama is *not* tragic, it is *not* antique, it *cannot be* Sophocles or Shakespeare—and everyone infers that it must be antithetical to tragedy. In just the same way, the more cheery and sparkling the toothpaste ads, the more mass eschatology lurks just behind the surface of the screen, adhering invisibly to it like a sort of emotional plaque. It needs only an occasional entrance on the evening news or a brief outburst of terror in a police drama for its unintended message to register. One of the more measurable effects of televised violence concerns the extent to which heavy viewers overestimate the amount of violence in the real world. Television tries to say: all is well with the world. We conclude: all is not well with the world.

Television is the perfect reification machine, but its dehumanizing and distinction-blurring messages tend to unravel and fall apart in the moment of their fabrication. The same quality of monolithic impenetrability coupled with internal cracks and weaknesses characterizes all industrialized mass culture. Above all, mass culture always offers a pretense of dialogue when it is in fact monologue imposed from above or outside the life of the individual "consumer." Jürgen Habermas describes one of the ways in which mass culture tends to call forth its dialectical negative when he writes:

> The gentle social control exercised by the mass media makes use of the spectacles of an undermined private sphere in order to make political processes unrecognizable as such. The depoliticized public realm is dominated by the imposed privatism of mass culture. The

40. Christopher Lasch, *The Culture of Narcissism: American Life in an Age of Diminishing Expectations* (New York: Norton, 1978), p. 106.

personalization of what is public is thus the cement in the cracks of a relatively well-integrated society, which forces suspended conflicts into areas of social psychology. There they are absorbed in categories of deviant behavior: as private conflicts, illness, and crime. These containers now appear to be overflowing.[41]

The fake privatization of public concerns together with the monologic denial of two-way or democratic communication cannot maintain its illusory hold over the consciousness of "the masses" or "the public" forever, and is perhaps always dimly perceived as inadequate, subhuman, undemocratic.

Partly through cracks in the mass media themselves, then, negative classicism has become the major myth of our time. Its development has been an important aspect of Western cultural history since about the time of the French Revolution. In order to understand its contemporary manifestations, I have followed it back as far as Gibbon and Burke, though I have also concentrated on some of its chief mythologizers in the nineteenth and twentieth centuries. These include Marx, Engels, and the Frankfurt Institute theorists on the left; existentialists from Kierkegaard and Nietzsche to Gabriel Marcel, Karl Jaspers, and Albert Camus; Freud, Jung, and the psychoanalysts; the "cyclical historians"; and Baudelaire, Flaubert, Matthew Arnold, T. S. Eliot, José Ortega y Gasset, down to Marshall McLuhan, Christopher Lasch, Richard Sennett, and Daniel Bell among cultural critics and theorists. Most of these figures partake to greater or lesser degree of the two classicisms, because most of them treat contemporary mass culture as the antithesis of some true way, whether that way involves an individual "leap of faith" as in Kierkegaard, proletarian education and revolution as in Marx, the transcendence of the exceptional man as in Nietzsche, adherence to an Enlightenment ideal of reason as in Freud, Christianity plus a nostalgic authoritarianism not far from fascism as in Eliot, or the advocacy of democratic and communitarian ideals as in Lasch and Sennett. The list is far from complete, but these are among the most influential and representative shapers of the two classicisms and of contemporary theories of mass culture. An analysis of their thinking should suggest both that our present insistence upon

41. Jürgen Habermas, *Toward a Rational Society: Student Protest, Science, and Politics*, tr. Jeremy J. Shapiro (Boston: Beacon, 1970), pp. 42–43.

decadence and apocalypse, though extreme, is hardly new, and also that even in periods and writers who have seemed to believe most optimistically in the idea of linear progress, the undercurrent of negative classicism has run strong.

Just as varieties of liberalism have striven for release from the past, varieties of classicism have striven to restore its authority. From its beginnings in Renaissance humanism, modern classicism has measured a defective present against a largely utopian past. While the recollection of past cultural greatness has often helped to invigorate current strains of art, writing, and education, the act of recollection itself may suggest the "decadence" as easily as the innocent "rudeness" or "barbarism" of the present. Friedrich Schiller's distinction between "naive" and "sentimental" poetry involves a related contrast, but one that ought to present difficulties for any version of classicism.[42] "Naive" art is straight from the source, from "nature"; "sentimental" art longs for the condition of "naivete," but can do no better than imitate it. "Sentimentality" is thus always a symptom of the artist's fallen state, the inability to recapture lost innocence. Classicism as the defense of the high culture of the past against the supposedly mindless mass culture of the present wears the aspect of Schiller's "sentimentality." As such, it is itself a symptom of "decadence," or of the distance from our "naive," supposedly organic and healthful roots in the classical past. Here classicism and mass society with the mass culture that classicism rejects prove inseparable, parts of a single historical totality that may be called "modern civilization" or the "modern condition." Here, too, arises the paradox that classicism itself may be as sterile and empty as what it condemns, while mass culture in its latest manifestations—the cinema, radio, television, at least in their formative periods—may behave like Schiller's "naive" art, displaying perhaps a complete ignorance of past culture, but also displaying the creative energy and freshness that often accompany the births of new art forms and media. (Perhaps the fact that television grew upon ground already planted by motion pictures and radio explains why it has seemed less "naive" and vigorous than its predecessors. It inherited two very short but spectacular traditions,

42. Friedrich Schiller, *Über naive und sentimentalische Dichtung* (Oxford: Blackwell, 1957 [1795]).

and may thus have suffered under the burden of its own dimly recognized but oppressive classicism.)

As a form of utopian recollection and cultural "sentimentality," modern classicism is always a debate between the ancients and the moderns in which the ancients win—a debate between past "high culture" and present "mass," or "popular," or "democratic," or "totalitarian," or "commerical," or "bourgeois," or "secular," or "industrial" pseudoculture. Conservative and radical critiques both lead to identifications of mass culture with either "decadence" or "barbarism" or both. But from a third perspective, that of democratic liberalism, mass culture is sometimes seen as the last, best hope of civilization. The diffusion of culture—knowledge, an appreciation of the beautiful, perhaps wisdom—to the common man, even when it involves dilution or some loss of value or substance, is declared to be a new factor in history which should be viewed optimistically. Thus, according to Herbert J. Muller in *The Uses of the Past*, Roman analogies should be at least temporarily shelved, because "common men are having their first real chance in history, and have not had it long."[43] However that may be, in America as in Europe, especially after Vietnam and Watergate, the rising tide of social crisis literature with its catastrophic mass culture theories has all but drowned out voices of liberal caution such as Muller's.

The bread and circuses pattern cannot itself be seen as a major causal factor in the decline and fall of Rome; it may be symptomatic of decadence, but the sources of decay went deeper. Nevertheless, one frequent explanation for the decay of ancient civilization is at least related to bread and circuses. This is the idea that, as Rome grew from a city-state on the model of the Greek *polis* to an empire on the Alexandrian model, it took on the character of a mass society. Roman civilization was invaded from without by the barbarians, but it was also subverted from within by "the lower classes." In a passage that inspired Muller's defense of the common man, Mikhail Rostovtzeff presents this thesis at the end of *The Social and Economic History of the Roman Empire*. At some point in its development, classical civilization ceased to assimilate the masses. Whether they were internal

43. Herbert J. Muller, *The Uses of the Past* (New York: Oxford University Press, 1957 [1952]), p. 233.

or external barbarians, the masses instead began to impose their values on the ruling classes. Hence, bread and circuses. Hence, too, Christianity. According to Rostovtzeff:

> We may say, then, that there is one prominent feature in the development of the ancient world during the imperial age, alike in the political, social, and economic and in the intellectual field. It is a gradual absorption of the higher classes by the lower, accompanied by a gradual leveling down of standards. This leveling was accomplished in many ways. There was a slow penetration of the lower classes into the higher, which were unable to assimilate the new elements. There were violent outbreaks of civil strife: the lead was taken by the Greek cities, and there followed the civil war of the first century B.C. which involved the whole civilized world. In these struggles the upper classes and the city-civilization remained victorious on the whole. Two centuries later, a new outbreak of civil war ended in the victory of the lower classes and dealt a mortal blow to the Greco-Roman civilization of the cities. Finally, that civilization was completely engulfed by the inflow of barbarous elements from outside, partly by penetration, partly by conquest, and in its dying condition it was unable to assimilate even a small part of them.[44]

What Rostovtzeff believes to have occurred on a broad scale and over centuries in the ancient world is, to use José Ortega y Gasset's phrase, a "revolt of the masses." Mass culture in its classical form—bread and circuses—appears as one aspect of the failure of the best classical values to take root among common people. Civilization founders upon its inability to be a civilization for everybody. Through diffusion and dilution, it leads to its antithesis: barbarism, both external and internal. But there is some question of the extent to which Rostovtzeff projects the features of modern mass society backward upon ancient civilization. And there is also the question raised by Muller of the extent to which democratization has yet been allowed to take effect and to prove itself in modern conditions.

In the failure of the ancient world to civilize the masses, Rostovtzeff sees "a lesson and a warning" for the modern world. The first thing to

44. Mikhail Rostovtzeff, *The Social and Economic History of the Roman Empire*, 2d ed., 2 vols. (Oxford: Oxford University Press, 1967), I, 534. A useful compendium of modern theories about Rome's fall is Donald Kagan, ed., *The End of the Roman Empire: Decline or Transformation?* (Lexington, Mass.: Heath, 1978).

be learned is that "our civilization will not last unless it be a civilization not of one class, but of the masses." Obviously, unless the civilizing process can penetrate all levels of society without turning into its opposite, it will ultimately fail, and while it lasts it will continually be threatened by subversion from below or from outside. Rostovtzeff goes on to say that the second thing to be learned "is that violent attempts at leveling have never helped to uplift the masses. They have destroyed the upper classes, and resulted in accelerating the process of barbarization" (541). Ways must be found to disseminate civilization to the masses without diluting it. Upper-class elitism, Rostovtzeff thinks, must be combined with democracy. But how? The demise of ancient civilization presents us with no models of success, only failure. Thus it happens that bread and circuses reappears on the modern scene as a problem begging for solutions; the study of Roman ruins leaves Rostovtzeff with questions he cannot answer: "The ultimate problem remains like a ghost, ever present and unlaid: Is it possible to extend a higher civilization to the lower classes without debasing its standard and diluting its quality to the vanishing point? Is not every civilization bound to decay as soon as it begins to penetrate the masses?" (541).

Rostovtzeff's questions are basic to any consideration of mass culture as a symptom or a cause of social decadence, but one answer may be mass culture itself. Despite the bread and circuses analogy, there was no equivalent in the ancient world for the mass media, including the press, radio, television, cinema, and also no equivalent for systems of mass public education. The mythology of negative classicism tends to lump all these unprecedented features of modern life into one destructive category, defined under the aspect of bread and circuses as the undoing rather than as the potential salvation of modern civilization. For either capitalist or socialist democracy to work, intelligence, information, and humane values must either arise from or be bestowed upon the masses. But, Rostovtzeff fears, the very process of disseminating culture to the masses turns it into its opposite, into "mass culture" in the most negative sense. Meanwhile the masses themselves begin to impose their own crude, "barbaric" values on the entire society. "Bread and circuses" emerges from the dilution—or, better, dissolution—of high culture and from the worst instincts of the masses themselves. Like many other conservatives and conservative liberals, Rostovtzeff believes that the modern progress of civilization may have reached its high point in the partial, bourgeois democracies of the last century, and that the extenstion of freedom to everyone can only bring the cycle down from its peak, toward decadence, barbarism, disaster.

But what was the mechanism whereby the elites of the ancient world sought to disseminate high culture to the masses? The answer is that they had no such mechanism and that they did not even dream of civilizing the masses in the sense Rostovtzeff means. What the elites of the Roman world gave to the masses was "bread and circuses," in which the elites themselves participated with more or less enthusiasm. And the spread of Christianity, which may itself be interpreted as a form of civilizing the masses, from the beginning lay outside the control of the ruling elites. A truer analogy to modern mass culture may perhaps be found in the early Church than in "bread and circuses," though both have frequently been cited as examples of what is happening today, of our modern decline and fall.

Rostovtzeff's questions form the core of the conservative version of negative classicism. The radical version of the same mythology only reverses its terms, not the general pattern, laying blame for our downfall upon the ruling classes rather than upon the victimized masses. But perhaps something is happening throughout much of the modern world for which the past offers no analogies. In his various defenses of the mass media, especially the electronic mass media, Marshall McLuhan has effected one of the most complete, and certainly one of the most controversial, breaks from the two classicisms among recent theorists of culture. The terminology of McLuhanism, however, is no less eschatological than that of negative classicism. In his heady prophecies of the coming "global village" and the electronic "noösphere" or overmind, McLuhan leaves out of the picture whether the village will be civilized or not and whether the overmind will be intelligent or foolish. "The medium is the message" and, as far as McLuhan is concerned, the message is good. Despite his weaknesses, McLuhan offers a striking challenge to negative classicism. And there have been other, quieter theorists who have also challenged it, often on the grounds suggested by Herbert Muller.

The past never inscribes all the writing on the wall, and any application of classical analogies to the present must be questioned from the outset. In his account of "The Social Causes of the Decay of Ancient Civilization," Max Weber criticizes the idea that there is much to be learned about the modern world from Roman history:

> The interest of a story is always keener when the audience has the feeling: *de te narratur fabula* [the story is about them], and when the storyteller can conclude his yarn with a *discite moniti* [beware]! Unfortunately . . . we can learn little or nothing for our contemporary social problems from ancient history. A modern proletarian and a Roman slave would be as unable to understand one another as a European and a Chinese. Our problems are of a completely different character.[45]

Cautionary notes like Weber's, however, have not kept Roman ghosts from haunting the modern world. But the conclusion of his essay leads to another, perhaps harder question, about the value of what was lost and what gained in the transition from classical civilization to the Middle Ages. Weber refuses to weigh entire societies and eras in the meager scales of reason; nevertheless, his obituary on the ancient world leads to an idyllic description of the world that followed:

> So the threadbare wrap of ancient civilization disappeared, and the intellectual life of Western man sank into a long night. But that fall reminds us of that giant in Greek mythology who gained new strength whenever he rested on the bosom of mother earth. If one of the old classical authors had arisen from his manuscript in Carolingian times and had examined the world through the window of the monk's cell in which he found himself, his surroundings would have looked strange to him, indeed: the dung-heap odour of the manor-yard would have hit his nostrils. But those classics were in deep sleep now, as was all civilization, hidden away under the cover of an economic life which had returned to rural forms. Neither the songs nor the tournaments of feudal society roused it out of this sleep. Only when, on the basis of free division of labour and of commercial exchange, the *city* had arisen again in the Middle Ages, when, later still, the transition to a national economy prepared the ground for civil liberty and broke the fetters imposed by the external and internal authorities of the feudal age, only then the old giant arose and carried with him the intellectual inheritance of antiquity up to the new light of our modern middle-class civilization.[46]

45. Max Weber, "The Social Causes of the Decay of Ancient Civilization," 1896, in J.E.T. Eldridge, ed., *Max Weber: The Interpretation of Social Reality* (New York: Scribner, 1971), p. 256.

46. Ibid., pp. 274–75.

Similarly, it is as idyll or utopia that the "new Middle Ages" figures in many of the apocalyptic designs of negative classicists today: a place of rest after the *Sturm und Drang* of modern social existence. Negative classicism often turns out to be an ironically hopeful mode of thought: "decadence" and "barbarism" become the signs and portents of a longed-for transformation.

In the "new light" of "middle-class civilization," with its neoclassical government buildings, coliseums, and freeways, its Roman law codes and its institutions both republican and imperial, we can at least look back over the expanse of the Middle Ages and the ancient world and wonder: What indeed has been gained? And what lost? At the height of the Roman Empire, Juvenal felt that much had been lost. There were others, however, who contradicted him. Those most responsible for bread and circuses, the emperors and their cohorts, did not see anything amiss about Roman life. One has only to consult Augustus's *Res Gestae* to see the gap between emperor and satirist. Here is Augustus on the bread and circuses policy that he did much to make an imperial custom:

> To the Roman plebs I paid 300 sesterces apiece in accordance with the will of my father. . . . These largesses of mine reached never less than 250,000 persons. . . . In my thirteenth consulship I gave sixty *denarii* apiece to those of the plebs who at that time were receiving public grain; the number involved was a little more than 200,000 persons.
>
> . . . I gave a gladiatorial show three times in my own name, and five times in the names of my sons or grandsons; at these shows about 10,000 fought. . . . Twenty-six times I provided for the people, in my own name or in the names of my sons or grandsons, hunting spectacles of African wild beasts in the circus or in the Forum or in the amphitheaters: in these exhibitions about 3,500 animals were killed.[47]

And so forth. For Augustus, there is only a self-reflecting glory in the imperial spectacles and the dole. For the thousands of plebs who were the recipients of his bounty, there must have been a similar feeling of living at the pinnacle of history, in the most important city and at the most important time in the world. It is perhaps more difficult to

47. Augustus, *Res Gestae*, in Naphtali Lewis and Meyer Reinhold, eds., *Roman Civilization*, 2 vols., *Sourcebook II: The Empire* (New York: Harper and Row, 1966 [1955]), pp. 14 and 16.

imagine what the thousands of gladiators and victims of the arena thought, though the rebellion of Spartacus in 73 B.C. offers a clue. What Juvenal thought is clear.

Richard Gilman has recently argued that the word "decadence" should be discarded as illogical.[48] Perhaps so, but his essay itself attests to the importance of the word in contemporary discourse. Behind the word, moreover, lies the elaborate, pervasive, seductive mythology of negative classicism, with a history at least a century and a half long in European and American culture. Whereas Gilman would be satisfied if the word "decadence" were abandoned, I believe that the mythology of "bread and circuses" has influenced modern history and will continue to influence it profoundly. Whether or not it becomes the dismal reality of the future, the idea of decline and fall has acquired the force of a reality in the present. Perhaps our myths are always the things we take to be most real, and which therefore have the most real effects upon our lives. Historical *déjà vu* seems to be the order of the day, the substance of cultural modernism and even "post-modernism" themselves. According to John Lukacs in *The Passing of the Modern Age* (1970), "We live now amidst the ruins of a civilization: but most of these ruins are in our minds."[49] The ruins of the present may or may not be more mental than actual, but they seem doubly ruinous and inescapable when the failures of the past are projected onto them. Insofar as they partake of negative classicism, books on contemporary society, whether sophisticated ones like Daniel Bell's *The Cultural Contradictions of Capitalism* (1976) or more popular fare like Howard Ruff's cheerfully doleful bestseller, *How to Prosper during the Coming Bad Years* (1979), add up to a powerful imaging of the future in terms of the past. Myths of empire and decadence always point either toward a second coming of the barbarians or toward a second coming of religion. On the left appear the ideas of imperialism as the last stage of "late capitalism" and of the rejuvenating "barbarism" of the proletariat. On the right appears the

48. Richard Gilman, *Decadence: The Strange Life of an Epithet* (New York: Farrar, Straus, & Giroux, 1979).

49. John Lukacs, *The Passing of the Modern Age* (New York: Harper and Row, 1970), p. 4. Compare Sinai, *The Decadence of the Modern World*, p. 5: "We are living amidst the ruins of a civilization, with both its mental and material structures crumbling."

idea that we must have, to use Bell's term, a religious "instauration"—perhaps a revival of the old, perhaps the birth of a new faith—to save us from our secularized, spiritually dead-ended selves. These may be satisfying ways to round off prophetic stories, and they have the authority of the past behind them—the specific gravity, as it were, of all classicisms. But bringing a mythic pattern full circle cannot be the same as breaking out of that circle. As Marx declared, "A chapter on the decline of the Roman Empire which might read exceedingly well in Montesquieu or Gibbon would prove an enormous blunder if put in the mouth of a Roman senator, whose peculiar business it was to stop that very decline."[50]

"The decline, or aging, of the West is as much a part of our mental outlook today as the electron or the dinosaur," writes Northrop Frye, "and in that sense we are all Spenglerians."[51] Negative classicism, increasingly part of the content of mass culture itself, substitutes a catastrophic or a cyclic view of history for a progressive one. It holds truistically that society as we know it is passing away, to be succeeded by forms of social existence that will betray the features of a regression to earlier stages of history. According to this mythology, even the features of the present that seem most unlike the past—notably the mass media—are repetitions of classical patterns. Civilization does not lead to more perfect types of itself, but to decadence and barbarism. As Theodor Adorno and Max Horkheimer put it, "The curse of irresistible progress is irresistible regression."[52] Perhaps negative classicism itself is a part of the general regression, hastening "the end of our time." As myth, it may be no more rational than other forms of religious and apocalyptic thought, including those associated by it with mass culture. In *The Doomsday Syndrome*, John Maddox suggests that prophecies of doom may create an intellectual pollution that is just as dangerous as industrial pollution and nuclear fallout. At least myth should be recognized as myth, whether it comes from the mass media or from their intellectual critics. It seems clear, moreover, that

50. Karl Marx, "The Indian Question," *New York Daily Tribune*, 14 August 1857, reprinted in Marx and Engels, *On History and People*, vol. VII of the Karl Marx Library (New York: McGraw-Hill, 1977), p. 127.

51. Northrop Frye, "*The Decline of the West* by Oswald Spengler," *Daedalus*, 103 (Winter 1974), 7.

52. Theodor Adorno and Max Horkheimer, *Dialectic of Enlightenment* (New York: Seabury, 1972 [1944]), p. 36.

some social critics write themselves into their visions of present and future "triumphs of barbarism and religion," either as the would-be saviors of the old order or as the prophetic heralds of the new.

> And they cast dust on their heads, saying, Alas, alas that great city, wherein were made rich all that had ships in the sea by reason of her costliness! For in one hour is she made desolate. Rejoice over her . . . ye holy apostles and prophets.   [Rev. 18:19–20]

Besides the effort to see mythology for what it is (the main purpose of this book), a second effort is also necessary, to move beyond either skepticism or a fatalistic pessimism toward that political and cultural commitment most able to ensure that the liberation of "the masses" and the creation of "mass culture" will mean progress rather than decadence. The aim of all social and cultural theorizing just now should be to convert the ruins of our civilization, real or imagined, into a living community.

CHAPTER 2

The Classical Roots of
the Mass Culture Debate

*From my tutor: not to be a Green or a Blue partisan at the
races, or a supporter of the lightly armed or heavily armed
gladiators at the Circus.*

—MARCUS AURELIUS

i

PATTERNS of both "high" and "mass" culture can be drawn from
ancient history. The Athenians provide the core of what modern
classicists wish to preserve: not just Greek literature and works of art,
but above all the Greek example of intellectual transcendence and
objectivity. The Romans of the Empire provide, along with much
else, the pattern of negative classicism, bread and circuses, decadence
and barbarism.

Present in Greek and Roman political theories, moreover, are most
of the elements in modern critiques of mass culture and mass society.
Discussions of the types of government, as in Plato's *Republic*, foreshadow modern discussions of the possible relationships between political institutions, culture, and the masses. For modern classicists,
the political categories of Plato and Aristotle have a special significance: the terms of current discourse, already derived from the past,
are reinforced by reference to the authority of that same past. Further, hostility between men of ideas and ordinary people is as old as
Western philosophy. Thus, Heraclitus matches one of his modern
emulators, Friedrich Nietzsche, in his insistence that most people are
blind to or even actively hostile toward moral and cultural excellence:

Heraclitus am I. Why do ye drag me up and down, ye illiterate? It
was not for you I toiled, but for such as might understand me. One
man in my sight is a match for thirty thousand, but the countless
hosts do not make a single one.[1]

When about 500 B.C. the elder Ephesians banished Hermodorus,
Heraclitus thought that they "would do well to hang themselves and
leave their city to the boys," for Hermodorus "was the best man of
them," and their treatment of him proved their vulgar enmity toward
"the best." Heraclitus describes them as reasoning, or rather as failing
to reason, in the following manner: "We would have none among us
who is best; if there be such an one, let him be so elsewhere among
other people" (505). This may be the earliest extant version of the idea
that the masses prefer mediocrity to excellence. In other fragments,
Heraclitus expresses the same aristocratic scorn for the failure of most
people to value the high and noble: "For what mind or sense have
they? They follow the bards and use the multitude as their teacher,
not realizing that there are many bad but few good. For the best
choose one thing over all others, immortal glory among mortals, while
the many are glutted like beasts" (505).

Heraclitus presents in miniature two of the basic assumptions behind many later criticisms of democracy, the common man, and mass
culture, including those that underlie negative classicism. The first is
that whatever is common or average or many contradicts whatever is
good, true, and beautiful. The "best" is few or even singular and the
"bad" is many, as anyone who wishes to be a prophet and a critic of his
times must assert in some fashion. Heraclitus unconsciously projects
the properties of words onto the affairs of men, an error that philosophers have been committing ever since and that is apparent in much
contemporary theorizing about mass culture and society as unitary or
totalitarian phenomena. Of course the "best" tends to be rare or even
singular, but the "better" and the "good" are more clearly plural as
are the "worse" and the "bad," whereas the "worst" by such linguistic
reckoning must be just as rare or singular as the highest excellence.
Thus the word "mass" arises in modern discourse as a unifying concept at times synonymous with the "worst," even though the former is

1. Heraclitus, *On the Universe*, together with Hippocrates, IV, tr. W. H. S. Jones
(New York: Loeb Classical Library, 1931), pp. 467–68.

logically multitudinous and the latter singular.

Heraclitus's argument from words to things leads to the contradictory idea that the individual may be good, but that many individuals
taken together cannot be. Much the same idea shapes those modern
dystopian fantasies that depict a solitary character—Franz Kafka's
Josef K. or George Orwell's Winston Smith—struggling against the
implacable machinery of a vast bureaucratic state, fictional versions of
"mass society." It hardly matters that Winston Smith is himself very
much an "average man" with no outstanding qualities. He is "the
one," the everyman hero of a melodrama that pits a solitary individual
against a monolithic society, thereby reducing the archetypal conflict
between individual and society in the eighteenth- and nineteenth-
century novel to its barest elements.[2] In *The Trial*, Kafka comes
closer to the truth of the pattern by making the melodrama seem very
much the projection of the deranged imagination of his "average
man," Josef K. But the dystopian visions of both novelists depend on
the same idea that we see in Heraclitus: though the one may be good,
the many are evil.

The second aspect of Heraclitus's social thought that recurs often in
later cultural and political theory is his likening of "the multitude" to
animals, a common metaphoric equivalent for "barbarians." The "few
good" are spiritual beings, choosing "immortal glory among mortals";
but "the many are glutted like beasts." Here is one ancestor of
Nietzsche's "herd instinct" and T. S. Eliot's "apeneck Sweeney." It
appears to be an idea as old as civilization itself that the "uncivilized"
are "barbarians," little better than the "brute creation." Homer's
description of the cave-dwelling Cyclopes, "an unruly people, who
have no settled customs," suggest how men of the *polis* came to view
"barbarians."[3] Part of Heraclitus's originality may consist in his application of the same lycanthropic terminology to the civilized as well,
so that there are internal or "vertical barbarians" inside the city walls.
It follows that most people are either internal or external barbarians,

2. See Georg Lukács, *The Theory of the Novel* (Cambridge, Mass.: MIT Press,
1971).

3. For Homer on the Cyclopes, see Cosmo Rodewald, ed., *Democracy: Ideas and
Realities*, in the series "The Ancient World: Source Books" (London: Dent and Hak-
kert, 1975). See also Catherine H. and Ronald M. Berndt, *The Barbarians: An Anthropological View* (London: Watts, 1971).

because it is always difficult to live up to the highest standards of a culture—another way of saying that civilization is always at least a partial failure, undergoing decline and fall even at the moment of its highest development.

The Heraclitean assumption of the rarity of "the best" recurs often in Greek thought. In one of the earliest extant excursions into political theory, Herodotus describes the debate of three Persians about the relative merits of democracy, oligarchy, and monarchy. The hypothetical democrat, Otanes, proposes to "do away with monarchy and raise the People to power, for in the multitude all things are comprehended."[4] But the oligarchist contends that "there is nothing more unintelligent or more violent than a crowd; a crowd is good for nothing. To escape from a despot's violence only to be caught up in the violence of an unruly mob would be utterly intolerable. What a despot does, he does knowingly; the common folk do not even know what they are doing. How could they, since they are untaught and have had no experience of the finer things of life?" But it is the monarchist, Darius, who prevails; he asserts that the best state is the one ruled by the best man in it, an argument similar to Heraclitus's idea of the rarity of "the best." Democracy defeats itself anyway, Darius thinks, for "where commoners rule there cannot fail to be corruption."

Herodotus describes the auditors voting in favor of Darius and monarchy (there is no ironic intent in the democratic procedure followed in the debate). But the argument of Otanes in favor of democracy has its echoes in Greek literature, perhaps most notably in the funeral oration of Pericles in Thucydides, and also in *The Suppliants*, where Theseus defends democratic institutions against the criticisms of a herald from Creon. And in his *Politics*, while considering a range of arguments for and against democracy, Aristotle expresses the possibility that collective judgment may be superior to the judgment of an individual:

> It is possible that the many, no one of whom taken singly is a good man, may yet taken all together be better than the few, not individually but collectively, in the same way that a feast to which all contribute is better than one given at one man's expense. For where

4. Herodotus, *The Persian Wars*, tr. George Rawlinson (New York: Modern Library, 1942), Book III, chaps. 80–83.

there are many people, each has some share of goodness and intelligence, and when these are brought together, they become as it
were one multiple man with many pairs of feet and hands and many
minds.[5]

Aristotle goes on to assert that "the general public is a better judge of
works of music and poetry [than the few]; some judge some parts,
some others, but their joint pronouncement is a verdict upon the
whole." One might construe this passage as a description of how
classics become classics, not through the scrutiny of a handful of dis-
cerning critics, but through a much broader process of popular accep-
tance which spans decades and generations. Far from being elitist,
true classics are the common possessions of mankind. But though
Aristotle's "multiple man"—body politic or social organism—points
toward modern theories of public opinion, he had reservations about
his theory of the collective wisdom of the multitude. Not all collec-
tivities are alike; groups of animals do not generate group wisdom or
group virtue; "and some men are hardly any better than wild
animals."

The argument of Otanes, that "in the multitude all things are comprehended," is in one sense a truism: "the multitude" is everything
and everybody. In another sense, however, it merely reverses the
faulty social arithmetic of Heraclitus, as does Aristotle's tentative pos-
tulation of collective wisdom. For just as the individual may be either
wise or unwise, virtuous or evil, so the "multiple man" of society may
be either virtuous or evil—or both at different times, or even both
simultaneously. There is no guarantee in numbers that a democratic
society will govern itself rationally any more than there is that a despot
will be enlightened. Besides, it is easier to believe in the existence of a
single good man than in goodness distributed among a number of
ordinary men who have vices as well as virtues. To be operative, such
diffused goodness must somehow be channeled through institutions
capable of activating it. Until the American and French revolutions,
the possibility of creating such institutions received little attention
from social theorists, who more often than not merely rehearsed the
two axioms of Heraclitus's politics: virtue is rare; the multitude is

5. Aristotle, *The Politics*, tr. T. A. Sinclair (New York: Penguin, 1962), p. 123.

bestial; monarchy, oligarchy, and aristocracy are therefore the only viable forms of government. Contemporary theories of mass culture and society likewise often do little more than echo Heraclitus's axioms.

Another element in Greek political theory, not stemming from Heraclitus, shows up in modern conservative versions of negative classicism. Aristotle thinks of democracy as a decadent form of a better kind of government that he calls "polity" or "constitutional government," in which rule is "exercised by the bulk of the citizens for the good of the whole community." There are three basic kinds of government, each with a characteristic "deviation": as "tyranny" is the deviation from "kingship" and "oligarchy" from "aristocracy," so "democracy" is the deviation from "polity" (115–16). Aristotle seems to be echoing Plato's speculations about how forms of government succeed each other regressively rather than progressively. In the eighth book of *The Republic*, Socrates turns to the model of decadence in Hesiod, from the Golden Age through ages of silver and brass down to that of iron— the last a metaphor for the degenerate present. Socrates suggests that if the ideal state exists anywhere, it does not lie in the future but in the past, for types of government decline from better to worse: "timocracy" or "the government of honour" follows "aristocracy" or "the government of the best"; when the "timocratical man" falls prey to the pursuit of wealth, "oligarchy" arises, in which the pursuit of wealth makes the state even weaker. "And then the state falls sick, and is at war with itself." Socrates continues: "Then democracy comes into being after the poor have conquered their opponents, slaughtering some and banishing some, while to the remainder they give an equal share of freedom and power; and this is the form of government in which the magistrates are commonly elected by lot."[6]

Socrates has nothing but contempt for democracy, which he sees as a condition of mindless anarchy, though the form of government which succeeds it—"tyranny"—is undoubtedly worse. Socrates' description of democracy sounds very much like Edmund Burke's of the French Revolution or José Ortega y Gasset's of "the revolt of the masses": nobody pays any attention to traditional authority; the incompetent majority shoulder aside the competent minority; sons no

6. Plato, *The Republic*, tr. Benjamin Jowett (Cleveland: World, 1946), p. 302.

longer obey their fathers; even the animals are "infected" by the pursuit of liberty at all costs:

> No one who does not know would believe, how much greater is the liberty which the animals who are under the dominion of man have in a democracy than in any other State: for truly, the she-dogs, as the proverb says, are as good as their she-mistresses, and the horses and asses have a way of marching along with all the rights and dignities of freemen; and they will run at anybody who come in their way if he does not leave the road clear for them: and all things are just ready to burst with liberty. [310]

"The excessive increase of anything often causes a reaction in the opposite direction," says Socrates. And "the excess of liberty, whether in States or individuals, seems only to pass into excess of slavery." Thus he expresses a paradox familiar in modern conservative and liberal thought, from Burke and de Maistre through Tocqueville and Mill down to Spengler, Ortega, and beyond: "Tyranny naturally arises out of democracy, and the most aggravated form of tyranny and slavery out of the most extreme form of liberty" (311).

Greek intellectuals thus offer versions of most of the assumptions to be found in modern antidemocratic theory. Heraclitus and Plato, and, more tentatively, Herodotus and Aristotle, believe that "the many" are irrational or bestial; that they tend to be unruly and potentially revolutionary; and that excellence is rare and "noble" while evil and inferiority are "common" (or, to use a modern expression, "mass"). Further, Herodotus, Plato, and Aristotle all present the idea of the inevitable degeneration of democracy into tyranny, a theory echoed by Polybius. And from all of them may be inferred the existence of two antithetical cultures or teachings: that which meets the standards of the cultivated few and that which pleases the ignorant many. What the Greek philosophers include in either category, however, is quite different from what we now tend to classify as "high" and "mass" culture. Though Aristotle thinks that poets express universal truths, Plato banishes them from the Republic for defaming the gods and misleading the people, and he criticizes other representational artists for similar reasons. And Heraclitus speaks contemptuously of those who "follow the bards." Only the discipline of reason can escape the charge of mendacity which the more austere Greek philosophers level against the arts.

The Greek classics line the most prominent shelves in the library of high culture. They also contain many statements to support the aristocratic or elitist views of the defenders of high culture against the threats of the modern and the mass. It is at least easier to find in Greek literature arguments against democracy than arguments for it.[7] But the Greek heritage is ambiguous, for while it provides many precedents for the argument that culture can only be aristocratic, it also suggests that the healthiest cultures grow in democratic soil. Even in antiquity it was commonly assumed that there must have been some correlation between the flourishing of the arts and the relative freedom of Athenian institutions in the fifth century. In discussing the decay of eloquence and the other arts in his own age (either the first or the third century A.D.), Longinus asks:

> Are we to accept the well-worn view that democracy is the kindly nurse of great men, and that great men of letters may be said to have flourished only under democracy and perished with it? For freedom, they say, has the power to foster the imaginations of high-souled men and to inspire them with hope, and with it there spreads the keenness of mutual rivalry and an eager competition for the first place. Furthermore, by reason of the prizes which are open to all in republics, the intellectual gifts of orators are continually sharpened by practice and as it were kept bright by rubbing, and, as might be expected, these gifts, fostered in freedom, help to shed light on the affairs of state.[8]

Though such a view was less "well-worn" among the original makers of Hellenic culture, they too sometimes made the connection between the partially democratic institutions of Athens and its cultural greatness. Even Herodotus, who made the monarchist Darius prevail over the democrat Otanes, could write: "The Athenians went from strength to strength, thus proving that equality is an excellent thing."[9] And in his funeral speech, Pericles declares that "our city is an education to Greece"—an example of patriotic hyperbole which history has transformed into meager understatement. "Just as our political life is

7. A. H. M. Jones, *Athenian Democracy* (Oxford: Blackwell, 1969), especially chap. 3, "The Athenian Democracy and Its Critics." See also T. A. Sinclair, *A History of Greek Political Thought* (London: Routledge & Kegan Paul, 1951).

8. Longinus, in Cosmo Rodewald, ed., *Democracy: Ideas and Realities*, chap. 44.

9. Herodotus, *The Persian Wars*, pp. 407–8.

free and open," Pericles says, "so is our day-to-day life in our relations
with each other." And freedom extends to the cultivation of the arts:
"When our work is over, we are in a position to enjoy all kinds of
recreation for our spirits. There are various kinds of contests and
sacrifices regularly throughout the year; in our own homes we find a
beauty and a good taste which delight us every day and which drive
away our cares. Then the greatness of our city brings it about that all
the good things from all over the world flow in to us."[10] One might
suppose that freedom and cultivated leisure would make the Athenians unfit for war. Not so, says Pericles: "Our love of what is beautiful
does not lead to extravagance; our love of the things of the mind does
not make us soft" (118).

Although Marx cites the Greek experience to show "that certain
periods of highest development of art stand in no direct connection
with the general development of society," thus posing difficulties for
those of his followers who have wanted to assert that the connection is
always direct, other modern writers agree with Pericles and Longinus.[11] Hegel says that a "vital freedom" existed in Athens, "and a
vital equality of manners and mental culture." The key aspects of
Athenian character were "the independence of the social units and a
culture animated by the spirit of beauty."[12] And Matthew Arnold,
that key figure in the defense of the classics against the threats of
democracy and of "ignorant armies clashing by night," agrees:

> "We have freedom," says Pericles, "for individual diversities of
> opinion and character; we do not take offense at the tastes and habits
> of our neighbour if they differ from our own." Yes in Greece, in the
> Athens of Pericles, there is toleration; but in England, in the En-
> gland of the sixteenth century?—the Puritans are then in full
> growth. So that with regard to these characteristics of civilization of a
> modern spirit . . . the superiority . . . rests with the age of
> Pericles.[13]

10. Thucydides, *History of the Peloponnesian War*, tr. Rex Warner (Baltimore:
Penguin, 1954), Book II, chap. 4, pp. 115–23.

11. Karl Marx, *Introduction to the Critique of Political Economy*, section 8, in Lee
Baxandall and Stefan Morawski, eds., *Marx and Engels on Literature and Art* (St.
Louis: Telos, 1973), p. 134.

12. Georg Wilhelm Friedrich Hegel, *The Philosophy of History*, tr. J. Sibree (New
York: Dover, 1956), p. 260.

13. Matthew Arnold, "On the Modern Element in Literature," in *On the Classical
Tradition*, ed. R. H. Super (Ann Arbor: University of Michigan Press, 1960), p. 25.

One modern writer who insists that there is no correlation between democracy and the flourishing of Greek culture is Friedrich Nietzsche. In *The Birth of Tragedy*, he traces the origins of theater to the primitive synthesis of Apollonian and Dionysian tendencies in religious ritual. For the theory that sees an adumbration of Athenian democracy in the tragic chorus, he offers no comfort. The chorus was the original form of the drama; it was neither an "idealized spectator" nor a representative of "the populace over against" the nobility. "The latter interpretation, which sounds so grandly edifying to certain politicians . . . may have been suggested by a phrase in Aristotle, but this lofty notion can have had no influence whatever on the original formation of tragedy, whose purely religious origins would exclude not only the opposition between the people and their rulers, but any kind of political or social context."[14] Nietzsche thinks it is "blasphemous" to see in the chorus "a 'foreshadowing' of constitutional democracy, though others have not stuck at such blasphemy." On the contrary, he says, the death of tragedy occurred the moment a democratic note was sounded upon the stage, with the increased realism and secularism of Euripides. "Through him the common man found his way from the auditorium onto the stage." Through Euripides, too, Socratic skepticism found its way onto the stage, for he was "the first rational maker of tragedy" and "the poet of esthetic Socratism." With the appearance of these traits, there vanished the irrational, unashamedly noble Dionysian energy necessary to produce genuine tragedy. The age of Socrates was essentially "operatic" and inauthentic. Nietzsche offers a complicated analysis of the motives that he supposes drove Euripides unconsciously to undermine tragedy, but the result is simple enough: Greek drama "died by suicide" (69). But even if this disaster had not occurred, Nietzsche thinks, there would still be no reason to accept the thesis that democracy nurtured drama and the other arts, for "no ancient polity ever embodied constitutional democracy." What is more, "one dares to hope that ancient tragedy did not even foreshadow it" (47).

On this issue, however (as on many others), Nietzsche stands resolutely in the minority, for other students of Greece have continued to see a relationship between Athenian democracy and its culture. M. I. Finley says that "it would be foolhardy to make the . . . suggestion

14. Friedrich Nietzsche, *The Birth of Tragedy*, tr. Francis Golffing (Garden City N.Y.: Doubleday Anchor, 1956), p. 47.

that the link between tragedy and democracy was a simple, direct one." But that there was a complex, indirect link he does not doubt: "Evidently fifth-century Athens somehow provided the atmosphere in which this art could flourish."[15] Finley thinks that the link may lie "in the way the dramatists were encouraged . . . to explore the human soul," despite the ritualistic limits established by theatrical tradition.

> [The playwrights] could probe with astonishing latitude and freedom into the traditional myths and beliefs, and into fresh problems society was throwing up, such as the new Socratic emphasis on reason, or the humanity of slaves, or the responsibilities and corruption of power. They did so annually under the auspices of the state and Dionysus, before the largest gatherings of men, women and children (and even slaves) ever assembled in Athens. [86]

Less cautiously than Finley, the Marxist scholar George Thomson says that "Greek tragedy was one of the distinctive functions of Athenian democracy" and that Aeschylus was able "to take the tide of democracy at the flood."[16] According to Thomson, the first great tragedian "was a democrat who fought as well as wrote" (335). Thomson acknowledges that Athenian "democracy" was based on slave labor, which gradually eroded "free labor" and led to imperialist expansion and an increased reliance on money as a source of unity and power. "Such were the insoluble contradictions on which Athenian democracy wrecked itself" (338).

However that may be, both the right and the left have sought to enlist Greek culture and especially tragedy on their side of the ideological struggle. In this debate, which runs from our own time back through Nietzsche, Arnold, Marx, Hegel, and beyond, tragedy becomes a synecdoche for all that is highest and noblest in culture or civilization. As such, tragedy itself acts like a tragic hero with a thousand faces, repeatedly committing suicide and reviving from the time of Euripides forward. From one perspective or another, each new historical crisis is said to involve either the "death of tragedy" or its rebirth. By implication, at least, an age or a culture lacking "tragic vision" is an age or a culture decadent, hollow at the core. When he wrote *The Birth of Tragedy*, Nietzsche thought that the noblest of

---

15. M. I. Finley, *The Ancient Greeks: An Introduction to Their Life and Thought* (New York: Viking, 1964), p. 85.

16. George Thomson, *Aeschylus and Athens: A Study in the Social Origins of Drama* (New York: Grosset & Dunlap, 1968 [1941]), pp. 1 and 331.

ancient arts was being reborn in the works of Richard Wagner, an opinion that he soon repudiated with a vengeance. Wagner became for him the worst sort of artistic charlatan, mimicking the forms of the past in works that had none of their tragic content. In his later writings, Nietzsche equates Wagner with decadence and mass culture, the direct opposites of classical and tragic values: "Bayreuth is large-scale opera—and not even *good* opera. —The theater is a form of demolatry in matters of taste; the theater is a revolt of the masses, a plebiscite *against* good taste. —*This is precisely what is proved by the case of Wagner:* he won the crowd, he corrupted taste."[17]

Nietzsche proclaims the death of tragedy in the modern world as well as the death of God. Obituaries like his are frequent from the time of the French Revolution down to the present. The more recent the frame of reference, the more frequently the antithesis of tragedy turns out to be "mass culture"; the dramatic mass media—film, radio, television—are often held almost by definition to be destructive to tragic profundity. As Raymond Williams puts it, "In our own century, especially, when there has been a widespread sense of . . . civilisation being threatened, the use of the idea of tragedy to define a major tradition threatened or destroyed by an unruly present has been quite obvious."[18] In criticizing Nietzsche's theories, Williams also points out that Nietzsche transforms tragedy into an absolute, instead of into a historical series of genres or dramatic conventions that have evolved continuously and that are still adaptable to present conditions and media.

In *The Death of Tragedy* (1961), George Steiner, who like Nietzsche finds it difficult to believe that tragedy (or genuine culture) is alive and well in the modern era of democracy, industrialism, and bourgeois values, insists that "there is nothing democratic in the vision of tragedy."[19] Steiner argues that the democratization of the

17. Friedrich Nietzsche, *The Case of Wagner*, tr. Walter Kaufmann, together with *The Birth of Tragedy* (New York: Vintage, 1967), p. 183.

18. Raymond Williams, *Modern Tragedy* (Stanford: Stanford University Press, 1966), p. 16.

19. George Steiner, *The Death of Tragedy* (New York: Knopf, 1963), p. 241. Another well-known statement of the idea that tragedy is not possible in modern society is Joseph Wood Krutch, "The Tragic Fallacy," in *The Modern Temper: A Study and a Confession* (New York: Harcourt, Brace, 1929), pp. 115–43. For a refutation of Krutch, see Louis I. Bredvold, "The Modern Temper and Tragic Drama," *The Quarterly Review*, 61, 21 May 1955, pp. 207–13.

audience after the French Revolution has led to a decline in dramatic standards. Beset by secularization and commercialization, drama through the nineteenth century "was becoming what it is today: mere entertainment" (116). Again, Steiner is not far from Nietzsche, who interprets the entire span of modern history, from the advent of Christianity forward, as hostile to the tragic vision. Nietzsche's thinking about tragedy has at least two consequences for later theories of democracy and culture. One is to make "the tragic sense" an ideal attainable only by a few exceptional individuals, such as Nietzsche himself, "the first tragic philosopher." The other is to identify the artist or tragedian with the exceptional individual who understands the tragic, thus rendering the notion of an informed audience or a community of culture—a primary value in Raymond Williams's theories—extremely problematic. Both these consequences are evident in the elitist tendencies of the *fin de siècle* "decadent" and "symbolist" movements.

Steiner, like Nietzsche, identifies tragedy as almost exclusively Greek, with a few astonishing outcroppings and rebirths in the Renaissance, neoclassical France, and the era of Henrik Ibsen and August Strindberg. Like Arnold and Nietzsche, Steiner juxtaposes Hebraism and Hellenism, arriving at the idea that the entire Judeo-Christian tradition has contributed to the demise of tragedy. Because Judaism and Christianity insist on justice and on some ultimate divine compensation for suffering, tragedy is alien to them. Steiner, moreover, again like Nietzsche, identifies socialism with Hebraism: "Marxism is characteristically Jewish in its insistence on justice and reason, and Marx repudiated the entire concept of tragedy" (4).

But Marx had only praise for Greek tragedy. Paul Lafargue records of his father-in-law that "every year he read Aeschylus in the Greek original."[20] Steiner's assertion runs counter to the idea that Marx was an economist "with a sense of the tragic." Michael Harrington, who makes this observation in his "hopeful book about decadence," *The Accidental Century* (1965), also defends the possibility of tragedy in democratic, modern conditions: "Abundance and technology certainly threaten the aristocratic right to tragedy. They could level everyone down to a common denominator, sating material needs and creating a

20. Paul Lafargue in Baxandall and Morawski, eds., *Marx and Engels on Literature and Art*, p. 150.

spiritual hunger. But they could also raise everyone up to the level of the tragic. It is quite possible that a decent society in which men die from death rather than plagues and famines will have a stark sense of the tragic."[21] Like Harrington, Raymond Williams in *Modern Tragedy* offers definitions compatible with Marxism, liberalism, democracy, and, perhaps most important, modernity. Tragedy is not one thing, identified with an irretrievable ideal past. It is instead a complex set of traditions, conventions, attitudes, talents, beliefs, theories, appearing and reappearing through history in many shapes. Defining a single tragic vision in terms of modern readings of Greek drama and identifying this vision as the primary element in genuine culture are illogical on several grounds. According to Williams:

> For the last century and a half (significantly during the loosening of Christian belief) many attempts have been made to systematise a Greek tragic philosophy, and to transmit it as absolute. But it is not only that the tragedies we have are extremely resistant to this kind of systematisation, with evident and intractable differences between the three major tragedians. It is also that these precise issues—of Fate, Necessity and the nature of the Gods—were not systematised by the Greeks themselves: it is a culture marked by an extraordinary network of beliefs connected to institutions, practices, and feelings, but not by the systematic and abstract doctrines we would now call a theology or a tragic philosophy.[22]

In terms of its social basis, it is at least possible to say, as even Nietzsche acknowledges, that Greek tragedy was a communal, participatory, popular art form, though whether it might also be accurately described as "democratic" is a different question. The role of the audiences as judges of the plays is perhaps analogous to democratic procedures in the assembly, but both Plato and Aristotle believed that this was not the best arrangement. Aristotle says that dramatists who "pander to the taste of the spectators" are making a mistake.[23] And in *The Laws*, Plato writes: "The ancient and common custom of Hellas . . . did certainly leave the judgment [of tragedy] to the body of spectators, who determined the victor by show of hands. But this custom has been the destruction of the poets; for they are now

21. Michael Harrington, *The Accidental Century* (Baltimore: Penguin, 1966), pp. 162–63.

22. Williams, *Modern Tragedy*, p. 17.

23. Aristotle, *Poetics*, tr. T. S. Dorsch (Baltimore: Penguin, 1965), chap. 13, p. 49.

in the habit of composing with a view to please the bad taste of their judges."[24] Then as now, "giving the public what it wants" seemed an unsatisfactory method for producing lasting artistic achievement.

Despite such reservations, drama and the other arts were clearly and fully public in ancient Greece, crucial achievements and possessions of the commonwealth. In light of the communal basis of Greek drama, Aristophanes' comedy *The Knights* offers an ironic counterpoint. In the "new comedy" that emerged after Aristophanes, even more than in the tragedies of Euripides, Nietzsche sees an "ignoble" mentality marked by a "cleverness and cunning" which he associates both with "bourgeois mediocrity" and with "slave morality." Aristophanes escapes these charges partly because he is such an acute satirist of his age. *The Knights* is a satire upon democracy, no doubt much to Nietzsche's liking. Aristophanes invites his fellow Athenians to view themselves in the guise of the foolish Demos,

> hot
> Of temper, ignorant, full as full can be
> Of votes and motions, fretful, elderly,
> And slightly deaf. . . .[25]

The problem is that Demos has been misled by his slave, "a Paphlagonian tanner" who represents the Athenian demagogue Cleon. Two other slaves, representing the generals Demosthenes and Nicias, try to win Demos away from the Paphlagonian tanner by getting him to accept as his guide a despicable sausage-monger (who is later named "Agoracritus," or "chosen in the agora"). At first, modesty makes the sausage-monger reluctant:

> Just think of the eddication I ain't had—
> Bar letters; and I mostly learnt 'em bad!

But Demosthenes reassures him:

> The pity is you learnt such things at all.
> 'Tis not for learning now that people call,
> Nor thoughtfulness, nor hearts of generous make.
> 'Tis ignorance and no scruples—   [32–33]

24. Plato, *The Laws*, in *Dialogues*, tr. Benjamin Jowett, 4 vols. (Oxford: Clarendon, 1953), IV, 659.

25. Aristophanes, *The Knights*, ed. and tr. Gilbert Murray (London: George Allen and Unwin, 1956).

advice that leads to the successful substitution of Agoracritus for the Paphlagonian tanner in the fickle heart of Demos.

It would be easy enough to interpret *The Knights* as an anti-democratic satire and let it go at that. But it can also be interpreted as a play that expresses Aristophanes' desire for democracy to work better and for his fellow citizens to make wiser choices. Demos is well-meaning enough, just bumbling and vain. *The Knights* in any event stands as a remarkable testament to the freedom and vigor of Athenian institutions, for when it appeared in 424 B.C. Cleon, Demosthenes, and Nicias were all powerful men. And if Demos in the assembly could be misled by a demagogue like Cleon, Demos in the theater could laugh at itself for being foolish. Such freedom to criticize and to laugh at both leaders and led, both "the few" and "the many," suggests the rightness of Matthew Arnold's estimate:

> Now the culminating age in the life of ancient Greece I call, beyond question, a great epoch; the life of Athens in the fifth century before our era I call one of the highly developed, one of the marking, one of the modern periods in the life of the whole human race. It has been said that the "Athens of Pericles was a vigorous man, at the summit of his bodily strength and mental energy." There was the utmost energy of life there, public and private; the most entire freedom, the most unprejudiced and intelligent observation of human affairs.[26]

In the Athens of Pericles, Socrates, and Aristophanes, it first became possible, as Arnold says in his sonnet on Sophocles, to "see life steadily and see it whole." And the sometimes opposed but sometimes also united ideas of popular participation in and state encouragement of the arts could not have grown sturdier roots.

ii

The experience of democracy in Athens did not give rise to a coherent and forceful tradition of democratic theory. Indeed, the debate about the best kind of government went mostly the other way, as in Herodotus and Plato. And reinforcing what the decline of the Greek city-states seemed to show, the history of Rome strongly suggested

26. Arnold, "On the Modern Element in Literature," p. 23.

that democratic institutions, even if desirable, were not durable. Rome became both an enormous city and an enormous empire, unmanageable by popular rule. The transition from republican government to imperial dictatorship under Augustus has served political theorists ever since as a model for the inevitable declension of democracy into its opposite, as in Oswald Spengler's "Caesarism," the ancestor of "Bonapartism" and "Hitlerism." Even among supporters of the Roman Republic, there was no great fondness for democracy: in contrast to Longinus, Cicero believed that the decline of Greece was due to its democratic institutions: "All Greek states are governed by impulsive votes taken while public meetings are in session. And to say nothing of present-day Greece, which has long since been dragged down into misery by the Greeks' own mismanagement, it was this one evil, the unrestrained and extravagant freedom of their public meetings, that brought about the destruction of the power, prosperity and glory that the Greeks at one time enjoyed."27 In writing about ordinary men and women, most Roman intellectuals adhere to the contemptuous attitudes of Heraclitus. Ramsay MacMullen has culled a "lexicon of snobbery" from Roman writers.28 Horace might be speaking for Roman stoicism as well as for the entire tradition of Roman satire when he writes, "I loathe the crowd and I avoid it" (*Odes III*, i, 1). He also considers his contemporaries degenerate versions of their forefathers, so that everything "modern" appears to be on a downhill slide. In a passage quoted by Ortega in *The Revolt of the Masses*, Horace writes: "Our fathers, viler than our grandfathers, begot us who are even viler, and we shall bring forth a progeny more degenerate still" (*Odes III*, vi, 46–48). These attitudes are also expressed by Juvenal, though he combines hatred for "the crowd" with sympathy for the poor man from the country who is cheated and abused by city slickers. The mob "rails against the condemned" Sejanus, although, had his conspiracy against Tiberius succeeded, it would gladly have proclaimed him emperor. "The people that once bestowed commands, consulships, legions and all else, now meddles no more and longs eagerly for just two things—*panem et circenses!*"

Juvenal's acerbic commentary contains several elements that recur

27. Cicero, in Cosmo Rodewald, ed., *Democracy: Ideas and Realities*, p. 118.
28. Ramsay MacMullen, *Roman Social Relations, 50 B.C. to A.D. 284* (New Haven: Yale University Press, 1974), pp. 138–41.

in later assertions of the inability of ordinary people to manage their lives intelligently. These elements include: (1) contempt for the average person; (2) what might be called "decadentism," or the belief that things were once better than they are now; (3) the belief that ordinary people in fact have the capacity to make intelligent decisions, an idea that follows from decadentism (since people once did live more rationally than they do now) but that contradicts the first element in the list; (4) contempt for politics; (5) the idea that the average man follows no greater or wiser authority than fortune; (6) the idea that what the average man wants—to be fed and to be entertained—are not worthy ends. Above all, Juvenal suggests that the people who compose "the mob of Remus" do not know where their best interests lie, an axiom in all versions of political and cultural conservatism. With the exception of the third, these elements correspond closely to modern anti-democratic versions of negative classicism—for example, those of Nietzsche, Spengler, and Ortega.

But Juvenal is not merely expressing a conservative animadversion to the desires of the "mob," for he also makes clear that it was the conscious policy of the imperial administrators to encourage and to meet the mob's demands. Augustus established the imperial practice of providing both games and free distributions of grain, and both he and his successors (Tiberius was something of an exception) participated willingly in both. At Rome under Augustus, some sixty-six days a year were devoted to public games; the figure rose to one hundred and thirty-five under Marcus Aurelius, although he found the games boring; and to at least one hundred and seventy-five in the fourth century.[29] Regular attendance at the arena was necessary for an emperor to retain his popularity, though it is also clear that most of them enjoyed an exciting round of gladiatorial mayhem as much as any of their bloodthirsty subjects. There is also some reason to suppose that "circuses" were at least as important a part of the policy as "bread." "The excellence of a government is shown no less by its concern for pastimes than by its concern for serious matters," wrote Fronto. "The people are, all in all, less avid for money than for spectacles; and . . . though distributions of corn and foodstuffs are enough to satisfy men

---

29. Samuel Dill, *Roman Society from Nero to Marcus Aurelius* (London: Macmillan, 1911), p. 234.

as individuals, spectacles are needed to satisfy the people as a whole."[30]

The problem raised by Juvenal, then, was not simply that of a brutal populace demanding and receiving brutal entertainments from their rulers. The pattern was a much more symbiotic one, in which the ruling classes and the ruled developed between them forms of mass entertainment rooted in shared tastes and interests. That these tastes were debased and sadistic in the extreme only adds to the enormity of their unconscious collusion. "The two most quantitatively destructive institutions in history," Michael Grant writes, "are Nazism and the Roman gladiators."[31] In both cases, large segments of the population collaborated with their rulers in the institutionalization of mass murder, and in the case of the Roman games, mass murder was also served up as mass entertainment.

Juvenal's reaction, of course, is not the modern one of humanitarian horror, but that of the satirist railing against the fickleness of the mob, the loss of freedom, and the degeneracy of the age. But the Roman games and the dole can be interpreted as the customs of an imperial civilization at the height of its vitality, rather than as symptoms of decadence. In the fullest study of this aspect of ancient history, *Le pain et le cirque* (1978), Paul Veyne has challenged the leftist idea that "bread and circuses" involved a conspiracy of the ruling classes to bribe the masses into political acquiescence. *Panem et circenses*, Veyne believes, must instead be viewed in light of "the sociology of the gift" as an ancient example of public munificence or *évergétisme*, similar to the building of temples, roads, and aqueducts. The gladiatorial games may seem to us, as they seemed to Juvenal, a sign of the "depoliticization" of the masses and of the waning of public spirit. Not so, Veyne suggests: their provision by the emperors and the public demand for them show an engagement in the affairs of the city on at least a symbolic level. "The emperor's luxury was not only an egoistic consumption; it was also that of a public benefactor who gives specta-

30. Fronto quoted by Roland Auguet, *Cruelty and Civilization: The Roman Games* (London: George Allen and Unwin, 1972), p. 187.
31. Michael Grant, *Gladiators* (London: Weidenfeld and Nicholson, 1967), p. 8. The same judgment has been made by others—for example, by Simone Weil in "The Great Beast," *Selected Essays* (London: Oxford University Press, 1962), pp. 121 and 130.

cles to his subjects. The egoism of the potentate who drinks all alone
passed, wrongly, for the conduct of a tyrant; as an act of propaganda,
in the true sense of the word, Vespasian ordered the demolition of the
palace of gold that Nero had built for himself and erected on the site
the ampitheatre of the Coliseum, destined to receive the Roman people."[32] Veyne's study provides a good antidote for the easy assumption that "bread and circuses" was a Machiavellian strategy of the
Roman emperors or even that it necessarily corresponded to "decadence." Citing David Riesman and Thorstein Veblen on "conspiracy
theories" of mass culture, Veyne argues that the notion of exchanging
absorption in circuses for political responsibility is historically inaccurate, and also that the high point of "bread and circuses" corresponds
to the high point of the Roman Empire and not to its decline.[33] But
that there was a sort of decadence in the development of "bread and
circuses" is evident from Veyne's own analysis of the evolution from
the duties of the wealthier citizens of the Greek city-states, who were
expected to raise, equip, and feed armies and erect public works, to
the *liberalitas* of the Roman emperors and nobles, who supported and
entertained the unemployed urban masses through a cloying combination of welfare and spectacle which helped to undermine the
imperial economy and ultimately their own power.

If there was not a conscious conspiracy on the part of the rulers to
bribe the masses, there was still an unconscious collusion through
which the emperors and the urban "rabble" gradually weakened the
position of the senatorial nobles. In his *Considerations on the Causes
of the Greatness of the Romans and Their Decline*, Montesquieu gives
an account of this collusion:

> The people of Rome, who were called *plebs*, did not hate the worst
> emperors. After they had lost their power, and were no longer
> occupied with war, they had become the vilest of all peoples. They
> regarded commerce and the arts as things fit for slaves, and the
> distributions of grain that they received made them neglect the land.
> They had been accustomed to games and spectacles. When they no
> longer had tribunes to listen to or magistrates to elect, these useless
> things became necessities, and idleness increased their taste for

32. Paul Veyne, *Le pain et le cirque: Sociologie historique d'un pluralisme politique*
(Paris: Seuil, 1976), p. 681 (my translation).
33. Ibid., p. 85.

them. Thus Caligula, Nero, Commodus, and Caracalla were lamented by the people because of their very madness, for they wildly loved what the people loved, and contributed with all their power and even their persons to the people's pleasures. For them these rulers were prodigal of all the riches of the empire, and when these were exhausted, the people—looking on untroubled while all the great families were being despoiled—enjoyed the fruits of the tyranny. And their joy was pure, for they found security in their own baseness. Such princes naturally hated good men: they knew they were not approved of by them. Indignant at meeting contradiction or silence from an austere citizen, intoxicated by the plaudits of the populace, they succeeded in imagining that their government produced public felicity, and that only ill-intentioned men could censure it.[34]

It would be difficult to compose a better commentary on Juvenal than Montesquieu's, or for that matter a better description of one sort of mass tyranny.

That no Roman citizen thought of the gladiatorial combats as murder goes without saying. Juvenal is silent on the matter, but his contempt for gladiators, women gladiators, and aristocrats who follow the games too avidly suggests that his view is probably close to the one expressed by Tacitus. Describing the gladiatorial games given in honor of Germanicus and Drusus, Tacitus complains that "the latter was abnormally fond of bloodshed." But he adds: "Admittedly it was worthless blood."[35] There could be no grounds for humanitarian protest when it was felt that the victims were not fully human. In his gruesome celebration of the games, *De Spectaculis*, Martial speaks of the "dangerous crowd" of "the guilty" being so numerous that "the huge arena" cannot hold them all; they deserve what they get. Martial thinks it quite wonderful to see a criminal crucified and torn to shreds by a "Caledonian bear." The criminal's "mangled limbs lived, though the parts dripped gore, and in all his body was nowhere a body's shape." Martial continues in this vein for some thirty-three sections, praising Caesar and extolling spilled blood and guts as signs of Rome's

34. Montesquieu, *Considerations on the Causes of the Greatness of the Romans and their Decline*, tr. David Lowenthal (New York: The Free Press and Collier-Macmillan, 1965), p. 137.

35. Tacitus, *The Annals of Imperial Rome*, tr. Michael Grant (New York: Penguin, 1977), p. 75.

greatness.[36] In contrast to Pericles' funeral oration, here is patriotic hyperbole that history has caused to look grossly inflated. As W. E. H. Lecky wrote in his *History of European Morals*, Martial's *De Spectaculis* "is not more horrible from the atrocities it recounts than from the perfect absence of all feeling of repulsion or compassion it everywhere displays."[37]

In contrast to Lecky, Nietzsche sees no reason to criticize the games on moral grounds, except as symptoms of social and esthetic decadence. He can even mention them in the same breath as tragedy, claiming both to be motivated by the lust for cruelty. He seems to contradict his more frequent and characteristic insistence on the uniqueness, profundity, and cultural primacy of tragedy when he rejects the Aristotelian ideas of catharsis and "tragic pity":

> What constitutes the painful voluptuousness of tragedy is cruelty; what seems agreeable in so-called tragic pity, and at bottom in everything sublime, up to the highest and most delicate shudders of metaphysics, receives its sweetness solely from the admixture of cruelty. What the Roman in the arena, the Christian in the ecstasies of the cross, the Spaniard at an auto-da-fe or bullfight, the Japanese of today when he flocks to tragedies, the laborer in a Parisian suburb who feels a nostalgia for bloody revolutions, the Wagnerienne who "submits to" *Tristan and Isolde*, her will suspended—what all of them enjoy and seek to drink in with mysterious ardor are the spicy potions of the great Circe, "cruelty."[38]

Perhaps all culture has sadomasochistic roots, as Nietzsche here contends. If so, how is one to claim primacy for tragedy over other forms of cruelty, including the Roman games? Instead of occupying a transcendent, ideal category, tragedy blurs into the general ruck of cultural production, with nothing to distinguish it from the kind of bloody spectacle celebrated by Martial. This is hardly the tendency in Nietzsche's other writings about tragedy, in which he gives it the status of the highest, rarest, least accessible value.

---

36. Martial, *De Spectaculis Liber*, in *Epigrams*, tr. Walter Ker, 2 vols. (Cambridge, Mass.: Loeb Classical Library, 1919), I, pp. 7–9.

37. W. E. H. Lecky, *The History of European Morals from Augustus to Charlemagne*, 2 vols. (New York: Appleton, 1910), I, 280, n. 3.

38. Friedrich Nietzsche, *Beyond Good and Evil*, tr. Walter Kaufmann (New York: Vintage, 1966), pp. 158–59.

As the Roman games grew more popular, the fine arts declined. Longinus was not alone in worrying about "the decay of eloquence" which marked his age. In the *Satyricon*, Petronius has Eumolpus say: "As for our own times, why, we are so besotted with drink, so steeped in debauchery, that we lack the strength even to study the great achievements of the past. One and all we traduce the dead and slander our great tradition."[39] How much of the decadence that Petronius records can be blamed on the bread and circuses policy is uncertain, but it is at least clear that "the influence of the games gradually pervaded the whole texture of Roman life."[40] One of the victims of the arena was the theater. Tragedy and comedy had to compete with gladiatorial combats and chariot races for spectators, and the arena won a slow victory over the stage. Terence had audiences walk out of his plays to watch rope dancers and gladiators.[41] The theaters themselves came to be used for combats and displays of wild beasts. Cruder types of dramatic entertainment, pantomime and farce, evolved partly to meet the competition of the games, and these relied heavily on stage effects, obscenity, and other forms of sensationalism. Gradually the viciousness of the stage approximated the viciousness of the arena. It is no wonder that Juvenal and other writers treat actors and actresses with as much contempt as they treat gladiators; if anything, they see the stage as even more corrupt and corrupting than the arena.[42]

Christianity eventually brought about the abolition of gladiatorial combats (and of the persecution of Christians); it also caused the closing of the theaters.[43] Before its spread, humanitarian protests against the bloodshed in the arenas were rare. Of the few that were made, the most forceful was Seneca's. He especially disapproved of the slaughter of defenseless criminals and other non-gladiators who were merely herded into the arenas between main performances and mowed down like cattle. "In the morning they throw men to the lions and the bears; at noon, they throw them to the spectators." Seneca

39. Petronius, *Satyricon*, tr. William Arrowsmith (Ann Arbor: University of Michigan Press, 1959), p. 90.
40. Lecky, *History of European Morals*, I, 274.
41. Margarette Bieber, *The History of the Greek and Roman Theatre* (Princeton: Princeton University Press, 1939), p. 312.
42. Dill, *Roman Society from Nero to Marcus Aurelius*, p. 86.
43. Bieber, *The History of the Greek and Roman Theatre*, p. 428.

believed that these gruesome proceedings devalued life and brutalized the characters of the audience. "Man is a thing which is sacred to mankind. But nowadays he is killed in play, for fun!"[44]

As Roman stoicism generally foreshadows the ascetic ideals of Christianity, so Seneca's protest foreshadows the more effective protests of the church fathers. Special credit in this regard must go to the monk Telemachus, who in 404 A.D. entered an arena to stop a gladiatorial combat:

> A sudden strength from heaven,
> As some great shock may wake a palsied limb,
> Turn'd him again to boy, for up he sprang,
> And glided lightly down the stairs, and o'er
> The barrier that divided beast from man
> Slipt, and ran on, and flung himself between
> The gladiatorial swords, and call'd "Forbear
> In the great name of Him who died for men,
> Christ Jesus!" For one moment afterward
> A silence follow'd as of death, and then
> A hiss as from a wilderness of snakes,
> Then one deep roar as of a breaking sea,
> And then a shower of stones that stoned him dead,
> And then once more a silence as of death.
> His dream became a deed that waked the world.[45]

This event, described here in Tennyson's poem "St. Telemachus," caused the emperor Honorius to prohibit gladiatorial contests, though this prohibition was not very effective and though other games—chariot racing, animal baiting—continued wherever there were arenas and audiences.

One who agreed with Telemachus that the games were an abomination was Salvianus, the presbyter of Marseilles. About 450 A.D., Salvianus recorded his sorrow and rage against those of his fellow Christians who, in the midst of barbarian depredations, continued to demand circuses.

44. Seneca's protest is cited and commented upon by Michael Grant in *Gladiators*, pp. 117–18.

45. Alfred, Lord Tennyson, "St. Telemachus," in Christopher Ricks, ed., *The Poems of Tennyson* (New York: Norton, 1969), pp. 1431–33.

Do you then seek public shows, O citizen of Treves [capital of Gaul]?
Where, pray, are they to be given? Over the pyres and ashes, the
bodies and blood of the dead? For what part of your city is free from
these? Where has blood not been shed, where are bodies and mangled limbs not strewn? Everywhere the city's appearance betrays its
capture, everywhere are the horror of captivity and the image of
death. The remains of a most unhappy people lie on the graves of
their dead, yet you ask for circuses; the city is blackened by fire, yet
you put on a festive countenance![46]

The image of the decadent citizens of Treves reveling at the circus
while the barbarians pound down the gates sums up the association of
"bread and circuses" with social calamity which is usually at least
implicit in modern literature. To this image, Salvianus adds an idea
that also recurs through the ages: the coming of the barbarians may be
preferable to urban decadence and wantonness, a necessary scourge or
cleansing, God's just wrath visited upon the wicked imperial capitals
as it had once been visited upon the cities of the plain. For the
barbarians, though pagan, are innocent of civilized corruptions: "I
must return again to my oft-repeated contention, what have the barbarians like this? Where in their lands are circuses, where are theaters, where those other wicked vices that are the ruin of our hope and
salvation? Even if they had such things, being pagans, their error
would involve less offence to what is sacred" (168). Salvianus's praise
of barbarian innocence has recurred in many contexts through the
ages, down to Byron's "Childe Harold's Pilgrimage" and beyond.

"Mark well, O Christian, how many unclean names have made the
circus their own."[47] Telemachus and Salvianus were not the only early
Christians who protested against the circuses and gladiatorial games.
In his *De Spectaculis*, the most energetic and sweeping of all the
protests made by the church fathers against the public amusements
and games of the ancient world, the "gloomy Tertullian" writes: "If we
can plead that cruelty is allowed us, if impiety, if brute savagery, by all
means let us go to the amphitheatre." There one would see as many

---

46. Salvianus, *On the Government of God*, tr. Eva M. Sanford (New York: Columbia University Press, 1930), pp. 184–85.

47. Tertullian, *Apology and De Spectaculis*, tr. T. R. Glover (New York: The Loeb
Classical Library, 1931), p. 253.

demons as men reveling in violence and the pleasures of the flesh. The public shows are "idolatry"; they "belong to the devil, his pomp and his angels." Tertullian acknowledges that Saint Paul had referred not unfavorably to the Greek games at Tarsus (1 Cor. 9:24), but he condemns boxing, wrestling, and all athletic contests anyway. The fact that the Greek games had involved public participation but that the Roman games had become purely "spectator sports" had caused as much concern among the Romans as any of the games' other features, and may have been the origin of the maxim "Many spectators and few men."[48] But this is not a distinction that Tertullian cares to make. Nor does he distinguish between gladiatorial combats and chariot races on the one hand, and theatrical and musical entertainments on the other: "tragedies and comedies" are just as "bloody and lustful, impious and prodigal" as gladiator shows; they also "teach outrage and lust." *De Spectaculis*, then, condemns all forms of public amusement: "*Omne enim spectaculum sine concussione spiritus non est*" (There is no public spectacle without violence to the spirit) (268–71).

On the surface, at least, Tertullian's *De Spectaculis* could not be more opposed to the crass sadism of Martial's *De Spectaculis*. The contrast illustrates the extremes of moral viewpoint which existed in the ancient world. Both Martial and Tertullian were educated men—intellectuals of sorts—but their attitudes toward "spectacles" were hardly restricted to the intellectual elites. Martial's brutality had its obvious reflection in the brutality of the mass audiences that filled the arenas, whereas Tertullian's opposition to that brutality had its reflection in the mass movement of Christianity. The examples of Martial and Tertullian should help to dispel any facile division of people, ancient or modern, into brutalized masses and sensitive elites, for it is usually the case that the worst and the best *moral* features of a culture appeal to everyone, whether educated or not. In contrast to literacy, philosophical and scientific ideas, and perhaps esthetic sensibility (though this is much more dubious), morality has never been the monopoly of an aristocratic or intellectual elite.

At about the time that Telemachus was martyred, Saint Augustine recorded the seduction of his friend Alypius by the games. It is a familiar story, retold with countless variations, perhaps most fre-

48. Cited by Auguet, *Cruelty and Civilization*, p. 195.

quently in puritanical pamphlets and sermons (themselves staples of popular culture in all ages), warning the innocent against the seductiveness of wine, women, song, games, gambling, plays, dancing, painting, novels. One thinks of Don Quixote's seduction by romances, although Alypius falls prey to something obviously more pernicious than *Amadis of Gaul.* A more exact analogy with Augustine's account would be the innumerable recent studies of the deleterious effects of televised violence on our own society of spectators. Because of its suggestiveness as a pattern, I quote it in its entirety:

> [Alypius] went to Rome ahead of me to study law and there, strange to relate, he became obsessed with an extraordinary craving for gladiatorial shows. At first he detested these displays and refused to attend them. But one day during the season for this cruel and bloodthirsty sport he happened to meet some friends and fellow-students returning from their dinner. In a friendly way they brushed aside his resistance . . . and carried him off to the arena.
>
> "You may drag me there bodily," he protested, "but do you imagine that you can make me watch the show and give my mind to it? I shall be there, but it will be just as if I were not present, and I shall prove myself stronger than you or the games."
>
> He did not manage to deter them by what he said, and perhaps the very reason why they took him with them was to discover whether he would be as good as his word. When they arrived at the arena, the place was seething with the lust for cruelty. They found seats as best they could and Alypius shut his eyes tightly, determined to have nothing to do with these atrocities. If only he had closed his ears as well! For an incident in the fight drew a great roar from the crowd, and this thrilled him so deeply that he could not contain his curiosity. Whatever had caused the uproar, he was confident that, if he saw it, he would find it repulsive and remain master of himself. So he opened his eyes, and his soul was stabbed with a wound more deadly than any which the gladiator, whom he was so anxious to see, had received in his body. He fell, and fell more pitifully than the man whose fall had drawn that roar of excitement from the crowd. The din had pierced his ears and forced him to open his eyes, laying his soul open to receive the wound which struck it down. This was presumption, not courage. The weakness of his soul was in relying upon itself instead of trusting in You.
>
> When he saw the blood, it was as though he had drunk a deep draught of savage passion. Instead of turning away, he fixed his eyes upon the scene and drank in all its frenzy, unaware of what he was doing. He revelled in the wickedness of the fighting and was drunk

with the fascination of bloodshed. He was no longer the man who had come to the arena, but simply one of the crowd which he had joined, a fit companion for the friends who had brought him.

Need I say more? He watched and cheered and grew hot with excitement, and when he left the arena, he carried away with him a diseased mind which would leave him no peace until he came back again, no longer simply together with the friends who had first dragged him there, but at their head, leading new sheep to the slaughter. Yet you stretched out your almighty, ever merciful hand, O God, and rescued him from this madness.[49]

In 1972, under the aegis of Senator Richard Pastore's Senate Communications Subcommittee, the United States Surgeon General's Office issued a report titled *Television and Growing Up.* Having surveyed hundreds of supposedly scientific studies, the report concluded that too much televised violence makes our society more violent and more frightening than it would be without televised violence. Ten years later a second government report reached the same conclusion. These reports seem doomed to be historically tautological; Augustine anticipated them by fifteen centuries.

Before the influence of Christianity closed the arenas and the theaters, the views expressed by Suetonius in his *Lives of the Caesars* were probably typical of those held by the majority of Romans. When he complains about Caligula's cruelty, Seutonius has in mind cruelty to the public rather than to the victims of the arena. The idea seems to be that Caligula did not restrict his sadism within the limits of decency and that he violated the standards for bread and circuses established by Augustus: "During gladiatorial shows he would have the canopies removed at the hottest time of the day and forbid anyone to leave; or cancel the regular programme, and pit feeble old fighters against decrepit criminals; or stage comic duels between respectable householders who happened to be physically disabled in some way or another. More than once he closed down the granaries and let the people go hungry."[50] Suetonius finds nothing more monstrous than Caligula's willful reversals of Augustus's policy, depriving his subjects both of food and of well-managed, sufficiently gory amusements. Suetonis goes on to list numerous instances of Caligula's "bloody-

49. Augustine, *Confessions*, tr. R. S. Pine-Coffin (Baltimore: Penguin, 1961), Book VI, part 8, pp. 122–23.

50. Suetonius, *The Twelve Caesars*, tr. Robert Graves (New York: Penguin, 1957), p. 163.

mindedness," but his grounds for doing so are not clearly humanitarian. He is more disturbed by Caligula's capriciousness, his dangerous unpredictability, than by his sadism. With a few notable excep-
tions such as Commodus, most of the other emperors were less
irregular in their administration of cruelty than Caligula. But it cannot
be doubted that cruelty was institutionalized in the Roman games and
that it formed the basis of a pattern of mass entertainment that lasted
for centuries. The idea of state-sponsored mass culture could not have
had a worse beginning.

Though Greek and Roman writers offer numerous arguments
against democracy, the actual record of ancient history offers little
support to those theorists who seek to combine aristocratic elitism
with literary classicism. Greek culture flourished in conditions of communal participation and equality—conditions that approximated democracy even though based on slavery. In contrast, the political and
cultural decadence of imperial Rome Juvenal blames on "the mob of
Remus" who want only "bread and circuses." But Juvenal also believes decadence to be linked to the forfeiture of popular power and
responsibility in the transition from the Republic to the Empire.
Bread and circuses is not a result of democracy, but of the destruction
of republican (that is, of partially democratic) institutions through the
triumph of Caesarism. The ancient legacy, then, suggests in several
ways that democracy and cultural greatness are not antithetical but
may instead be symbiotic. From the perspective of the two classicisms, however, democracy is only a prelude to tyranny, as it is according to Plato and Polybius. "Bread and circuses" becomes a name
for the process by which democracy turns into its opposite, the Republic into the Empire, the aristocratic Senate giving way to the
urban mob—or, in modern terms, the process by which a liberal
though hierarchical society, with its "creative elites" protected by
class institutions, turns into "mass society." But it has never been
apparent that democracy contains the seeds of its own destruction,
and its preservation and extension may be the only means of continuing the work of cultural growth and averting the disasters foreseen by
negative classicism. That the Athenian precedent of communal participation in cultural greatness was short-lived suggests only how easily a culture shared by both the few and the many can be corrupted by
tyranny, greed, poverty, and the machinery of empire.

CHAPTER 3

"The Opium of the People"

We, too, at this moment of world history which is perhaps symmetrical with the Roman decadence . . . seem caught in the same dilemma as the Romans of the IVth century: —either faith, or anarchy. Without faith, morality crumbles, for we cannot, up to the present at least, conceive of an ethics apart from a mysticism. . . . But, on the other hand, it is difficult for the Europeans of today, as it was for the hellenized Romans of the time of Julian the Apostate, to have the faith in dogma of younger races. —Must then we too put our hopes in the coming of the Barbarians?

—Fernand Gregh, preface to Alfred de Vigny's *Daphné*
(1913)

THEORIES of mass culture usually lead to the problem of religion. The social and industrial processes that have created the modern mass media seem intrinsically bound up with secularization. But mass culture also can be viewed as a substitute for mythology or even as an ersatz religion. Nineteenth and twentieth-century ideas about the relations between religion and culture range from the view that religion is the foundation of culture to the view that they are antithetical. An offshoot of the latter idea is the thesis that religion is essentially proletarian, of or for the masses; though for entirely opposite reasons, Marx and Nietzsche both maintain that the system of illusions embodied in religion is incompatible with enlightenment or genuine culture. But a separation of religion and culture is also possible from a theological point of view, as Kierkegaard shows. Both the Marxist and the existentialist traditions, moveover, attempt in their conflicting ways to show how the need for religion has been transformed under modern conditions into secular mass culture. For conservatives who believe that culture is dependent upon or even identical with religion, industrialized mass culture is anathema, the Antichrist. For radicals who believe that religion is mystification or the systematic delusion of the masses, the ersatz religion of mass culture is mystification of a new, perhaps more insidious kind.

During the gradual breakdown of ancient civilization, the bloody mayhem of the arenas gave way to the ceremonial observances of the Church as the center of most people's cultural attention. Bread and circuses met their nemesis in Christianity. Eusebius's account of the "spectacular" fates of the early Christian martyrs cannot easily be used to support Roman analogies for modern mass culture:

> Maturus, Sanctus, Blandina . . . were led forth to the wild beasts, to the public, and to the common exhibition of the inhumanity of the heathen, for the day of fighting with beasts was specially appointed for the Christians. Maturus and Sanctus passed through all torture in the amphitheater. . . . Blandina was hung on a stake and offered as a prey to the wild beasts that were let in. . . . Then, when none of the beasts would touch her, she was taken down from the stake and brought back into the jail. . . . Caesar wrote that they should be tortured to death, but that if any should recant they should be let go.[1]

In such a passage, are the modern masses forshadowed by the amphitheater spectators or by the martyred Christians, the unwilling entertainers? If such analogies are at all logical, the answer must be a double one. For if, as Nietzsche argues, the early Christians prefigure the modern masses and Christianity is an early form of mass culture based on the psychology of *ressentiment,* then the new religion itself may be as symptomatic of decadence as is the arena's appetite for martyrdom. Gibbon, after all, referred to barbarism *and* religion as the twin causes of the downfall of ancient civilization. And Hegel points out that the passion for religious disputation became just as decadent as the passion for circuses in the Byzantine Empire: "Streams of blood flowed as the result. . . . To all these religious

1. Eusebius, *Ecclesiastical History,* Book v, i, 39, from the translation in Naphtali Lewis and Meyer Reinhold, eds., *Roman Civilization,* 2 vols., *Sourcebook II: The Empire* (New York: Harper and Row, 1966 [1955]), p. 593.

contentions was added the interest in the gladiators and their combats, and in the parties of the blue and green color, which likewise
occasioned the bloodiest encounters; a sign of the most fearful degradation, as proving that all feeling for what is serious and elevated is
lost, and that the delirium of religious passion is quite consistent with
an appetite for gross and barbarous spectacles."[2]

Although religious fanaticism obviously can contribute to cultural
degeneracy, perhaps the most frequent kind of objection to public
amusements through the ages has been religious. Tertullian and Salvianus are only the forebears of thousands of good Christians who have
decried decadence and sought to clean up corrupt public morals,
down to the American "Moral Majority" of the 1980s. But whether for
good or evil, creatively or destructively, religion operates on a mass
basis, and can itself be seen as a form of mass culture. Before the
emergence of modern, secular, industrialized mass culture, Christianity was the main antithesis to classical civilization. The identity
between religion and mass culture, moreover, is possible not just
because there are and have always been multitudes of believers, or
because prayerbooks, hymnals, sermons, and the Bible achieve enormous circulations, but also because religion per se can be viewed as
"for the many" or even as fundamentally "proletarian" and set over
against a category of arts and sciences defined both as "for the few"
and as classical. Religion and "high culture" are often held to be
interdependent or even identical, but they are also often held to be
opposites, as in those theories—Nietzsche's prominent among them—
which define religion as proletarian and culture as aristocratic. In his
monumental theodicy *A Study of History*, Arnold Toynbee sees the
relationship between religion and culture in both ways. He contends
that during the decline of all civilizations there arises a "Universal
Church" that is both the death of the old culture and the source of a
new one. Such a "Universal Church" is invariably the work of an
"internal proletariat," as "barbarism" or the *Völkerwanderung* is the
work of an "external proletariat." Toynbee thus attributes to the
masses—his two "proletariats"—an immense power to be both the
destroyers and the creators of culture through religion, much as Marx

2. G. W. F. Hegel, *The Philosophy of History*, tr. J. Sibree (New York: Dover,
1956), p. 339.

attributes power to destroy and to create to the industrial proletariat without religion.

More acutely than any of the other church fathers, Tertullian poses the problem of the relationship between Christianity and culture. His version of that relationship involves the complete negation of culture. Christ appears as the supreme anarchist, the original of Rousseau, denying the validity of all efforts at civilization. *"Quid Athenae Hierosolymis?"* he asks. "What has Athens to do with Jerusalem?" Just as Tertullian rejects the public amusements of the ancient world even in their most harmless forms of theater and music, so he rejects all earthly authority in matters of government: "It is impossible to serve two masters, God and Caesar." Such a statement seems far removed from Christ's injunction to "render unto Caesar the things that are Caesar's"; Tertullian wants to render nothing unto Caesar. But Tertullian's theological anarchism goes even deeper than rejection of the state and of worldly amusements, for, in his assertions of belief in spite of and even because of the "absurd" impossibility of Christianity, he rejects classical philosophy's legacy of rationalism: "Tell me, what is the sense of this itch for idle speculation? What does it prove, this useless affectation of a fastidious curiosity, notwithstanding the strong confidence of its assertions? It was highly appropriate that Thales, while his eyes were roaming the heavens in astronomical observation, should have tumbled into a well. This mishap may well serve to illustrate the fate of all who occupy themselves with the stupidity of philosophy."[3]

It is tempting to imagine that, had "the zealous African" strayed too near a well while casting a theological eye on the heavens, he too might have tumbled in. But it is at least clear that his opposition to the things of this world is as total as he can make it. Tertullian thus creates difficulties for those modern theorists who, like Matthew Arnold and T. S. Eliot, seek to combine "Hellenism" with "Hebraism," or to be both classicists and Christians, and who believe that culture is fundamentally and necessarily religious. Against the view that holds, with Eliot, that "no culture has appeared or developed except together with a religion," the example of Tertullian suggests that religion—

3. Tertullian quoted by Charles Norris Cochran, *Christianity and Classical Civilization: A Study of Thought and Action from Augustus to Augustine* (London: Oxford University Press, 1957), p. 222.

Christianity, at least—may be radically incompatible with any version of "high culture."

At the same time, Tertullian can serve as a focus for understanding the two main branches of negative classicism. On the one hand, there are those modern theories, most of them conservative, which cite "bread and circuses" as an analogy for contemporary, secular mass culture. On the other hand, there are those theories—Marxist, existentialist, Freudian—which stress the mass-culture character of early Christianity and, indeed, of all religious movements. For Marx, religion is "the opium of the people." The problem of political liberation—as later the problem of psychological liberation for Freud—is partly to be solved by demystification, removing the chains of illusion from the masses. But for Nietzsche, in contrast, the socialism proclaimed by Marx is only the secular, modern version of the mass movement of Christianity, based on proletarian envy and "slave morality."

Largely because of his extreme rejection of the things of this world, Tertullian figures in two modern, ironic accounts of the opposition between Christianity and classical culture. In both Gibbon's *Decline and Fall of the Roman Empire* and Nietzsche's *On the Genealogy of Morals*, Christianity is identified with the hostility of oppressed groups ("vertical barbarians" in Ortega's phrase, "internal proletariats" in Toynbee's) toward the established order and values of ancient civilization. Rather than as the necessary foundation of culture, working in favor of conservative interests, Christianity appears as a kind of revolutionary counterculture, expressing the *ressentiment* of the oppressed. Out of the ruins of the city of the world, built by the brilliance of pagan civilization, rises the City of God, built by the subversive longings of the masses.

Gibbon finds in Tertullian an example of the affinity between those two ravagers of Rome, barbarism and religion. Gibbon quotes *De Spectaculis* to show the "resentment and spiritual pride" into which the primitive Christians were "sometimes seduced" "by the power of the pagans."[4] He extracts from its conclusion a passage that juxtaposes the abominated earthly "spectacles" with "the greatest of all spectacles, the last and eternal judgment of the universe." In this passage,

---

4. Edward Gibbon, *Decline and Fall of the Roman Empire*, 6 vols. (New York: Everyman's Library, 1954 [1910]), I, 457.

Tertullian waxes as sadistic as Martial, though no doubt in a better cause. He imagines himself as an angelic spectator peering down into an infernal arena:

> How shall I admire, how laugh, how rejoice, how exult, when I behold so many proud monarchs, and fancied gods, groaning in the lowest abyss of darkness; so many magistrates, who persecuted the name of the Lord, liquefying in fiercer fires than they ever kindled against the Christians; so many sage philosophers blushing in red-hot flames with their deluded scholars; so many celebrated poets trembling before the tribunal, not of Minos, but of Christ; so many tragedians, more tuneful in the expression of their own sufferings; so many dancers—[5]

Knowing that he has captured Tertullian (and, indeed, Christianity itself) in a deliciously wicked moment of self-contradiction, Gibbon stops with "dancers" (or, in the original, with *histriones*). "The humanity of the reader will permit me to draw a veil over the rest of this infernal description," Gibbon says, "which the zealous African pursues in a long variety of affected and unfeeling witticisms."

Gibbon's critical stance toward Christianity has its ancient analogues, for Celsus, Julian the Apostate, Porphyry, and other pagan critics accused the new religion both of irrationality and of appealing to slaves, criminals, and riffraff. Gibbon speaks of the "very odious imputation . . . that the new sect of Christians was almost entirely composed of the dregs of the populace," an "imputation" that he ironically counters by pointing out that, "as the humble faith of Christ diffused itself through the world, it was embraced by several persons who derived some consequence from the advantages of nature or fortune," such as Cyprian, Justin Martyr, and Tertullian (1:495). Gibbon appears to think of these educated converts as traitors to rational enlightenment. In general, his attitudes toward Christianity agree with those of other Enlightenment intellectuals, who tend to see religion as a system of illusions—"priestly tricks"—mainly useful for keeping the lower classes in order.[6]

5. Tertullian quoted and translated by Gibbon, I, 457.
6. Ironically, A. O. Lovejoy finds in Tertullian affinities to eighteenth-century deism. In some ways, says Lovejoy, "he appears less an Early Father of the Latin Church than an Early Father of the deism" of the seventeenth and eighteenth centuries. But Lovejoy also acknowledges that in some other ways Tertullian is "a partial precursor of Kierkegaard." See "'Nature' as Norm in Tertullian," *Essays in the History of Ideas* (Baltimore: Johns Hopkins University Press, 1948), pp. 308–48.

A little more than a century after Gibbon, Nietzsche quoted the same passage from *De Spectaculis* to illustrate the same thesis of the "resentment and spiritual pride" of the primitive Christians. In *On the Genealogy of Morals*, he serves up Tertullian as the example par excellence of the Judeo-Christian psychology of *ressentiment*. Like other men of "slave morality," Tertullian is "neither upright nor naive nor honest and straightforward with himself": "His soul *squints*." It was a great mistake, Nietzsche thinks, for Dante to put over the gateway to Hell the inscription "I too was created by eternal love." At least Dante should have countered that paradox by inscribing over the gateway to Heaven "I too was created by eternal *hate*." With that as a preface, Nietzsche quotes the same infernal "spectacle" passage that Gibbon quotes, only he draws no ironic veil over its conclusion, in which, after roasting wrestlers and charioteers, Tertullian expresses gratitude for the future "favour of seeing and exulting" in the holo-caust of the damned.[7]

Though agreeing with Gibbon's analysis of Tertullian's motives, Nietzsche goes beyond the great historian in linking the psychology of *ressentiment* in Christianity to modern, secular culture. Gibbon could treat Christianity ironically, seeing it as a partially destructive force equivalent to "barbarism," for his own faith lay in progress through reason and the sciences. In contrast, Nietzsche has none of Gibbon's Enlightenment faith. If the gradual emancipation of the common peo-ple from their "masters" has meant advancement, it has been an advancement only of "poison through the entire body of mankind." And now that this poisonous "progress" has become secularized, translated from the unreal world to the real one, it "seems irresis-tible."[8] Nietzsche sketches the secularization of *ressentiment* from Tertullian down to the present. Democracy and socialism are the modern forms of the "slave morality" expressed in *De Spectaculis* and the Bible. "The 'redemption' of the human race (from 'the masters,' that is) is going forward; everything is visibly becoming Judaized, Christianized, mob-ized (what do the words matter!)." And "the dem-ocratic movement is the heir of the Christian movement."[9]

7. Friedrich Nietzsche, *On the Genealogy of Morals*, tr. Walter Kaufmann and R. J. Hollingdale (New York: Vintage, 1967), pp. 48–52.

8. Ibid., p. 36.

9. Friedrich Nietzsche, *Beyond Good and Evil*, tr. Walter Kaufmann (New York: Vintage, 1966), p. 116.

No doubt Tertullian's "squinting" was easy game for Gibbon and Nietzsche, but the questions raised by his example cannot be easily dismissed. The idea that Christianity arises from and answers the needs of the masses, and especially of the poor, the humble, the oppressed, is as old as Christianity itself. "Blessed are ye poor for yours is the kingdom of God" (Luke 6:20). Nothing could be plainer than that, though that is where the difficulties of reconciling religion and culture start. H. Richard Niebuhr writes: "Christian exaltation of the lowly offends aristocrats and Nietzscheans in one way, champions of the proletariat in another. The unavailability of Christ's wisdom to the wise and prudent, its attainability by the simple and by babes, bewilder the philosophical leaders of culture or excite their scorn."[10]

It is possible to avoid the problem of the proletarian nature of Christianity either by seeing culture as evolving out of religion without replacing it, or by seeing religion and culture as representing two opposed but equally necessary and timeless principles, faith and reason. Matthew Arnold takes the latter approach when he constructs a model of high culture that combines "Hellenism" and "Hebraism." It is the task of criticism—which in his case often amounts to Anglican "Broad Church" or liberal theology—to select and emphasize the best elements of both, thus forming a continuous tradition of values to be transmitted through the Church, through literature, and through state-funded "liberal education." Though in *Culture and Anarchy* Arnold argues that Great Britain in 1867 needs to "Hellenize" more than to "Hebraize," he aims to achieve balance. In *Literature and Dogma*, where his purpose is to rescue the Bible from the stultifications of orthodoxy and to counteract the secularizing tendencies that have driven the masses away from the Church, he asserts that "the Muse of righteousness" is "far more real, and far greater" than the Greek "Muse of art and science." The latter is "the Muse of the gifted few," but the former is "the Muse of the work-day, care-crossed, toil-stained millions of men,—the Muse of humanity."[11]

For Arnold, Tertullian represents a spirit of uncompromising hostility toward the world which violates both Christianity and culture. In his sonnet "The Good Shepherd with the Kid," Arnold presents "the fierce Tertullian" upholding the doctrine of the Montanists ("that

10. H. Richard Niebuhr, *Christianity and Culture* (New York: Harper, 1951), p. 9.
11. Matthew Arnold, *Literature and Dogma*, in *Dissent and Dogma*, ed. R. H. Super (Ann Arbor: University of Michigan Press, 1968), p. 317.

unpitying Phrygian sect"), according to which sins committed after baptism could not be forgiven. Tertullian had criticized the painters of the catacombs who showed the Good Shepherd carrying a kid instead of a lamb:

> *He saves the sheep, the goats he doth not save.*
> So rang Tertullian's sentence, on the side
> Of that unpitying Phrygian sect which cried:
> "Him can no fount of fresh forgiveness lave,
>
> Who sins, once washed by the baptismal wave."
> So spake the fierce Tertullian. But she sighed,
> The infant Church! of love she felt the tide
> Stream on her from her Lord's yet recent grave.
>
> And then she smiled; and in the Catacombs,
> With eye suffused but heart inspired true,
> On those walls subterranean, where she hid
>
> Her head 'mid ignominy, death, and tombs,
> She her Good Shepherd's hasty image drew—
> And on his shoulders, not a lamb, a kid.[12]

For Arnold as for Gibbon and Nietzsche, Tertullian stands for the opposite of Christian love and mercy. But Arnold, perhaps more fairly than Gibbon and Nietzsche, makes him the spokesman for the Montanist heresy rather than for Christianity in general. So the example of "the zealous African" does not suggest to Arnold anything problematic about his own attempt to reconcile Hellenism and Hebraism.

To Arnold's belief that criticism—or liberal theology—can bring the two "Muses" together in the construction of a tradition of high culture may be contrasted those theories that find in Christianity the sort of hostility to the things of this world—including culture—which Tertullian expresses. From classical times forward, many theorists have asserted the impossibility of bringing culture to the masses, who must settle for the comforting illusions of religion, or who express their hostility to culture through religion. The friends of religion, the masses are said to be the enemies of art and science, and the two Muses, as in Nietzsche's antitheology, are engaged in perpetual strife

---

12. Matthew Arnold, "The Good Shepherd with the Kid," in Kenneth Allott, ed., *The Poems of Matthew Arnold* (New York: Norton, 1965), p. 491.

(that this strife is often fruitful, according to Nietzsche, does not alter their irreconcilability).

Echoing Gibbon and anticipating Nietzsche, Ludwig Feuerbach declared that "the decline of [classical] culture was identical with the victory of Christianity."[13] Against the hard-won findings of reason and the triumphs of art in the here-and-now, the new religion presented a view of the world that satisfied all wishes in the hereafter and that appealed especially to the uneducated:

> The Apostles and Evangelists were no scientifically cultivated men. Culture, in general, is nothing else than the exaltation of the individual above his subjectivity to objective universal ideas, to the contemplation of the world. The Apostles were men of the people; the people live only in themselves, in their feelings; therefore Christianity took possession of the people. *Vox populi vox Dei.* Did Christianity conquer a single philosopher, historian, or poet of the classical period? The philosophers who went over to Christianity were feeble, contemptible.[14]

Feuerbach stands midway between Enlightenment exposés of religion as "priestcraft" and "superstition" and Nietzsche's "slave morality" antitheology. His *Essence of Christianity* (1841), with its thesis that theology is anthropology turned upside down, also served as the cornerstone for Marx's critique of religion.

Marx agrees with Feuerbach that religion is only the image of this world projected onto the clouds. "Feuerbach starts out from the fact of religious self-alienation, of the duplication of the world into a religious, imaginary world and a real one. His work consists in resolving the religious world into its secular basis."[15] Marx carries Feuerbach's work forward by arguing that, once religion has been brought back to earth, "the chief thing still remains to be done." The static, individualistic materialism implicit in Feuerbach must be transformed into a dynamic, social materialism that will enable people to repossess all the aspects of life that they have alienated from themselves, mirrored darkly in the illusions that they project skyward. The demolition

13. Ludwig Feuerbach, *The Essence of Christianity*, tr. George Eliot (New York: Harper Torchbooks, 1957), p. 132.
14. Ibid.
15. Karl Marx, "Theses on Feuerbach" (1845), in Robert C. Tucker, ed., *The Marx-Engels Reader* (New York: Norton, 1972), p. 108.

of religion will necessarily involve the demolition of the unjust society that supports it and that is supported by it. Liberation from theological illusions and liberation from political and economic oppression will form a single process. For "the criticism of religion is the premise of all criticism."[16] Into Feuerbach's analysis of Christianity, moreover, Marx inserts a psychological element that emerges again strongly in Nietzsche: the idea that the function of religious illusions is to reconcile men to an unjust social order. "Religious suffering is at the same time an expression of real suffering and a protest against real suffering. Religion is the sign of the oppressed creature, the heart of a heartless world, and the soul of soulless conditions. It is the opium of the people."[17]

The attempts by Feuerbach and Marx to resolve religion into its "secular basis" can be seen as extensions of Enlightenment critiques. The *philosophes* viewed Christianity as mystification imposed on the "canaille" to keep them deluded and pacified. Paul Henri d'Holbach anticipated Marx's opium phrase when he wrote: "Religion is the art of making men drunk with enthusiasm, to prevent them thinking about the oppressions committed by their rulers."[18] Voltaire said that he would be cheated and cuckolded less by his servants if their faith remained firm, and David Hume's *Natural History of Religion* is largely a history of "superstition" and its prevalence among "the greatest part of uninstructed mankind."[19] Such ideas are ancient: versions of them can be found in Lucretius, Epicurus, Plato, and Critias. But the modern critique of religion as ideology derives from the Enlightenment, and reaches its fullest nineteenth-century elaborations in Marx and Nietzsche.

For the *philosophes*, Christianity appeared as the reflex of collective ignorance, that which fills the minds of the vast majority of people who lack culture. In an age when literacy and education were necessarily restricted to a minority, culture tended to be viewed in aristo-

16. Karl Marx, "Contribution to the Critique of Hegel's *Philosophy of Right*" (1844), in Tucker, *The Marx-Engels Reader*, p. 11.
17. Ibid., p. 12.
18. D'Holbach quoted by Owen Chadwick, *The Secularization of the European Mind in the Nineteenth Century* (Cambridge: Cambridge University Press, 1975), p. 49.
19. David Hume, *The Natural History of Religion*, in Frank Manuel, ed., *The Enlightenment* (Englewood Cliffs, N. J.: Prentice Hall, 1965), p. 51.

cratic terms even by those with radical political leanings. Even though it looked forward to the emergence of the majority of people from intellectual childishness (Kant's *Unmündigkeit*), the idea of progressive enlightenment carried with it an implicit cultural elitism, as Marx recognized when he wrote that "this doctrine necessarily arrives at dividing society into two parts, one of which is superior to society."[20] For the first time in history, a large class of professional intellectuals saw themselves in opposition to "priestcraft" and the Church, and either competing for the minds of ordinary people or abandoning them as incapable and perhaps unworthy of knowledge. The great project of the *Encyclopédie* might have as its ultimate goal a complete liberation from "superstition" and ignorance, but Denis Diderot could still write that "the general mass of the species is made neither to follow, nor to know, the march of the human spirit."[21]

During and after the American and French revolutions, radical intellectuals transformed Diderot's apparent pessimism about "the general mass of the species" into optimism. Agreeing that mankind had been deluded by "priestcraft," Thomas Paine calls for the complete overthrow of the "nobility and clergy." In *The Rights of Man*, Paine distinguishes three types of government, the earliest based on "priestcraft," the next on "power," and the third on "reason" or on the scientific enlightenment of the "public." The first two governments have combined historically into that system of oppression that the American and French revolutions have overthrown in favor of government by "reason." The name for this combination of "priestcraft" and "power" or "fraud" and "force" is "Church and State." "The key of St. Peter and the key of the Treasury became quartered on one another, and the wondering cheated multitude worshipped the invention."[22] Here is the reverse of Edmund Burke's nightmare, in which "the nobility and the clergy," and with them "learning," are "trampled

20. Karl Marx, "Theses on Feuerbach," in Tucker, *The Marx-Engels Reader*, p. 108.

21. Denis Diderot, "The Encyclopedia," in *Rameau's Nephew and Other Works*, tr. Jacques Barzun and Ralph H. Bowen (Indianapolis: Bobbs-Merrill, 1964), pp. 289–90. For the Enlightenment idea of religion as for the common people, see Peter Gay, *The Science of Freedom* (New York: Knopf, 1969), especially "A Faith for the Canaille," pp. 517–528.

22. Thomas Paine, *The Rights of Man*, in *The Essential Thomas Paine*, ed. Sidney Hood (New York: New American Library, 1969), p. 153.

under the hooves of a swinish multitude."[23] Paine is sure that if most people belong to an "ignorant multitude," that is because they have been "cheated" out of their birthrights to freedom and knowledge by "force and fraud." What is more, the people themselves must be the ultimate source of true learning or culture, something perhaps rare in the past but to be looked forward to in the democratic future.

Marx's opium metaphor can be seen in embryo in Paine's "force and fraud." But whereas Paine implies that people have simply had mystification foisted upon them by their rulers (rather like the brainwashing that totalitarian propagandists are often said to practice), Marx suggests that the self-alienated images that compose religious illusions are fundamentally necessary as unconscious compensations for injustice. Here he anticipates Nietzsche. Religion arises organically and spontaneously out of every oppressive social situation. "The abolition of religion as the illusory happiness of men, is a demand for their real happiness. The call to abandon their illusions about their condition is a call to abandon a condition that requires illusions."[24] Napoleon had arrived at something like this idea when he claimed to see "in religion the whole mystery of society." By "mystery" he did not mean the Incarnation nor any of the other dogmas of the Church, but rather the way in which religion functions as a kind of social cement, binding together what would otherwise fly apart into class warfare:

> I hold . . . that apart from the precepts and doctrines of the Gospel there is no society that can flourish, nor any real civilization. What is it that makes the poor man take it for granted that ten chimneys smoke in my palace while he dies of cold—that I have ten changes of raiment in my wardrobe while he is naked—that on my table at each meal there is enough to sustain a family for a week? It is religion which says to him that in another life I shall be his equal, indeed, that he has a better chance of being happy there than I have.[25]

Despite his own disillusionment, Napoleon cannot imagine social institutions existing on a purely secular basis. But that is what both

23. Edmund Burke, *Reflections on the Revolution in France* (Baltimore: Penguin, 1976), p. 173.

24. Karl Marx, "Contribution to the Critique of Hegel's *Philosophy of Right*," in Tucker, *The Marx-Engels Reader*, p. 12.

25. Napoleon quoted by Alec R. Vidler, *The Church in an Age of Revolution, 1789 to the Present Day* (Baltimore: Penguin, 1961), p. 19.

Paine and Marx say is inevitable, although the social institutions will no longer be oppressive and the secular civilization or culture of the future will be radically different from the culture of the past. Rather than arising from the false consciousness embodied in religion, the future secular culture will consist of true consciousness or democratic enlightenment—all the alienated aspects of mankind called home, as it were. Marx agrees with Pierre Joseph Proudhon that "man is destined to live without religion," which is the same as saying that man is destined to be free.

In contrast, Nietzsche's claim that democracy and socialism are the offspring of Christianity suggests that, though people may be able to construct a culture free of transcendental illusions, they will still smuggle religious irrationality into it. This irrationality Nietzsche links to the psychology of *ressentiment*. Feuerbach had claimed that Christianity was an inverted anthropology, but Nietzsche claims that socialism is an inverted Christianity, brought down to earth and made all the more destructive because of its translation of plebeian envy into politics. The masses can never build anything, they can only tear down what their masters have built. Nietzsche sees both Christianity and its modern offspring as inimical to culture or "noble values," defined largely in terms of tragic vision and the classical experience. As a consequence, his idea of ancient decadence blends into his idea of modern decadence, and his interpretation of the fall of the Roman Empire becomes a prophecy of the demise of modern mass society. What the Christians did to Rome, Nietzsche thinks, the socialists, anarchists, and other democratic "rabble" are repeating today: "The Christian and the anarchist: both decadents, both incapable of having any effect other than disintegrating, poisoning, withering, bloodsucking; both the instinct of mortal hatred against everything that stands, that stands in greatness, that has duration. . . . Christianity was the vampire of the *imperium Romanum*: overnight it undid the tremendous deed of the Romans—who had won the ground for a great culture *that would have time*."[26] The Roman Empire "was firm enough to withstand bad emperors," says Nietzsche, "but it was not firm enough against the *most corrupt* kind of corruption, against the *Chris-*

26. Friedrich Nietzsche, *The Anti-Christ*, in *The Portable Nietzsche*, ed. and tr. Walter Kaufmann (New York: Penguin, 1976), p. 648.

tians."27 The disintegrating horror of modern mass culture begins
with Tertullian, or rather with Jesus and the entire Hebraic tradition,
and leads to Proudhon and Marx. Gibbon had argued that a combination of barbarism and religion destroyed Rome; Nietzsche detects a
new synthesis of "internal" or "vertical" barbarism and secularized
religion in the democratic and socialist movements of his age. And the
more secular, rationalized, and democratic modern culture appears to
be, the more Nietzsche sees it as disguised religion and the enemy of
the authentic culture of the rare, "noble" individual who alone is
capable of complete freedom and creative disillusionment.

There have been many attempts besides Nietzsche's to show that
socialism is a disguised religion, and that Marx in particular cloaks
Judeo-Christian eschatology in secular garb. Insofar as Marxism is a
demand for the earthly fulfillment of the illusory happiness painted in
the clouds by religion, such analyses may be perfectly logical. Marx
himself saw that communism involves translating Jesus' radical but
other-worldly message into the politics of this world, or realizing the
utopia that is embedded in the Bible. As he wrote in 1843, "Creations
of fantasy, dreams, the postulates of Christianity . . . all these become, in democracy, the tangible and present reality, secular maxims."28 The Christian myth of prelapsarian life, like the Greek myth of
the Golden Age, contains the seeds of egalitarianism. Augustine
seems to anticipate Marx by fourteen centuries when he writes:
"Without justice, what are kingdoms but great robberies?" And Augustine's great teacher, Ambrose, held that "the Lord God specially
wanted this earth to be the common possession of all, and to provide
fruits for all; but avarice produced the rights of property."29 Similar
secularizations of Jesus' unearthly politics (or perhaps sacralizations of
earthly politics) have cropped up through the centuries, in eschatological heresies and peasant revolts and in the teachings of such
millenarian prophets as Joachim of Fiore, John Ball, and Thomas
Münzer.

27. Ibid.
28. Karl Marx, *Early Writings,* ed. and tr. T. B. Bottomore (New York: McGraw-
Hill, 1964), p. 20.
29. Augustine, *The City of God,* tr. Marcus Dods (New York: Modern Library,
1950), Book IV, section 4; Ambrose quoted by Norman Cohn, *The Pursuit of the
Millennium* (New York: Harper Torchbooks, 1957), p. 203.

> When Adam delved and Eve span,
> Who was then a gentleman?

As Norman Cohn argues in his study of medieval eschatology, *Pursuit of the Millennium,* the radical content of Christianity, transferred from the other world to this one, has been a powerful factor in the thinking of common people for ages.

This traditional connection between religion and politics emerges in various ways in modern socialist thought, from direct assertions that Christ was the first democrat or the first communist, as in Wilhelm Weitling's claim that "all democratic ideas sprang from Christianity,"[30] to the conservative brands of "Christian socialism" which Marx and Engels attack in the *Communist Manifesto:* "Nothing is easier than to give Christian asceticism a Socialist tinge. . . . Christian Socialism is but the holy water with which the priest consecrates the heart-burnings of the aristocrat."[31] Nevertheless, Marx and Engels themselves are eager to celebrate the radical contents of religion when these seem to issue in revolutionary action, as in the case of Thomas Münzer. As Cohn points out, "From Engels down to the Communist historians of today . . . Marxists have inflated Münzer into a giant symbol, a prodigious hero in the history of the 'class war.'"[32] And much the same kind of "inflation"—or celebration—occurs in William Morris's *Dream of John Ball.* Cohn considers such celebrations both naive and dangerous, because they express the same "eschatological phantasies" that so often misled the medieval peasantry to their destruction.

Cohn's thesis that the eschatological irrationality that motivated medieval jacqueries also motivates modern mass totalitarian movements is an updated and historically more detailed version of Nietzsche's *Genealogy of Morals.* I do not mean that Cohn rejects

30. William Weitling quoted by Chadwick, *The Secularization of the European Mind,* p. 78.

31. Marx and Engels, *The Communist Manifesto* (1848), in Tucker, *The Marx-Engels Reader,* p. 354. See also Erich Fromm, *The Dogma of Christ, and Other Essays on Religion, Psychology and Culture* (London: Routledge & Kegan Paul, 1963), pp. 1–69.

32. Cohn, *Pursuit of the Millennium,* p. 271. See also Ernst Bloch, *Thomas Münzer als Theologe der Revolution* (Frankfurt: Suhrkamp, 1962) and Friedrich Engels, *The Peasant War in Germany* (1850).

democratic and socialistic ideals as does Nietzsche, or that he sub-
scribes to Nietzsche's brand of antitheology. But Cohn also argues that
both eschatological Christian sects and modern fascistic and socialistic
movements are based on an irrational "slave morality" that is more
destructive than creative. Cohn is the historian of those "many times
when needy and discontented masses" have been "captured by some
millennial prophet" (xiv), including the recent past, in Fascist Italy,
Nazi Germany, and Soviet Russia. Marxism thus appears as one of the
"derivatives" of "Jewish apocalyptic." To arrive at *Das Kapital*, Cohn
thinks, one need only substitute "proletariat" for "chosen people" and
"classless society" for "Kingdom of Saints."

Viewed with enough ironic detachment, all secular ideologies can
be shown to be concealed and inverted religions, just as these same
ideologies show religions to be concealed and inverted politics or
anthropology. Cohn and Nietzsche treat nineteenth- and twentieth-
century ideologies much as Carl Becker treats the Enlightenment
faith in progress in his *Heavenly City of the Eighteenth-Century Philosophers* (1932). Hegelian idealism, moreover, is manifestly a theodicy and also the point of origin for both Feuerbach and Marx. And
the founder of Positivism and sociology, Auguste Comte, proposed
the creation of a new "religion of humanity"—all strictly "scientific,"
of course—the "priesthood" of which would be made up of Positivist
intellectuals like Comte himself. As earlier in the rites and holidays of
the French Revolution, here one sees a conscious attempt to pattern a
secular ideology on a religious model.

Aware of the religious character of all ideologies and philosophical
systematizings, Nietzsche makes only the most extreme, though perhaps also the most profound, of the many attempts to show that the
various brands of modern secular politics are religion burying its head
in the sand. After Nietzsche, among the more important exposés of
socialism as disguised religion are the recantations in Richard Cross-
man's *The God That Failed* (1949), Raymond Aron's *The Opium of the
Intellectuals* (1955), and Jacques Ellul's *The New Demons* (1973). For
Ellul, not just left-wing ideology but all forms of secular political
"faith" function as ersatz religions. Ideologies spring up on both the
left and the right to fill the void left by decaying Christianity. The
content of these ideologies Ellul defines as "modern myths," which he
identifies with mass culture or, as he calls it in other essays, "propa-

ganda," the inescapable product of "the technological society": "Myth is . . . the condition of loyalty of the mass of the people to a certain civilization and to its procedures in development or in crisis. It is also an explanation of man's permanence within this civilization."[33] Having believed ourselves to be enlightened, we discover that mythology flourishes in our desacralized world. "Obviously, religious sentiment is capable of focusing on something other than formal deity" (92). In the case of political ideologies, it focuses on leaders, parties, and the nation or state. In the case of commercial propaganda or mass culture, it focuses on stars, products, images, fragmentary news "events," and "human interest stories." The mass media play the leading role in the reinsertion of mythology into the modern world; the "television announcer" has served as the new mythology's most characteristic voice.

> The transformations produced in the modern psyche by the mass media, the disconnected order of the discourse, the reappearance of global mythical thinking, the rejection of rational logic, the instant seizure of the real, etc., that has all been thoroughly shown . . . by Marshall McLuhan. This is surely the best possible refutation of the idea that contemporary man is rational and scientific, and that we are in a demythicized society. Our historic situation involves a recourse to myth. Our means of acting in the world, and on reality, produce myth of themselves. How could we escape it? [97]

Ellul speaks of the modern "return to myth," suggesting that the creation of mass culture entails decadence or historical regression. Further, because it seems wholly secular and economically rationalized, modern mythology is difficult to recognize for what it is, making it doubly irrational and dangerous. And it is irrational, too, Ellul believes, because it secretly takes over the function of religious transcendence while projecting only the most mechanical, most transitory, and least transcendent values.

Ellul's position is in sharp contrast to that of his apparent mentor McLuhan, who thinks of the mass media and of the "myths" generated by them as beneficial. With his penchant for mistaking apples for oranges, McLuhan says that the various media of communication themselves are "macromyths," and so are languages. Thus "we can

---

33. Jacques Ellul, *The New Demons*, tr. C. Edward Hopkin (New York: Seabury, 1975 [1973]), p. 95.

regard all media as myths and as the prolific source of many subordi-
nate myths."[34] Despite their differences, however, both Ellul and
McLuhan contribute to the tradition that regards secular mass culture
as the primary modern replacement for religion and mythology. For
McLuhan, the substitute seems to be just as good as the original. In
any case, he pays little attention to content (since the form is the
content). For Ellul, however, the substitute involves a fall from grace
or at least from innocence and a filling up of the void left by the decay
of genuine religion with fraudulent "modern myths" and "new
demons."

A third figure in the tradition of likening secular mass culture to
religion is Roland Barthes, who in his *Mythologies* explores many
facets of contemporary mass culture: films, ads, wrestling matches,
plastics, cars, fashions, travel guides, the Eiffel Tower, and so on.
Perhaps because of his quasi-Marxist insistence that "statistically,
myth is on the right," Barthes does not meet with Ellul's approval.[35]
But with his structuralist emphasis on the primacy of language, codes,
and communication systems, Barthes seems at times like a French
version of McLuhan; he would certainly have agreed with McLuhan's
anthropologist collaborator Edmund Carpenter in describing the mass
media as "new languages, their grammars as yet unknown."[36] In any
case, the structuralist project in France involves Lévi-Strauss's attempts to construct a science of mythology based on his studies of
American Indians and other "primitives" on the one hand and Barthes's excursions among the latest technological and media fare on the
other. One result of these twin emphases on the primitive and on
modern mass society is that the latter comes by implication to represent a regression back to a "mythological" stage of consciousness, just
as Ellul speaks of the modern "return to myth." Although this implication may be only the reflex of the assumption of a universal, ahistorical
structure to human thought (Jacques Lacan's "Symbolic Order," for
instance), it is also apparent that Barthes's dissections of modern "my-

34. Marshall McLuhan, "Myth and Mass Media," in Henry A. Murray, ed., *Myth
and Mythmaking* (Boston: Beacon, 1968), p. 295.

35. Roland Barthes, *Mythologies*, selected and tr. by Annette Lavers (New York:
Hill and Wang, 1972), p. 148.

36. Edmund Carpenter, "The New Languages," in Edmund Carpenter and
Marshall McLuhan, eds., *Explorations in Communication* (Boston: Beacon, 1966), p.
162.

thologies" are similar to Marxist analyses of bourgeois ideology. Fredric Jameson sums up one aspect of the structuralist interest in mass culture as social decadence when he writes:

> If the Symbolic Order is the source of all meaning, it is also and at the same time the source of all cliché, the very fountainhead of all those more debased "meaning-effects" which saturate our culture, the very seat and locus of the inauthentic in Heidegger's sense. This is an aspect of the doctrine which has perhaps been obscured by the emphasis in structural research on pre-capitalistic and indeed pre-individualistic materials such as folklore and myth, causing us to forget that the equivalents in our own society for the "myth" or "pensée sauvage" of cold societies or primitive cultures are neither Joyce nor Husserl, but rather the bestseller and the advertising slogan, the Barthean "mythologie." So it is that our possession by language, which "writes" us even as we imagine ourselves to be writing it, is not so much some ultimate release from bourgeois subjectivism, but rather a limiting situation against which we must struggle at every instant. Thus the Symbolic Order can only be said to represent a psychic conquest from the vantage point of that imaginary stage which it supersedes: for the death of the subject, if it might be supposed to characterize the collective structure of some future socialist world, is fully as characteristic of the intellectual, cultural, and psychic decay of post-industrial monopoly capitalism as well.[37]

In this passage as in Barthes, mythology is synonymous with bourgeois ideology, which is in turn the main product of the communications revolution. Following Marx's theories of ideology and reification, Barthes argues that "myth is depoliticized speech" (143) and also that there is "one language which is not mythical . . . the language of man as a producer. . . . This is why revolutionary language proper cannot be mythical" (146). In contrast, Ellul thinks of "revolutionary language" as among the leading myths or "new demons" of modern society, although he also thinks that all secular ideologies, whether left, right, or center, are religious irrationality dressed up in pseudo-scientific disguises.

The tradition of regarding secular mass culture as covert religion has many ramifications. Quite apart from the problems of ideological

---

37. Fredric Jameson, *The Prison-House of Language: A Critical Account of Structuralism and Russian Formalism* (Princeton: Princeton University Press, 1972), p. 140.

perspective, analogies for the mass media drawn from religious experience proliferate in contemporary discourse. At least two recent books elaborate upon these analogies, though neither of them gets much beyond a metaphoric level of analysis. These are William Kuhns, *The Electronic Gospel: Religion and Media* (1969) and Gregor T. Goethals, *The TV Ritual: Worship at the Video Altar* (1981). According to Kuhns, "The media now draw people with the magnetic strength the churches once held."[38] He believes that "the entertainment milieu is the contemporary counterpart of the religious milieu" (26). The parallels between the two milieus Kuhns sets forth in much paradoxical detail: the celebrity or star system is like an earthbound pantheon; the old movie palaces are like Byzantine cathedrals; products in commercials are like magic talismans; talk show hosts are like priests; daily and weekly schedules for TV are like daily and weekly rituals; and "prime time" on television is even like "primal time" in Mircea Eliade's theory of mythology. There are, of course, differences; above all, "in the entertainment milieu there is no transcendent. Entertainment reflects man's own world and his earthbound hopes back to him. Nor is there in any strict sense a parallel to the transcendent" (27). But if this is the case, how can we possibly accept the substitution of "entertainment" for "religion"? From a theological perspective like Ellul's, the substitution can signify only a massive historical fraud, a diabolic invasion of the "inauthentic." Kuhns is not so worried about this problem as Ellul, but he clearly also believes that a kind of worldwide hoax or fraud is being perpetrated by the mass media: "The sustaining language of the religious milieu is total faith. The sustaining language of the entertainment milieu is the put-on" (33). Fortunately, Kuhns seems to imply, nobody quite believes in the mass media "put-on."

On one level, thinking of mass culture as ersatz religion is only another way of asserting that modern society is decadent; pushed to the extreme, the analogy to religion or mythology suggests that we are regressing into a new Dark Age via the mass media. Here again, it is important to observe that the mass media themselves are contributing to this idea: as Kuhns and Goethals show, commercial television in

38. William Kuhns, *The Electronic Gospel: Religion and Media* (New York: Herder and Herder, 1969), p. 16.

particular has opted for patterns of ritual and mythological content that reinforce the feelings of impending doom or mass eschatology which viewers extract from the medium as one of its subliminal messages. But treatments of mass culture as ersatz religion also run the risk of overlooking the diversity and rationality of many of the products of television and the film industry which pull in an opposite direction, toward enlightenment or the demythification of experience. This is a problem that mere analogizing and generalizing about myth and ideology overlook.

Similarly, attempts to demystify secular ideologies by showing that they have theological roots tend to be logically circular. They reverse the path the secular ideologies have already traveled, for the first victories for demystification belong to the ideologies themselves. Even if Marx's thinking is partly eschatological, he starts from the unmasking of Christianity as "opium," as mass delusion. Furthermore, though the problem of religious elements in Marxism may embarrass many Marxists, anti-Marxists seldom ask whether those elements are logically valid—the usual assumption is that they are not. But the claim that Hegelianism is a theodicy does not invalidate it: it must first be shown that theodicies are invalid. And the discovery of traces of "Jewish apocalyptic" in Marx does not invalidate his theories, but only raises the prior question as to the validity of Jewish apocalyptic. It has been left to a few highly interesting Marxist theorists—perhaps they should be called Marxist theologians—to try to demonstrate how the utopian-eschatological elements shared by both religion and socialism may achieve realization. According to Leszek Kolakowski, "The question whether eschatology is possible—regardless of whether the answer is negative or positive—is one of the central problems of what we may call philosophical anthropology, which today includes most of the vital issues of philosophy."[39] Similarly, that most theological of Marxists, Ernst Bloch, writes:

> Epicurus, Lucretius, the French Encyclopaedists, Marx and Engels are the salients of a portrayal of religion as little more than the product of ignorance and fear: scarcely (in view of the many Hate-lights in religion) a wholly false picture. Hence Marx called religion

39. Leszek Kolakowski, *Toward a Marxist Humanism* (New York: Grove, 1969), p. 11.

the opium of the people; and, as the decking of man's chains with
imaginary flowers, the best way to keep him in chains: hardly (in
view of the relation between baptism and sword, altar and throne,
and despite Thomas Münzer and the Peasants' War for Jesus' sake)
a complete misrepresentation. Of course Marx did extend the metaphor of flowers and chains, for he said the desired end was that man
might "throw off the chains and pluck the living flower." But in
practice the Church so often denied this *religious* end (no poppy of
oblivion, no opiate haze, no empty promise), that in Marx it remained a perceptive judgment, became in Social Democracy a matter of private opinion, and in Bolshevism was all but put out.[40]

It is the apocalyptic-utopian possibility of "plucking the flower" of
ultimate liberation which Bloch's theories seek to rescue both from
the ambiguities of Marx and from the mechanical stultifications of
"Bolshevism." His new heresy involves resurrecting the ghost of eschatology that dogmatic materialists believe they have laid to rest.

For many non-Marxists like Jacques Ellul, meanwhile, the idea of
an entirely secular or materialist culture is either an impossibility or a
monstrosity, the latest invention of the Antichrist. "Religions have
high claims to be regarded as the mothers of culture," wrote Nietzsche's friend Jakob Burckhardt. "Indeed, religion is a prime condition
of any culture deserving the name, and hence may coincide with the
sole existing culture."[41] In primitive societies, the sacred is omnipre-
sent. "Modernization" or "progress" involves the gradual separation
of a secular sphere from the sphere of the sacred, a progress that
Comte described in his thesis of the three stages of history. From the
viewpoint that identifies religion with culture, when the process of
secularization is complete (historically, perhaps, when Nietzsche can
declare that "God is dead"), then culture, too, is dead.

The idea of secularization as the death both of genuine or high
culture and of God has been explored by many theologians. It is a
main theme, for example, in the works of the Catholic historian
Christopher Dawson, who influenced T. S. Eliot's thinking about
religion and culture. "The world religions have been the keystones of
the world cultures," Dawson writes, "so that when they are removed

40. Ernst Bloch, *Man on His Own* (New York: Herder and Herder, 1971), pp.
111–12.
41. Jakob Burckhardt, *Force and Freedom* (New York: Meridian, 1955), p. 165.

the arch falls and the building is destroyed."[42] For Dawson as for Eliot, the waning of religious faith means the waning of the creative energy that generates culture. Neither mass culture nor science can take the place of religion. "The world of reason has become more arid and spiritually void, and the world of the soul has lost the consecrated ways by which it expresses itself in the world of culture and has been left at the mercy of the forces of darkness which are the negative and destructive aspects of the Unconscious."[43] As in Ellul, secularization leads to totalitarianism. Dawson speaks of the "disintegration of modern civilization between a science without significance and the spirit which can only express itself in self-destruction" (21). The substitution of material for spiritual values and the translation of religious into political authority produce cultural sterility. According to Dawson: "If we accept the principle of social planning from the bottom upwards without regard for spiritual values we are left with a machine-made culture which differs from one country to another only in so far as the process of mechanization is more or less perfected. To most people, this is rather an appalling prospect, for the ordinary man does not regard the rationalization of life as the only good."[44] Man does not live either by reason or by technology alone. Dawson concludes that "wherever modern mechanized mass culture obtains, even in countries of liberal tradition, we find the freedom of the personality threatened by the pressure of economic forces, and the higher cultural values sacrificed to the lower standards of mass civilization" (76). Eliot, drawing upon Dawson's essays and upon such similar works as Jacques Maritain's *True Humanism* (1938), concludes that "the only hopeful course for a society which would thrive and continue its creative activity in the arts of civilisation, is to become Christian."[45]

The arguments of Eliot and Dawson, based on the idea of an organic connection and even identity between religion and high culture, do not exhaust the resources of modern theology in its warfare against secularization and mass culture. Indeed, the contrary idea of an antag-

42. Christopher Dawson, *Religion and Culture* (London: Sheed and Ward, 1948), p. 22.

43. Ibid., p. 21.

44. Christopher Dawson, *The Dynamics of World History* (New York: Sheed and Ward, 1956), pp. 75–76.

45. T. S. Eliot, *The Idea of a Christian Society*, in *Christianity and Culture* (New York: Harcourt, Brace and World, 1968 [1940]), p. 19.

onism between religion and culture, central to the thinking of secularists of both the Marxist and the Nietzschean varieties, was powerfully
resurrected in a theological form by Søren Kierkegaard, who in this
respect as in others may be looked upon as the modern Tertullian.
Kierkegaard, in fact, considers Tertullian "the unconditionally most
consistent and most Christianly two-edged of all the Church Fathers."[46] In response to those tolerant theologians who, like Lessing,
want to be against "fanaticism" but also for Christianity, Kierkegaard
imagines that Tertullian might have defended Christianity by defining
it as "fanaticism" and Christ as "the greatest fanatic of all," a "lofty and
audacious" approach with which Kierkegaard sympathizes.[47]
Kierkegaard reverses the liberal values in Arnold's "Good Shepherd"
sonnet by approving of the uncompromising way in which Tertullian
rejects the world.

For Kierkegaard, the opposite of Christianity is not atheism or
agnosticism or any other species of overt secularism so much as
"Christendom," which is, however, secularism pretending to be religious. "It transforms Christianity into something entirely different
from what it is in the New Testament, yea, into exactly the opposite;
and this is the Christianity of 'Christendom,' of us men."[48] The opposition between genuine Christianity and bourgeois Christendom in
Kierkegaard is similar to that between genuine culture and "herd
culture" in Nietzsche. The genuine can be reached only by an individual brave enough to confront the absolute; it cannot be reached by
"us men." Kierkegaard's existentialist rejection of the things of this
world is as complete as Tertullian's, partly because he categorizes all
social pluralities as hostile to the truth or to individual authenticity. As
Nietzsche's would later, Kierkegaard's extreme individualism expresses itself in a constant Heraclitean barrage against "the herd,"
"the public," "the masses," "the bourgeois mind," "the press," "us
men," "Christendom." His thinking is characterized by a sort of
Christian elitism that is logically parallel to Nietzsche's cultural
elitism:

46. Søren Kierkegaard, *Journals and Papers*, 4 vols. (Bloomington: Indiana University Press, 1971), I, 222.
47. Kierkegaard, *Journals and Papers*, III, 30–31.
48. Søren Kierkegaard, *Attack upon 'Christendom'*, in *A Kierkegaard Anthology*,
ed. Robert Bertall (New York: Modern Library, 1946), p. 445.

In the New Testament the Saviour of the world, our Lord Jesus Christ, represents the situation thus: The way that leadeth unto life is straitened, the gate narrow—few be they that find it!

—Now, on the contrary, to speak only of Denmark, we are all Christians, the way is as broad as it possibly can be, the broadest in Denmark, since it is the way in which we all are walking, besides being in all respects as convenient, as comfortable as possible; and the gate is as wide as it possibly can be, wider surely a gate cannot be than that through which we all are going *en masse.*   [442]

Instead of a religion for the masses, Christianity here appears as a religion for the few, or rather for only one—the solitary individual struggling to save himself from the shipwreck of the world.

Kierkegaard's rejection of philosophical "systems"—and especially of "the System," namely Hegel's—is also a result of his extreme individualism. Only the individual is alive, real; the social, the collective, the abstract is inauthentic, dead. "The systematic Idea [in Hegel] is the identity of subject and object, the unity of thought and being. Existence, on the other hand, is their separation" (205). It follows that "an existential system is impossible" (201). It follows, too, that faith—genuine Christianity—is supremely irrational. Kierkegaard revives Tertullian's "credo quia absurdum" in his own doctrine of the absurd.[49] Faith is "absurdity, held fast in the passion of inwardness" (220). There can be no rational approach to faith through philosophy, or through theology, or indeed through any of the other forms of culture, which are simply irrelevant, as they were for Tertullian. "For the absurd is the object of faith, and the only object that can be believed" (221).

Under the categories of Christendom and the bourgeois public, Kierkegaard treats all culture as other theorists treat only mass culture. That is, he draws no distinction between an inferior sort of culture for the masses and a superior sort for an intellectual elite. Everything is lumped together in his absolute condemnations of collective mediocrity, as in the satiric history of boredom with which he opens "The Rotation Method" in *Either/Or:*

The gods were bored, and so they created man. Adam was bored . . . so Eve was created. Thus boredom entered the

49. Kierkegaard, *Journals and Papers,* IV, 135.

world . . . then Adam and Eve and Cain and Abel were bored *en
famille*; then the population of the world increased, and the peoples
were bored *en masse*.   [22–23]

To overcome boredom, mankind invents a variety of diversions.
"What was it . . . that delayed the fall of Rome?" Kierkegaard asks.
"Was it not *panis* and *circenses*?" And what is being done today in the
bread and circuses line, he wonders. Society demands "public entertainment," otherwise it will yawn itself to death. Thus, Kierkegaard
envisages a future mass culture designed to overcome boredom,
which he has just shown to be the main driving force of social change.
This future mass culture, moreover, will be nothing more nor less
than the antithesis of religious faith and the expansion of present,
secular, bourgeois, industrial culture.

> Let us celebrate the millennium in a riot of merriment. Let us place
> boxes everywhere, not, as at present, for the deposit of money, but
> for the free distribution of money. Everything would become gratis;
> theaters gratis, women of easy virtue gratis, one would drive to the
> park gratis, be buried gratis, one's eulogy would be gratis.   [23]

Kierkegaard offers an ironic modernization of Tertullian's *De Spectaculis*, according to which "boredom is the root of all evil" and consequently also the root of all culture, whether it be for the bored aristocrat or for the equally bored man of the crowd.

For theorists on both the right and the left in the nineteenth century, industrialized leisure came to appear as it does to Kierkegaard:
as identical to the problem of boredom—or as it does to Marx: as
identical to mere recuperation before renewed labor. Similarly, education came increasingly to seem a mere adjunct to labor or, to use
Marx's phrase, as "a mere training to act as a machine." Bourgeois
industrialism seemed unable to manufacture anything higher than a
shallow profit-motive culture based on "commodity fetishism" and
economic demand. Social roles tended to shrink into economic ones:
sellers and buyers, producers and consumers—or, even more prob-
lematically, workers and owners. And everything that could not be
marketed or converted back into labor appeared valueless, even
though the very processes of marketing and of industrial labor seemed
from any transcendentalist perspective to render everything
valueless.

Kierkegaard makes these problems central to his attack on "the public" in *The Present Age* (1846); his tract on the spiritual nullity of bourgeois society is like the obverse side of what Marx and Engels say two years later in the *Communist Manifesto* about the revolutionary potential of the masses. A creature of the egalitarian principle of envy, "the public" appears on the world-historical scene as the driving force of "the abstract levelling process, that self-combustion of the human race," which is blowing through the age like "a trade wind" and is bound to "consume everything." For Kierkegaard, the public is not a collection of irrational individuals like Nietzsche's "herd" or Gustave Le Bon's "crowd"; it is instead "a monstrous abstraction," an over-rationalized and over-systematized category into which "the individual" disappears altogether. "The public is a monstrous nothing," a "phantom" or "mirage," conjured out of thin air by another ghostly abstraction, "the press."[50] All that may be good about "the public" or the "levelling process" from which it arises, Kierkegaard thinks, is that it allows the individual to exercise a species of existential resistance against it and so to become an individual, or in other words to complete one's "religious education" by freeing oneself from it. "The public" is the necessary though utterly negative ground for self-realization, a nearly dialectical process, phantom totality versus concrete person, despite Kierkegaard's opposition to Hegel. Kierkegaard recognizes that the concepts of the free individual and the all-determining, all-devouring mass society arise from the same historical circumstances: liberation from the crowd can occur only where there is a crowd. Nietzsche's position forty years later is similar, though perhaps based on a more cynical assessment of human nature: "Public opinions—private lazinesses." And Nietzsche's Zarathustra says: "Life is a well of joy; but where the rabble drinks too, all wells are poisoned."[51]

Kierkegaard is aware that public opinion cannot be explained in terms of the psychology of the individual, and that to personify it after the manner of Rousseau's "general will" is to falsify it. But he indulges in ironic personifications of it anyway, to show just what sort of "phantom" it is: "bloodless," but also all-powerful unless something real, concrete, and alive can be put in its place. "If I tried to imagine the public as a particular person . . . I should think of one of the Roman

50. Søren Kierkegaard, *The Present Age*, tr. Alexander Dru (New York: Harper, 1962).

51. Nietzsche, *The Portable Nietzsche*, pp. 63 and 208.

Emperors, a large well-fed figure, suffering from boredom, looking only for the sensual intoxication of laughter, since the divine gift of wit is not earthly enough. And so he wanders about, indolent rather than bad, but with a negative desire to dominate" (65). Because he is the product of the leveling of all individual excesses into mediocrity, this metaphoric emperor is, no doubt, better behaved than Caligula, but morally inferior to Marcus Aurelius. Also, it is entirely appropriate that he is Caesar, and yet the mirror image of the complacent bourgeois whom Kierkegaard loves to taunt. As the public, he is everybody and nobody, the idle spectator in search of a spectacle, who yet has such a bloated self-conception that he believes himself to be Caesar, the representative of God and sovereign executive of everything. Kierkegaard concludes his fantasy on a somewhat ominous note: "Every one who has read the classical authors knows how many things a Caesar could try out in order to kill time."

Between Marx's alienated masses and Kierkegaard's imperial public there seems little to choose. In many twentieth-century analyses of "the mass public"—sometimes as destructive "crowds" and "mass movements," sometimes as passive audiences for the "propaganda" and electronic "kitsch" of the mass media, the raw material for the "industrialization of consciousness"—the nightmare qualities of both are joined together. Ortega, Karl Jaspers, Herbert Marcuse, and many other modern theorists of mass society make no distinction between "public" and "masses." The masses have apparently not been transformed into an enlightened public, but the public has come increasingly to wear the aspect of masses and to merge with such categories as "mass society" and the "mass audience" for Hollywood and television spectaculars. This result has nothing to do with lack of education or even of esthetic sensibility on the part of the people now included in "the public" or "the masses" in the Western democracies. On the contrary, never before have so many people been so literate and well-educated. But education has been powerless to prevent the production of alienated masses and equally alienated artists and intellectuals in modern society, perhaps the primary fact underlying much of our recent literature of social crisis.

Modern existentialism, whether of the Christian variety that looks back to Kierkegaard or of the atheistic variety that looks back to Nietzsche, is a philosophy of ethical confrontation and extreme individualism. What it confronts is not so much the deaths of God and of culture as the death of the individual in mass society. In *Man against Mass Society*, Gabriel Marcel rejects "the spirit of abstraction" much as Kierkegaard rejects Hegelian system making, seeing in it the roots of totalitarianism and "mass violence."[52] Products of "the spirit of abstraction," the modern mass media, including the press and radio, belong to totalitarian "techniques of degradation." What Marcel has to say about the effects on "the average man" of these techniques of degradation, even in their most innocuous forms as mass entertainment, is close to the views put forward by Ortega in *The Revolt of the Masses* or, more recently, by Jacques Ellul in *Propaganda* and *The Technological Society*:

> Does not the invasion of our life by techniques to-day tend to substitute satisfaction at a material level for spiritual joy, dissatisfaction at a material level for spiritual disquiet? And do not the satisfied and the unsatisfied tend to come together in a common mediocrity? . . . I am bearing in mind also that this generalized comfort, with its appurtenances—standardized amusements, and so on—seems the only possible way to make life tolerable, when life is no longer considered as a divine gift, but rather as a "dirty joke." [42]

Here again mass culture is what seems to fill the void left by the decay of religion. But for Marcel, the ideas conveyed by the mass media are hardly consoling: "The existence of a widely diffused pessimism, at the level of the sneer and the oath rather than that of sighs and weeping, seems to me a fundamental given fact about contemporary humanity" (42). In place of a religion-based culture that values life, there emerges an industrialized pseudoculture that despises life and despises itself. Marcel's philosophy becomes a rescue mission for "the individual," seeking to lead him away from "masses" and "abstractions" and dehumanizing "techniques" such as the mass media, back to the particular and the authentic.

Much the same rescue mission is attempted by the other existentialists, as when, in *Man in the Modern Age*, Karl Jaspers writes: "An appeal to the idea of the masses is a sophistical instrument for the maintenance of vain enterprises, for fleeing from onself, for evading

52. Gabriel Marcel, *Man against Mass Society*, tr. G. S. Fraser (Chicago: Henry Regnery, 1952), p. 2.

responsibility, and for renouncing the attempt to climb towards true humanhood."[53] Between the leveling *ressentiment* of "mass man" on the one hand and the reduction of the ideal of universal enlightenment to technical expertise on the other, there has arisen "an enmity to culture" which is "grinding to powder all that has hitherto existed" (129–30). And, once pulverized by "the titanic apparatus of the mass-order," culture is replaced by mere entertainment—catchwords, advertisements, pastimes—and the potentially authentic individual is converted into a robotized "mass man," similar to the alienated worker of Marxism, who finds his only identity through merging with "the crowd." Marcel and Kierkegaard could turn from the confrontation with mass society to the confrontation with God. For Jaspers, however, the prospect of the annihilation of culture leads to a despair that partly echoes Nietzsche's loathing for the sub-morality and sub-intellection of "the average European of the present day": "There seems to be really no hope—in an epoch when the influence of the mass man is decisive—that the nobility of human existence shall persist in the form of a ruling minority" (212–13). Jaspers cannot think of a political solution to this dilemma, but only of an individual one, which he finds in his precarious doctrine of transcendence, situated somewhere between theology and Nietzsche's cultural heroism.

For Marx, religion of any sort was "the opium of the people." But industrialization was producing a new narcotic or pseudo-religion, a secular culture for the masses that soon appeared to pose the main threat to the salvationist schemes of both the Marxists and the existentialists.

53. Karl Jaspers, *Man in the Modern Age*, tr. Eden and Cedar Paul (Garden City, N.Y.: Doubleday Anchor, 1957 [1931]), p. 77.

CHAPTER 4

Some Nineteenth-Century Themes: Decadence, Masses, Empire, Gothic Revivals

In spite of all our protests, in spite of all our anger, we belong by our way of speaking to the same literary, scientific, and political society that we would ruin. . . . We are at the same time the corpse and the prosecutor of the old world; that is our vocation. The death of the old world will carry us away also; there is no salvation possible; our sick lungs can breathe no other than infected air. We are being hurried to inevitable ruin. It is altogether legitimate and indispensible; we feel that soon we shall be in the way; but, in disappearing with the old world, we shall be aware of the fatality that has bound us to it, and shall still deliver the most ferocious blows to it amid disaster and chaos; we shall passionately acclaim the new world— that world which does not belong to us—crying towards it our: "Caesar, the dying salute thee!"

—ALEXANDER HERZEN

Nero and Narcissus are always with us.

—OSCAR WILDE

i

NOT just Marxists and existentialists, secularists and theologians, but artists and writers of every persuasion have been profoundly affected by the development of industrialized mass culture. Over the last two centuries, painters, poets, sculptors, novelists, and playwrights have all been either the beneficiaries or the victims of the forces of massification: democratization, commercialization, the techniques of mass production. Nietzsche sums up one aspect of the complicated, often tortured relationship between the artist and modern society when he writes: "That is an artist as I love artists, modest in his needs; he really wants only two things, his bread and his art—*panem et Circen.*"[1] The meaning of the aphorism depends on the understanding that the society of bread and circuses, as Nietzsche knew from his own experience, did not allow artists to enjoy their bread and art without paying dearly. Central to Nietzsche's philosophy, moreover, is the paradox that the seeming progress of society really signifies its decadence, a paradox that is also basic to the "decadent movement" of artists and poets. "Nothing avails: one *must* go forward—step by step further into decadence (that is *my* definition of modern 'progress')."[2] Here is the formula of all decadent avant-gardes and modernist classicisms in the arts, as also of all decadent "transvaluations of values" in philosophy. "'Progress' is merely a modern idea, that is, a false idea" (571). The discoveries of the philosopher and the innovations of the avant-garde artist take on the appearance of delvings in a charnel house, using all the latest equipment. "It is a painful, horrible spectacle that has dawned on me," writes Nietzsche in *The Anti-Christ.* "I have drawn back the curtain from the *corruption* of man. . . . I understand corruption . . . in the sense of decadence: it is my contention that all the values in which mankind now sums up its supreme desiderata are *decadence-values*" (572). For Nietzsche, there are always new frontiers to cross, new boundaries to violate, even of disease. The "progress"—that is, "decadence"—of modern society forces the artist and philosopher of genius to be also "progressive," avant-garde, modernist—that is, "decadent."

The first modern versions of negative classicism were the declarations of decadence issued by Théophile Gautier and his Bohemian contemporaries in the 1830s; these were the deliberate antitheses of bourgeois assertions of progress through industry. The Chevalier d'Albert in Gautier's *Mademoiselle de Maupin* (1835) set the pattern by likening both his ennui and his pleasures to those of the Roman emperors: "Thy gilded house, O Nero! is but a filthy stable beside the

1. Friedrich Nietzsche, *Twilight of the Idols,* "Maxims and Arrows 17," in *The Portable Nietzsche,* ed. and tr. Walter Kaufmann (New York: Penguin, 1976), p. 468.
2. Ibid., p. 547.

palace I have built myself; my wardrobe is better stocked than yours, Heliogabalus, and it is infinitely more magnificent. My circuses are bloodier and more roaring," and so forth.[3] Nevertheless, says d'Albert, "nothing I can do has the least attraction for me." His mock distress points toward that hedonistic, solipsistic, "decadent" lifestyle that is both celebrated and satirized in later fiction: for example, in Joris-Karl Huysmans's *A Rebours,* Walter Pater's *Marius the Epicurean,* and Oscar Wilde's *Picture of Dorian Gray.*

"We are all emperors of the Lower Empire," said Théophile de Ferrière, also in 1835. "For are we not in decadence?"[4] Since the 1830s decadent artists and poets have thought of themselves as forming an avant-garde of esthetic modernism in the midst of historical backsliding, hastening the downfall of a moribund society by pushing art beyond the limits of bourgeois tolerance. This esthetic decadence contrasted a perversely ideal antiquity—Rome or Byzantium both as the capital of all pleasure and as necropolis, the ultimate dead end of history—to the sterility of industrial modernity. Rome or Byzantium could be at once utopia and dystopia, a model of decadent behavior to be admired and imitated but also an exemplar of imperial hubris and futility—the ironic mirror of the decadents' own bourgeois, industrial, imperial society which, they declared, was rapidly becoming another tottering empire like the one that had fallen. They condemned the decadence of their times; they also paraded the decadence of their own art works and lifestyles. The famous first line of Paul Verlaine's "Langueur" sums up this delicious contradiction, shared by many of the artists and writers who shaped artistic modernism in opposition to industrial modernism: "Je suis l'Empire à la fin de la décadence" (I am the Empire at the end of the decadence).

The chief factors that the decadent movement reacted against were progress in the guise of industrialization and the failures and inconsistencies that plagued democratization. In France, decadent posturing was inspired partly by the declines and falls that followed the revolutions of 1789, 1830, and 1848: the democratic promise of 1789 snuffed out by Napoleonic imperialism and the Bourbon Restoration; the

3. Théophile Gautier, *Mademoiselle de Maupin,* tr. Joanna Richardson (New York: Penguin, 1981), p. 143.

4. Théophile de Ferrière quoted by Koenraad Swart, *The Sense of Decadence in Nineteenth-Century France* (The Hague: Martinus Nijhoff, 1964), p. 77, n. 1.

promise of democracy in 1830 leading only to the July Monarchy and bourgeois industrialism; and the "socialist revolutions" across Europe in 1848 ending with the victory of reactionary forces, including, in France, the Second Empire of Napoleon III. Even more devastating was the "debacle" of the Franco-Prussian War followed by the bloody suppression of the Paris Commune in 1871, which Gustave Flaubert, for one, saw as an unmitigated catastrophe and the end of French civilization: "What barbarism! What a disaster! I was hardly a progressive and a humanitarian in the past. Nevertheless, I had my illusions! And I did not believe that I would see the end of the world. But this is it. We are witnessing the end of the latin world."[5]

After the setbacks suffered by the democratic movements throughout the nineteenth century, many artists and intellectuals adopted pessimistic, cynical, often reactionary positions. Toward the end of Emile Zola's *Germinal* (1885), Etienne Lantier, who has gone through the hell of a miner's life and who has seen the innocent "savagery" of the working class crushed by the "cannibalism" of the bourgeoisie, continues to dream of liberation. Etienne imagines the proletariat as the fittest species, overcoming a decadent bourgeoisie (Marxism for Etienne and perhaps also for Zola is a branch of social Darwinism). In the same passage, he also imagines the future revolution in terms of a Roman analogy:

> For if one class had to be devoured, surely the people, vigorous and young, must devour the effete and luxury-loving bourgeoisie? A new society needed new blood. In this expectation of a new invasion of barbarians regenerating the decayed nations of the old world, he rediscovered his absolute faith in a coming revolution, and this time it would be the real one, whose fires would cast their red glare over the end of this epoch even as the rising sun was now drenching the sky in blood.[6]

Etienne marches off into the bloody sunrise of the Paris Commune of 1871.

Zola could not have given his novel a more pessimistic conclusion. Marx viewed the Paris Commune as the harbinger of the final revolu-

---

5. Gustave Flaubert quoted by Swart, *The Sense of Decadence in Nineteenth-Century France*, p. 124.
6. Emile Zola, *Germinal*, tr. L. W. Tancock (Baltimore: Penguin, 1954), p. 496.

ion, only temporarily checked by the forces of repression. But, closer
o Flaubert, Zola interprets the Commune and its aftermath as one
nore inevitable disaster for the unfit masses, visited upon them by the
itter bourgeoisie and the extremely fit Prussians. In *Germinal*, all the
·evolutionary efforts of the miners end in calamity. The novel reaches
i climax in the desperate machine-breaking riot that also breaks the
ack of the strike. The sabotage of the Le Voreux mine by the anar-
:hist Souvarine kills only miners. Etienne himself emerges from the
ordeal of being buried alive a white-haired skeleton. When he
narches off full of hope toward the bloody "debacle" of 1871, he
eaves nothing but disaster in his wake and is headed only toward a
still greater catastrophe.

The entire Rougon-Macquart series of novels, anatomizing life un-
ler the Second Empire, points deterministically toward the catastro-
ohes of 1870–71. Zola's naturalism, supposedly applying the latest,
nost progressive "experimental" methods to the novel, explores the
lecadence of France after 1848 through the disasters and degenera-
:ions visited upon his characters. Even the more successful side of the
'amily tree, the Rougons, eventually produces imbeciles and de-
'ormed specimens. The counterfeit imperialism of Napoleon III also
·epresents a degenerate falling away from that of the first Napoleon.
No wonder that Max Nordau, in his massive exposé of the corruption
of his times, *Degeneration* (1893), includes Zola and other "realists"
ilongside esthetes, impressionists, and symbolists as exemplars of
lecay. The anatomist of decadence turns out himself to be decadent:
Zola "constantly practices . . . that atavistic anthropomorphism and
symbolism . . . which is found among savages . . . and among the
whole category of degenerates. . . . Machines are horrible monsters
lreaming of destruction; the streets of Paris open the jaws of Moloch
to devour the human masses; a *magasin de modes* is an alarming,
supernaturally powerful being."[7] There is much truth in Nordau's
issessment. But by identifying the critique of decadence with dec-
idence itself, Nordau adopts a line of argument that ought to condemn
his own treatise as an example of degeneracy. More to the point,
lespite his superficial antagonism to art-for-art's sake, Zola approximates the many "decadent" poets and symbolists who are Nordau's

7. Max Nordau, *Degeneration* (New York: Appleton, 1895), p. 494.

chief anathema: both the naturalists and the "decadents" create works of art that revel in the same regressive qualities they expose and condemn.

Dissecting the decadence of his society, Zola was frequently attacked by other anatomists of decay. "Zolaism is a disease. It is a study of the putrid. . . . No one can read Zola without moral contamination."[8] Condemnations of the "leprous character" and "sheer beastliness" of Zola's novels became rampant in the British press in the late 1880s, at the time of the Vizetelly censorship trial. When the matter of Victor Vizetelly's English translations of Zola came before Parliament in 1888, an M.P. wondered: "Were they to stand still while the country was wholly corrupted by literature of this kind? Were they to wait until the moral fibre of the English race was eaten out, as that of the French was almost? Look what such literature had done for France. It overspread that country like a torrent, and its poison was destroying the whole national life. France, to-day, was rapidly approaching the condition of Rome in the time of the Caesars."[9] This was to attribute, of course, great corruptive if not constructive power to literature, a belief that "decadent" writers were quite willing to encourage by making style their sovereign value, even while they disengaged themselves as completely as possible from social responsibility. The arguments against Zola, moreover, follow the general pattern of arguments against mass culture as corruptive and decadent. The same M.P. had no difficulty in associating Zola with the literary "garbage on which the children of London fed . . . the penny dreadful and the penny novelette." This literature of the masses is poisoning the entire national life; it constitutes a "terrible pestilence . . . spreading throughout the country."

The association of literary naturalism with negative classicism and also with the decadent movement is not fortuitous. Both Huysmans, whose *A Rebours* served as the pattern book and "breviary" for the decadent movement, and George Moore, the only British novelist who tried to be faithful to Zola's naturalism, began as imitators of Zola and ended by adopting decadent poses and styles. Zola himself de-

8. The National Vigilance Association, "Pernicious Literature" (1889), in George J. Becker, ed., *Documents of Modern Literary Realism* (Princeton: Princeton University Press, 1963), p. 381.
9. Ibid., p. 355.

clared his preference for "the works of decadence where a sort of sickly sensibility replaces the robust fertility of classical epochs."[10] And a number of other writers, Flaubert prominent among them, combine naturalistic and decadent traits.

With his hatred of things utilitarian, industrial, and bourgeois, Flaubert may be taken as representative of the decadent movement in France. The opposite of Homais, that smug, detestably progressive apothecary and citoyen who ironically wins the medal of the Legion of Honor at the end of *Madame Bovary*, is perhaps Heliogabalus. The sadistic, antique splendors of *Salammbô* are as inimical to bourgeois, industrial values as the clichés of *Bouvard et Pécuchet* are ironically expressive of them. And Flaubert has his cult of Nero, as Oscar Wilde and the *fin de siècle* decadents have theirs of Domitian, Salome, and Byzantium. Flaubert cultivates "the love of things Roman branching out into all madnesses, expanding into all lubricities, by turn Egyptian under Antony, Asiatic at Naples with Nero, Indian with Heliogabalus, Sicilian, Tartar and Byzantine under Theodorus, and always mingling some blood with its roses, and always displaying its red flesh under the arcade of its grand circus where the lions roared, where the hippopotamuses swam, where the Christians died."[11]

At the same time that Flaubert exemplifies many of the themes and attitudes of the decadent movement, he also points toward that extreme development of realism which Zola called naturalism. He denied being a realist, and would also have denied being a decadent, a naturalist, or anything else programmatic. But *Salammbô* reveals the axis along which naturalism and the decadent movement are joined. Flaubert's agonizingly precise realistic techniques are lavished upon a story that is essentially nihilistic. *Salammbô* comes close to fulfilling Flaubert's ambition to write "a book about nothing, a book without external attachments, which would hold together by itself through the

10. Zola quoted by Swart, *The Sense of Decadence in Nineteenth-Century France*, p. 112.

11. Gustave Flaubert quoted by Mario Praz, *The Romantic Agony* (New York: Oxford University Press, 1951), p. 182 (my translation). For Flaubert's Neronian cult, see the entire series of quotations in Praz. And compare Verlaine: "J'aime le mot de décadence, tout miroitant de pourpre et d'ors," quoted by Swart, *The Sense of Decadence in Nineteenth-Century France*, p. 165. See also A. E. Carter, *The Idea of Decadence in French Literature, 1830–1900* (Toronto: University of Toronto Press, 1958).

internal force of its style."[12] Just as much as Zola in *Germinal*, Flaubert is dealing with a historical cul-de-sac. The sadistic triumphs and lapidary splendors of Carthage lead nowhere but to treachery and destruction, the decimation of the barbarians who seem at least to embody some wild freedom, and the torture and death of Mâtho by the entire "civilized" population of the capital. Also, of course, Carthage itself is doomed to destruction in an even more ruinous and final way than Rome. Rome at least, as Sainte-Beuve declared, points toward "the whole future of civilization"; but Carthage is only a necropolis, devoid of hope.

Flaubert's Carthage represents in extreme form the futility, cruelty, and desolation of all empires; the entire history of civilization takes on the aspect of a death factory. *Salammbô* belongs partly to the *memento mori* genre exemplified by Constantin François Volney's *Ruins*; Flaubert populates the ruins with a horde of cruel, exotic ghosts. But as Georg Lukács suggests in *The Historical Novel* (1962), *Salammbô* resolutely refuses to be a political statement or to point a finger out of the past at the crimes of the present. The historical dead end of Carthage is mirrored in the total disjunction between Flaubert's narrative and immediate social concerns: the novelist refuses to judge; the work of art exists in a state of hermetic splendor; the supreme value is style. Flaubert's is the stance of the decadent practitioner of art-for-art's sake, although the stance itself is in an important way political: a decadent estheticism, by which art no longer connects with anything but art, is obviously antithetical to anything like mass art, anything manufactured for consumption by the masses. *Salammbô* is thus an implicit condemnation of the decadent, bourgeois, industrial society that casts the arts into the outer darkness of a modish alienation. Only across the barricade of Flaubert's deliberate isolation can Hamilcar's prophecy of the downfall of Carthage, for example, be read as pointing also to modern France: "You will lose your ships, your lands, your chariots, your hanging beds, the slaves who rub your feet! Jackals will lie down in your palaces, the plough will turn up your graves. Nothing will remain but the eagles' cry and heaps of ruins. You will fall, Carthage!"[13]

12. Flaubert quoted in Becker, *Documents of Modern Literary Realism*, p. 90.
13. Gustave Flaubert, *Salammbô*, tr. A. J. Krailshamer (New York: Penguin, 1977), p. 115.

Flaubert's Carthage nevertheless mirrors the Paris of the Second Empire, although of course less directly than Yvetot and Tostes mirror provincial France in *Madame Bovary*. Lukács argues that *Salammbô*'s "frozen, lunar landscape of archaeological precision" betrays a false "modernization of history"; a dead Carthage is made to stand in the place of a dying modernity. Lukács finds the result not far removed from naturalism: "Only in Flaubert's imagination does Mâtho embody ancient love. In reality, he is a prophetic model of the decadent drunkards and madmen of Zola."[14] The treacheries, triumphs, and disasters of the Carthaginians are no different in kind from those of modern France. History is both static and endlessly repetitious for Flaubert, because human nature never progresses. Flaubert's frequent descriptions of jewels and precious metals as features of clothing and architecture, the ornaments of a cruelly static necropolis petrified in the sands of the past, are also suggestive of the way history always works: imperializing civilization seems inevitably to transform the raw materials of humanity into piles of useless wealth, and then again into piles of bones and ruins. Like the golden bird in Yeats's Byzantium poems, the lapidary brilliance of Carthage seems to exist outside of time, beyond "the fury and the mire" of history. But whereas Yeats's Byzantium represents at least the mirage of eternality, the chief god of Flaubert's Carthage is Moloch the Devourer, to whom belongs "men's existence, their very flesh," and to whom frequent sacrifice must be made "to still his fury." Flaubert might just as well have said that Mammon is the chief god of his fellow Parisians; in *L'education sentimentale*, we are told that after the revolution of 1848, despite "the most humanitarian legislation ever passed in France . . . property was raised to the level of Religion and became indistinguishable from God."[15]

From the outset the decadent movement was profoundly anti-bourgeois, anti-industrial, and also antidemocratic. The antithesis of a genuine work of art is whatever can be understood and consumed by "the public," "the masses," "the canaille." According to that decadent impressionist, James McNeill Whistler, great artists are always ge-

---

14. Georg Lukács, *The Historical Novel*, tr. Hannah and Stanley Mitchell (New York: Humanities, 1965 [1937, English trans. 1962]), p. 192.

15. Gustave Flaubert, *Sentimental Education*, tr. Robert Baldick (New York: Penguin, 1964), p. 295.

niuses isolated in the midst of dull publics that fail to comprehend them: "There never was an Art-loving nation."[16] History has been a declension from the days when heroic artists could forge their will against the unwitting mediocrity of the masses down to modern times, when the bourgeoisie with their factories and their profit mongering have made the pursuit of the beautiful nearly impossible:

> The world was flooded with all that was beautiful, until there arose a new class, who discovered the cheap, and foresaw fortune in the facture of the sham.
> Then sprang into existence the tawdry, the common, the geegaw.
> The taste of the tradesman supplanted the science of the artist, and what was born of the million went back to them, and charmed them, for it was after their own heart; and the great and the small, the statesman and the slave, took to themselves the abomination that was tendered, and preferred it—and have lived with it ever since!
> And the artist's occupation was gone, and the manufacturer and the huckster took his place.[17]

This is the central myth of the esthetic decadents, expressed in one form or another in all of their manifestoes and works of art. It follows that a novel like *Salammbô* stands as a deliberate if implicit protest against any idea of art as a utilitarian or profitable or progressive or industrial activity. Like many later modernist artists and writers, the decadents aimed to produce works of art that were completely anti-thetical to mass culture, or to whatever seemed vulgar and cheap enough to be appreciated by the bourgeoisie and the masses below them.

If *Salammbô* is attached to the present only by indirection, Huysmans's *A Rebours* is very much a novel about contemporary decadence: the decline and fall of Des Esseintes, victim of urban-industrial malaise, ennui, and syphilis, reflects in miniature the fate of modern civilization. The decadent hero suffers from "that peculiar malady which ravages effete, enfeebled races." Des Esseintes represents a moribund aristocracy, which there is no hope of reviving: "The decayed nobility was done for; the aristocracy had sunk into imbecility or depravity. It was dying from the degeneracy of its scions, whose

16. James McNeill Whistler, "The Ten O'Clock," in Robert L. Peters, ed., *Victorians on Literature and Art* (New York: Appleton-Century-Crofts, 1961), p. 143.
17. Ibid., p. 145.

faculties had deteriorated with each succeeding generation till they now consisted of the instincts of gorillas at work in the skulls of grooms and jockeys."[18] Huysmans's language is unmistakably both Darwinian and Zolaesque; he applies an evolutionary but degenerative determinism to entire classes and societies. Huysmans did not leave naturalism behind to write decadent "breviaries"; rather, he found the theme of decadence ready-made in Zola and the Goncourt brothers and applied it to the upper end of the social register. *A Rebours* portrays the other side of the landscape of social disaster depicted in *Germinal*: both Des Esseintes and Etienne Lantier, both aristocracy and working class, are doomed at least metaphorically to be eaten alive by the fittest species, the bourgeoisie. "What point of contact," Des Esseintes wonders, "could there possibly be between him and that bourgeois class which had gradually climbed to the top, taking advantage of every disaster to fill its pickets, stirring up every sort of trouble to command respect for its countless crimes and thefts?" The commercialism of the bourgeoisie devours everything that stands in its way, like the cannibal god of capital in *Germinal*. "Overbearing and underhand in behavior, base and cowardly in character, [the bourgeoisie] ruthlessly shot down its perennial and essential dupe, the mob, which it had previously unmuzzled and sent flying at the throats of the old castes." The impact on culture of bourgeois domination and crassness, needless to say, has been catastrophic: "the suppression of all intelligence, the negation of all honesty, the destruction of all art" (218). Des Esseintes's attempt to create a sanctuary of esthetic sensation, walled off from the cultural depredations of the bourgeoisie, prefigures the pattern of many later attacks upon mass culture as sham, disease, or commercial cannibalism, an apocalyptic category of decline and fall.

In an important way, however, Des Esseintes does not merely despair of the future; he delights masochistically in his own deterioration and in the idea of the ultimate downfall of society at large. Inspired by reading Dickens, Des Esseintes conjures up a vision of London and even sets off on a trip to visit it, though he gets no farther than Paris. His London vision is replete with dockside scenes, street traffic, fog, the roar and bustle of business and industry, and it ends on

---

18. Joris-Karl Huysmans, *Against Nature*, tr. Robert Baldick (New York: Penguin, 1959), p. 214.

this note: "Des Esseintes shuddered with delight at feeling himself lost in this terrifying world of commerce, immersed in this isolating fog, involved in this incessant activity, and caught up in this ruthless machine which ground to powder millions of poor wretches" (134). Here is the atavistic world of *Germinal,* in which "machines are horrible monsters dreaming of destruction," but viewed through an opera glass of esthetic sensation.

The same sense of perverse enjoyment characterizes the theme of negative classicism in Huysmans's story. Des Esseintes's evocations of the crepuscular style of Latin decadence, which lead him to recount the decline and fall of ancient civilization, are high on his list of pleasures. He is especially fond of Petronius's *Satyricon,* which he reads as a "realistic novel, [a] slice cut from Roman life in the raw"; of Claudian, who "calls Antiquity back to life" while "the Western Empire crumble[s] to its ruin all about him"; and of Tertullian, that *sine qua non* of negative classicism, who "had gone on calmly writing his sermons . . . while the Roman Empire tottered" (45). Not that Des Esseintes pays heed to the content of the gloomy African's sermons: while Tertullian was preaching "carnal abstinence, frugality of diet, sobriety of dress . . . Elagabalus was treading in silver dust and sand of gold, his head crowned with a tiara and his clothes studded with jewels, working at women's tasks in the midst of his eunuchs, calling himself Empress and bedding every night with a new Emperor, picked for choice from among his barbers, scullions, and charioteers." Des Esseintes, we are told, delights in this contrast, but of course it is Heliogabalus upon whom he models his own behavior. Even more than the behavior of perverse emperors, however, it is the literary style of the Roman decadence that Des Esseintes admires. He is enamored of "that special gamy flavour which in the fourth century— and even more in the following centuries—the odour of Christianity was to give to the pagan tongue as it decomposed like venison, dropping to pieces at the same time as the civilization of the Ancient World, falling apart while the Empires succumbed to the barbarian onslaught and the accumulated pus of ages" (46).

Des Esseintes's fondness for decadent Latin is anything but pedantic. Far from a quiet rummaging among old books, his account of linguistic decadence leads to passages of bloodthirsty, apocalyptic lyricism, reaching a crescendo in this evocation of the barbarian invasions:

On the banks of the Danube, thousands of men wrapped in ratskin cloaks and mounted on little horses, hideous Tartars with enormous heads, flat noses, hairless, jaundiced faces, and chins furrowed with gashes and scars, rode hell-for-leather into the territories of the Lower Empire, sweeping all before them in their whirlwind advance. . . . Civilization disappeared in the dust of their horses' hooves, in the smoke of the fires they kindled. Darkness fell upon the world and the peoples trembled in consternation as they listened to the dreadful tornado pass by with a sound like thunder. The horde of Huns swept over Europe. . . . The earth, gorged with blood, looked like a sea of crimson froth; two hundred thousand corpses barred the way and broke the impetus of the invading avalanche which, turned from its path, fell like a thunderbolt on Italy, whose ruined cities burned like blazing hay-ricks. [49]

If Zola had written a novel about the fall of the Roman Empire, it would have sounded like this. In any case, Des Esseintes's love of decadence clearly also involves a love of barbarism and scenes of destruction. Huysmans leads us on an ironic path from his protagonist's fastidious and eccentric bibliophile tastes to images of the smashing of civilizations. What is the connection between the two? Perhaps only the meanderings of Des Esseintes's depraved imagination. But the very insistence on style as the supreme value seems to lead to scenes of desolation; it functions like a kind of vampirism, leaving the world symbolically incoherent, ravaged, falling into ruins.

The emphasis on style is evident in every important decadent manifesto. The decadents were far from being linguistic purists, however, seeking to prop up a tottering civilization by improving its rhetoric. The styles they valued most were themselves supposedly diseased, corrupt. Their classicism was primarily negative; their avant-garde modernism resuscitated the writers of a twilight age. In his preface to *Les fleurs du mal*, Gautier defines Baudelaire's "style of decadence" as "nothing other than art reaching the point of extreme maturity determined by the oblique suns of aging civilizations: a style ingenious, complicated, knowing, full of nuances and affectations."[19] He proceeds to compare Baudelaire's style to the "decomposing" language of falling Rome and of "the Byzantine school." Baudelaire, he says, preferred to the language of Virgil and Cicero that of "Apuleius,

19. Théophile Gautier, preface to Charles Baudelaire, *Les fleurs du mal* (Paris: Michel Lévy, 1868), p. 17.

Petronius, Juvenal, Saint Augustine, and that Tertullian whose style
has the black sound of ebony" (18). Gautier quotes a statement that
Baudelaire attached to a Latin poem in *Les fleurs du mal*: "Does it not
seem . . . that the language of the final Latin decadence—supreme
sigh of a robust person already transformed and prepared for the life of
the spirit—is singularly able to express the passion which the modern
poetic world understands and feels?" Out of their impotence and rage
in the face of bourgeois hegemony, decadent writers sought their
revenge by declaring style, that seemingly least powerful value, to be
their private monopoly, off limits to the bourgeoisie. Style was a
mystery beyond the ken of ordinary mortals. The effect of so treating
it, however, was like removing, at least in imagination, the keystone
from the grand arch of civilization. Here was a whole generation of
writers who might have been singing the praises of the French Second
Empire or of the British Empire, but who declared instead that those
empires were doomed. They even seemed to be hastening decline
and fall by imitating the decadent Romans and by cultivating linguistic
corruptions and eccentricities, like magical incantations against the
powers-that-be. And one and all they subscribed to the heresy that
modern society was not following the path of progress, but its
opposite.

ii

Just as much as the failures and disillusionments attendant upon
democratization, industrialization was a cause of dismay for many
nineteenth-century artists and intellectuals. The idea that machinery
is destructive of art and culture arose with the factory system. The full
history of how artists have responded to the threats of specific new
machine techniques—steam printing and linotyping, lithography,
photography, the telegraph and telephone, radio, cinema, television—has yet to be written, but it would deal with everything that we
now categorize as mass media. Flaubert again can serve as an example: "Let us cry against imitation silk, desk chairs, economy kitchens,
fake materials, fake luxury, fake pride. Industrialism has developed
the ugly to gigantic proportions. . . . The department store has rendered true luxury difficult . . . we have all become fakers and char-
latans. . . . Our century is a whorish century . . . the least pros

tituted are the real prostitutes."20 The equation of machinery with
degeneration rather than with progress, paradoxically central to many
versions of literary and artistic modernism, was in part a defensive
reaction to the displacement of traditional arts and crafts by methods
of mechanical reproduction.21 Zola's naturalism also shows the industrial present as retrograde, brutal, destructive of humane values and
of the masses who, though inevitably the victims of history, still sometimes exhibit tragic or heroic qualities. Both the decadent movement
and naturalism are anti-industrial, and the former at least is thoroughly antidemocratic as well: no good is to be expected either from
mass production or from the masses, the two main ingredients in the
modern idea of mass culture.

George Moore, that Irish-Parisian mimic of all late-nineteenth-cen-
tury fads and isms, including both naturalism and decadence, can
condemn the degeneracy of modern industrial society in one passage
and invoke the macabre splendors of falling Rome in the next. In his
Confessions of a Young Man (1888), Moore writes: "Oh, for the silence of marble courts, for the shadow of great pillars, for gold, for
reticulated canopies of lilies; to see the great gladiators pass, to hear
them cry the famous 'Ave Caesar,' to hold the thumb down, to see the
blood flow, to fill the languid hours with the agonies of poisoned
slaves! Oh, for excess, for crime!"22 No doubt this is the decadent
movement at its most jejune, but the same double purpose occurs in
the other celebrators of Roman degeneracy, from Gautier and
Flaubert to Huysmans and Wilde. As antique decadence is praised, so
modern decadence, supposedly caused by industrialization and democratization, is condemned. "The world is dying of machinery," says
Moore; "that is the great disease, that is the plague that will sweep
away and destroy civilization; man will have to rise against it sooner or
later." Moore is perhaps echoing William Morris when he adds: "I say
the great and the reasonable revolution will be when mankind rises in
revolt, and smashes the machinery and restores the handicrafts" (113).

As Raymond Williams has shown in the British case, similar anti-

20. Flaubert quoted by César Graña, *Bohemian versus Bourgeois* (New York: Basic,
1964), p. 108.

21. See my comments on Walter Benjamin's "The Work of Art in the Age of
Mechanical Reproduction" in chapter 7, pp. 238–40.

22. George Moore, *Confessions of a Young Man*, ed. Susan Dick (Montreal:
McGill–Queen's University Press, 1972), pp. 125 and 113.

industrial attitudes, together with the idea that the factory system (if
not society as a whole) was doomed to collapse, can be found in the
first critics of mass production, particularly the romantic poets (Blake,
Southey, Coleridge, Wordsworth) and their Victorian descendants
(Carlyle, Arnold, Ruskin, Morris). "A Machine is not a Man nor a
Work of Art," wrote William Blake; "it is destructive of Humanity &
of Art."[23] As early as 1804, Blake condemned England's "dark satanic
mills" for destroying the original Eden or Jerusalem of "England's
green and pleasant land," while in 1829 Robert Southey could write
that "everything connected with manufactures presents . . . features
of unqualified deformity." Like Blake's, Southey's rejection of the
factories was as much esthetic as economic and humanitarian. Samuel
Taylor Coleridge also thought that industrialism, at least if allowed to
regulate itself according to the self-justifying laws of political economy, was a menace to culture and to "human personality." Spinning an
archaeological fantasy, Coleridge said of the new science of economics
that "it would dig up the charcoal foundations of the temple of
Ephesus to burn as fuel for a steam-engine."[24]

   In France, a similar hostility toward industrialism appears at least
by the 1830s. Long before Baudelaire attacked "the fanaticism of
utensils," Stendhal decried "industrialism, second cousin to charlata-
nism"; Sainte-Beuve anatomized the "industrialization of literature";
and Balzac's *Illusions perdues* (1837–43) exposed the destructive effects of commercial and industrial techniques on poetry. "We shall die
by that which we believed would bring us life," writes Baudelaire in
one of his *Fusées*. "Mechanization will have so thoroughly Ameri-
canized us, progress will have so thoroughly atrophied the entire
spiritual side of us, that nothing among the bloody, sacrilegious, or
antinatural dreams of the utopians will be comparable to these positive results." Therefore, "the world is coming to an end."[25]

   23. William Blake quoted by Morris Eaves, "Blake and the Artistic Machine,"
PMLA, 92 (October 1977), p. 903.
   24. William Blake, preface to *Milton*; Robert Southey, *Sir Thomas More: or, Collo-
quies on the Progress and Prospects of Society* (London: John Murray, 1827), I, 174;
Samuel Taylor Coleridge, *Table Talk*, 20 June 1834, *Complete Works*, 7 vols., ed. W.
G. T. Shedd (New York: Harper, 1884), VI, 516.
   25. Charles Baudelaire, *Oeuvres complètes*, 15 vols. (Paris: Louis Conard, 1952),
XI, pt. 2, 74. See also Albert George, *The Development of French Romanticism: The
Impact of the Industrial Revolution on Literature* (Syracuse: Syracuse University
Press, 1955).

For Baudelaire and many other artists and intellectuals, industrialization and the emergence of the masses as a threat to the social order formed one process. Three decades into the nineteenth century, Thomas Carlyle penned his first accounts of how "the huge demon of Mechanism" was calling forth "whole multitudes of workmen" who needed somehow to be "organized" and led by some principle higher than "Mammonism." The protagonists of Carlyle's *French Revolution, Chartism,* and *Past and Present* are the industrialized masses, looking for upper-class heroes and leaders. In *Chartism,* Carlyle applies a Roman analogy to the industrial scene of 1839, suggesting that new chieftains must arise to lead the new barbarian hordes abroad—thus anticipating by nearly a century Spengler's and Ortega's identifications of "masses" with "barbarism." "Now once more, as at the end of the Roman Empire, a most confused epoch and yet one of the greatest, the Teutonic Countries find themselves too full. On a certain western rim of our small Europe, there are more men than were expected."[26] Where, then, Carlyle asks, are the new "Hengsts and Alarics . . . who, when their home is grown too narrow, will enlist and, like fire-pillars, guide onwards those superfluous masses of indomitable living Valour; equipped, not now with the battle-axe and war chariot, but with the steam-engine and ploughshare?"

Just as much as the doctrine of "hero worship," such a solution to the Malthusian problem of "superfluous masses" makes Carlyle sound like a precursor of fascism, as H. C. Grierson and others have claimed him to be. The equation may be anachronistic, but it is still true that the Malthusian image of "masses," associated with industrial regimentation and unemployment, became tragically linked to rationalizations not just for emigration but also for imperialistic expansion, as in this 1904 German call for *Lebensraum*:

> A people needs land for its activities, land for its nourishment. No people needs it as much as the German people which is increasing so rapidly and whose old boundaries have become dangerously narrow. If we do not soon acquire new territories, we are moving towards a frightful catastrophe. . . . Once more, as 2000 years ago when the Cimbri and the Teutons were hammering at the gates of Rome,

26. Thomas Carlyle, *Chartism,* in *Essays: Scottish and Other Miscellanies,* 2 vols. New York: Everyman's Library, 1915), II, 200.

sounds the cry, now full of anguish and unappeased desires, now arrogant and full of confidence—sounds more and more strongly the cry, "We must have lands, new lands!"[27]

Throughout much of Western Europe the failure of industrial capitalism to organize the "superfluous masses" led to attempts to organize them through the extreme alternatives either of revolutionary socialism or of facism and National Socialism—alternatives which, viewed from the perspectives of many modern cultural theorists of all political persuasions, involved the destruction of civilization either through a revolution of working-class "slaves" or through an eruption of working- and middle-class "barbarians."

Malthusianism may seem unrelated to the concerns of the decadent movement. *Germinal,* however, with its blunt depiction of the sex lives of the proletariat, "germinating" children to add to the "superfluous masses," is very much a Malthusian novel. And, though in reverse, so is *A Rebours*: Des Esseintes represents the sexual dead end of the aristocracy, its failure to match the other classes in reproducing its own kind. In his influential tract on decadence, *Essais de psychologie contemporaine* (1880–83), Paul Bourget defines a society on the wane as one "which produces too large a number of individuals who are unsuited to the labours of the common life." These are the masses of the unemployed and the poorly employed, everyone from paupers and miners on strike to decadent poets like Baudelaire and depraved aristocrats like Des Esseintes, whom Bourget sees as visited by the same deadly and insatiable craving for sensation which plagued Nero and Heliogabalus. According to Bourget:

> A society should be like an organism. Like an organism, in fact, it may be resolved into a federation of smaller organisms, which may themselves be resolved into a federation of cells. The individual is the social cell. In order that the organism should perform its functions with energy it is necessary that the organisms composing it should perform their functions with energy, but with a subordinated energy. . . . If the energy of the cells becomes independent, the lesser organisms will likewise cease to subordinate their energy to

27. Quoted in Louis Synder, ed., *The Imperialism Reader* (Princeton: Van Nostrand, 1962), p. 89.

the total energy and the anarchy which is established constitutes the *decadence* of the whole.[28]

Bourget offers an early, Darwinian and Malthusian version of the theory of the atomization that takes place in a mass society. The same "law" which governs the disintegration of the social organism, moreover, also governs the disintegration of language: "A style of decadence is one in which the unity of the book is decomposed to give place to the independence of the page, in which the page is decomposed to give place to the independence of the phrase, and the phrase to give place to the independence of the word." Such was the style of the writers of the Latin decadence; and such is the style of the decadent writers of modern Europe. In *The Case of Wagner*, Nietzsche paraphrases this passage from Bourget and concludes that decadence appears "every time there is an anarchy of atoms."[29]

The Malthusian side of Bourget's theory, according to which a declining society throws up superfluous individuals, seems to conflict with an exactly contrary idea: that a state of decadence arises from a weakening of the sexual impulse and consequently from under- rather than from over-population. This is Huysmans's version of the decadence of the aristocracy. In its later stages, according to Bourget, "Roman society failed to produce enough children; it therefore could no longer put enough soldiers in the field. The citizens ceased to care for the routines of parentage" (27). Bourget goes on to defend decadence, partly in these terms: if the members of a declining society "are poor reproducers of future generations," they may turn instead to the reproduction of an "abundance" of "fine sensations" and "rarefied sentiments . . . sterilised but refined." By implication, the problem of overpopulation or of the production of superfluous masses is here taken out of the hands of the effete, declining civilization and attached instead to the image of barbarian hordes. "Certainly, a teutonic chief-

---

28. Paul Bourget, *Essais de psychologie contemporaine* (Paris: Alphonse Lemerre, 1893 [1881]), pp. 3–32. I have quoted the translated passages from Havelock Ellis, "A Note on Paul Bourget," in *Views and Reviews* (Boston: Houghton Mifflin, 1932), p. 52; the page numbers in parentheses are from Bourget's book.

29. See Walter Kaufmann, *Nietzsche: Philosopher, Psychologist, Antichrist* (Princeton: Princeton University Press, 1974), p. 73.

tain of the second century was more able to invade the empire than a
Roman patrician was able to defend it" (27).

In contrast to the romantics and decadents, the first political economists equate machinery with progress. But whereas they might be
expected to show how the masses can gradually be transformed into a
prosperous, democratic public through industrial expansion, they not
only rationalize the existing distribution of property but also fail to
show conclusively how capitalism can cure poverty. Indeed, Thomas
Malthus and David Ricardo seem to prove that the progress of society
does not mean and perhaps can never mean progress for the poor.
Malthus's *Essay on Population* (1798) negates all prospects for the
betterment of "the lower orders" through "systems of equality" and
through schemes of government relief like the poor laws.[30] Unless
"checked" by "moral restraint," population will always outgrow sub-
sistence only to be checked in harsher ways by warfare, disease, or
famine. At the same time, as Ricardo shows even more clearly than
Malthus, industrial expansion will not necessarily help the poor either. To Malthus's theory of overpopulation, Ricardo adds the problem of technological unemployment. Together, they suggest that even
under the best industrial conditions there will be unemployment, or,
to use Malthus's phrase, a "redundant population": "the poor ye shall
always have with you." No wonder that Carlyle calls the "science" of
bourgeois progress "dismal." At the heart of bustling rationalizations
of industrialism and free trade looms up the specter of "the masses" as
"redundant population," ominous, haggard, a hideous "swarm" casting its pall over England's green and pleasant land.

Just as much as against machinery and "the factory system," the
first romantics set themselves against Malthusianism. As early as
1803, Southey writes that Malthus's *Essay* has become "the political
bible of the rich, the selfish, and the sensual."[31] He sees at least dimly

30. Thomas Malthus, *Essay on the Principal of Population*, 2 vols. (London: Everyman's Library, 1932). Malthus also has his version of the decline and fall of empires.
Rome's fall was due to moral degeneracy including a failure to attend to agriculture.
"The pernicious custom of importing great quantities of corn to distribute, gratuitously
among the people," Malthus says, "had given it [agriculture? the Empire?] a blow
from which it never afterwards recovered" (1:149). Like all forms of relief to the poor,
the bread side of the bread and circuses policy Malthus regards as ruinous. A severe
moralist, he does not mention circuses.

31. Robert Southey quoted by Harold A. Bonar, *Hungry Generations* (New York:
King's Crown, 1955), p. 69.

the main fallacy in Malthus's argument, which is that poverty ante-
dates overpopulation and is the result of preexisting arrangements of
property and power, not of "imprudence." Wordsworth, Coleridge,
Byron, Hazlitt, Shelley, and Carlyle also lash out against "sophisms
like those of Mr. Malthus," which according to Shelley are "calculated
to lull the oppressors of mankind into a security of everlasting triumph."[32] There was in fact a torrent of anti-Malthusian literature
written between 1820 and 1850, much of it summarized in Harold
Bonar's able study *Hungry Generations*, which takes its title from
Keats's "Ode to a Nightingale":

> Thou wast not born for death, immortal Bird!
> No hungry generations tread thee down—

an allusion that suggests the extent to which romanticism and the new
political economy were incompatible with each other, but that also
suggests how much both groups of intellectuals, the romantics and the
economists, are troubled by the Malthusian specter of a "redundant
population" of the unemployed, uprooted poor.

Keats's lines point to the dilemma that other writers and artists—
John Ruskin, William Morris, Leo Tolstoy—explore more thoroughly
later in the century: the difficulty or perhaps impossibility of fulfilling
cultural ideals in the midst of injustice, poverty, class conflict, and
industrial regimentation and squalor. Even those intellectuals who
most vigorously deny the validity of Malthus's arguments of course do
not deny the existence of alienated masses of the dispossessed and
disfranchised. But often the romantics are thrown back upon solutions
to "the social question" which are not far from those advocated by
Malthus. In *The Excursion*, for example, Wordsworth rejects Malthus
but lamely recommends emigration as a cure for overpopulation. Britain should "cast off / her swarms" by shipping them overseas.[33] Similarly, Carlyle rains down wrath on Malthus, whom he accuses of
wanting to murder the poor (like "Marcus," the author of the notori-
ous *Book of Murder*—a nineteenth-century "Modest Proposal"). But
Carlyle also adopts the language of "swarms" and "masses" and a

32. Shelley, preface to *The Revolt of Islam*.
33. Wordsworth, *The Excursion*, Book IX, lines 377–78.

"surplus population" that must be drawn off through emigration—the original of the *Lebensraum* argument.

No matter how much hatred Malthus inspired, his notion of a "redundant population" of the unemployed poor became the central image in nineteenth-century social thought, and it has remained central ever since. It is obviously on the idea of the masses as alienated— "superfluous," unemployed or employed only as the tools of other people's tools—that Marxism is grounded. Industrialization devours the old class alignments and the natural environment as well, converting the potentially democratic "people" into rich and poor, and dehumanizing both classes in the process—"people" become capital and labor, owners and masses. Abstract or mechanical money relations— Carlyle's "cash nexus"—in urban industrial centers take the place of older, local, perhaps simpler and perhaps kindlier relations in natural or rural settings. The peasantry, wrenched from the land by the enclosure movement, by overpopulation, and by both aristocratic and bourgeois greed, is converted into a new and dangerous sort of industrial cannon fodder. The new factories spew out commodities, including the "most wretched of commodities," the proletariat. Marx summarizes: "The other classes decay and finally disappear in the face of Modern Industry; the proletariat is its special and essential product."[34] Thus the bourgeoisie manufactures its own undoing, "the masses" who, "crowded into the factory, are organized like soldiers." "The weapons with which the bourgeoisie felled feudalism to the ground are now turned against the bourgeoisie itself. But not only has the bourgeoisie forged the weapons that bring death to itself; it has also called into existence the men who are to wield those weapons— the modern working class—the proletarians" (340).

Throughout their writings, Marx and Engels often liken the masses to slaves and sometimes to barbarians on the Roman model; for Marx and Engels too, it appears, "the tradition of all the dead generations weighs like a nightmare on the brain of the living." Spartacus ranks high on the list of Marxist saints, and "barbarism" is cherished both for its destructive and for its rejuvenative powers. In one of Engels's last essays, moreover, the revolutionary masses are not just the destroyers of an old civilization, but the founders of a new one:

34. Karl Marx, *Communist Manifesto* (1848), in Robert C. Tucker, ed., *The Marx-Engels Reader* (New York: Norton, 1972), p. 344.

It is now, almost to the year, sixteen centuries since a dangerous party of overthrow was likewise active in the Roman Empire. It undermined religion and all the foundations of the state; it flatly denied that Caesar's law was the supreme law; it was without a fatherland, was international; it spread over all countries of the empire, from Gaul to Asia, and beyond the frontiers of the empire. It had long carried on seditious activities in secret, underground; for a considerable time, however, it had felt itself strong enough to come out into the open. This party of overthrow was known by the name of Christians.[35]

No doubt Marx would have approved of Engels's Roman analogy only in the sense that communism seeks to realize in this life the ideals of freedom and equality disembodied and inverted in Christian eschatology. The promise of religion becomes the promise of the liberation and humanization of the masses, their "de-reification," but outside the churches, without benefit of clergy, who cannot accept the transmutation of theological illusions into materialistic goals. In much the same way, whatever is valid—that is, aiming toward the construction of a just society—in the culture of the past will remain valid, although outside the elitist institutions and without benefit of clerisy or of the critics, artists, and professors who insist that the class culture to which they are devoted is all-sufficing or that it can resolve the injustices of a class-divided society.[36] To Marx and Engels, the choice was clear: "either barbarism or socialism." Citing Engels as the source of this phrase, Rosa Luxemburg could write in the midst of World War I:

This world war means a reversion to barbarism. The triumph of imperialism leads to the destruction of culture, sporadically during a modern war, and forever, if the period of world wars that has just begun is allowed to take its damnable course to the last ultimate consequence. Thus we stand today, as Friedrich Engels prophesied . . . before the awful proposition: either the triumph of imperialism and the destruction of all culture, and, as in ancient Rome, depopulation, desolation, degeneration, a vast cemetery; or, the victory of socialism, that is, the conscious struggle of the international proletariat against imperialism, against its methods, against

35. Friedrich Engels, "The Tactics of Social Democracy" (1895), in Tucker, *The Marx-Engels Reader*, pp. 422–23.

36. See the discussion of the allegedly humanizing properties of culture in the Frankfurt Institute, *Aspects of Sociology* (Boston: Beacon, 1972), p. 94.

war. This is the dilemma of world history, its inevitable choice, whose scales are trembling in the balance awaiting the decision of the proletariat.[37]

From Luxemburg's perspective, imperialism and war are the worst, last results of the failure to organize the "superfluous masses" through socialism. From the perspective of the decadent movement, imperialism and the masses may seem like social problems to be resolutely ignored, but it is clear that a vision similar to Luxemburg's underlies all decadent invocations of Roman imperialism and barbarian invasions. Empire is the state of society before the final collapse, at the edge of the precipice, of barbarism, of the new Dark Age.

iii

Ten years before the start of World War I, in terms like Luxemburg's, Anatole France declared: "Imperialism is the most recent form of barbarism, the end of the line for civilization. I do not distinguish between the two terms—imperialism and barbarism—for they mean the same thing."[38] When France wrote, however, the paradoxical equation of barbarism with empire was less familiar than the view that overseas expansion coupled with industrial growth was leading to the gradual elimination of "barbarism" and "savagery" and to the installation of "civilization" around the world. From the perspective of the defenders of empire, the "barbarians" waiting to be transformed into their better selves might be the industrial masses, but were also and more obviously the "coloured," "inferior" races in Africa and Asia—the "new-caught, sullen peoples, / Half devil and half child," as Kipling called them. The rhetoric of a civilizing mission and "the white man's burden" was the basic stuff not only of imperialist or "jingoist" journalism, but also of much literature written from about 1880 down to World War I, the same period in which the decadent movement reached its peak. The languages of jingoism and of decadence, the praise of empires and the prophecies of their doom, are the contrary

37. Rosa Luxemburg, "The Junius Pamphlet" (1916), in *Rosa Luxemburg Speaks*, ed. Mary-Alice Waters (New York: Pathfinder, 1970), p. 269.

38. Anatole France, "La folie coloniale" (1904), in Synder, *The Imperialism Reader*, p. 155.

poles around which much turn-of-the-century European writing revolves.

Of the British writers who defended empire, none was more prominent than Kipling, who was, as George Orwell put it, "the prophet of British imperialism in its expansionist phase."[39] Kipling's reputation has inevitably been bound up with his position as an imperial propagandist, with critics taking sides in a dispute more ideological than esthetic. In an early attack on Kipling as "the voice of the hooligan," Robert Buchanan writes: "There is a universal scramble for plunder, for excitement, for amusement, for speculation, and, above it all, the flag of a Hooligan Imperialism is raised, with the proclamation that it is the sole mission of Anglo-Saxon England, forgetful of the task of keeping its own drains in order, to expand and extend its boundaries indefinitely, and, again in the name of the Christianity it has practically abandoned, to conquer and inherit the earth."[40] As in the days of ancient Rome, Buchanan thinks, the upper classes are bribing the working class with the cheap stuff of a "spectacular" patriotism, to which Kipling is contributing: "The mob, promised a merry time by the governing classes, just as the old Roman mob was deluded by bread and pageants—*panem et circenses*—dances merrily to patriotic war-tunes, while that modern monstrosity and anachronism, the conservative working man, exchanges his birthright of freedom and free thought for a pat on the head from any little rump-fed lord that steps his way and spouts the platitudes of cockney patriotism" (235). Buchanan offers us Juvenal redone into Victorian English. That Kipling is a defender of British imperialism is obvious, but his "hooliganism" is partly qualified by the fact that much of his propaganda takes the form of warnings to deal with empire responsibly, in the spirit of civilizing rather than exploiting: imperialists must "take up the white man's burden." This is the message underlying Kipling's own frequent comparisons of British with Roman imperialism, where the Roman decline serves as warning—for example, in the Roman Wall stories in *Puck of Pook's Hill.*

39. George Orwell, "Rudyard Kipling," in *A Collection of Essays* (Garden City, New York: Doubleday, 1954), p. 125.
40. Robert Buchanan, "The Voice of the Hooligan," *Contemporary Review* (1899), reprinted in Roger Lancelyn Green, ed., *Kipling: The Critical Heritage* (London: Routledge & Kegan Paul, 1971), p. 235.

Of the other early modern writers in Britain who took empire for a theme, the most important is Joseph Conrad, who has rarely been accused of jingoism, but often of a disturbing ambiguity about the expansionist practices of his adopted country. Especially in his African stories, based on his experiences in the Belgian Congo in 1890, Conrad appears to condemn civilization as skin-deep, a rapacious fraud. The two European traders in "An Outpost of Progress," Kayerts and Carlier, go mad in the jungle and destroy each other over a bit of sugar. Conrad tells us that these specimens of civilization "could only live on condition of being machines." They are mass men, whom civilization has protected and programmed and whom the wilderness has "liberated" to the horror of their own nothingness. The story clearly implies that between civilization and the savagery that worships fetishes and practices cannibalism there is little to choose. Similarly, in "The Heart of Darkness," the metamorphosis of Kurtz suggests that civilization is merely a veneer and that its vaunted superiority to savagery is a sham, like the lie that Marlow tells Kurtz's "intended" at the end of the story.

Rather than as indictments of imperialism in general, however, Conrad's African stories should perhaps be more narrowly interpreted as reflecting his Congo experiences. It is not clear, for example, that what he says in "The Heart of Darkness" about the Eldorado Exploring Expedition ("to tear treasure out of the bowels of the land was their desire, with no more moral purpose at the back of it than there is in burglars breaking into a safe") is aimed at a larger target than King Leopold II's murderous central African venture, which was a scandal to both the friends and the enemies of European expansion.[41] What is clear is that Conrad generally thinks of British as superior to other European imperialisms. When Marlow describes the African map in the company office in Brussels, "marked with all the colours of a rainbow," he says: "There was a vast amount of red—good to see at any time, because one knows that some real work is done in there," in contrast to all the other colors, including yellow for the Belgian Congo, "dead in the center." Conrad's tale tells us something of the "horror" that goes on in the yellow part of the map, equating imperialist rapacity with the "unspeakable rites" practiced by Kurtz.

Idol worship is the common denominator uniting Europeans and

41. Joseph Conrad, "The Heart of Darkness," in *Youth and Two Other Stories,* Malay Edition (Garden City, N. Y.: Doubleday, Doran, 1929), p. 55.

"savages" in "The Heart of Darkness." Not only is Kurtz worshiped as an idol, but he indulges in his own worship—or, what amounts to the same thing, in his own self-aggrandizement and the sacrifice of other lives to it. The "pilgrims" at the trading station worship ivory, money, advancement, and also Kurtz's reputation. And Kurtz's "intended" back in Europe worships her heroic image of Kurtz as civilizer. Even Marlow is not immune from fetishism, sitting cross-legged on deck like a Buddha as he expresses his own worship of Kurtz as a superior person able to confront "the horror" within us all. Of imperialism in general, Marlow thinks quite cynically: "The conquest of the earth, which mostly means the taking it away from those who have a different complexion or slightly flatter noses than ourselves, is not a pretty thing when you look into it too much." But he adds: "What redeems it is the idea only." A moral purpose, progress, a civilizing mission— these, presumably, can justify imperialism. Marlow-Conrad does not rest content with this justification, however; he equates the belief in a redeeming idea also with idol worship: "An idea at the back of it" justifies imperialism, but is also "something you can set up, and bow down before, and offer a sacrifice to. . . ."

This passage, which both gives and takes away one of the two justifications for imperialism that Marlow offers, comes at the end of an extended comparison between Roman and British imperialism, in which Marlow accuses the Romans of operating only by "brute force" and "robbery with violence, aggravated murder on a great scale, and men going at it blind," although he adds: "as is very proper for those who tackle a darkness." The British, however, are saved from being no better than the Romans by "efficiency—the devotion to efficiency"—or does "devotion" suggest idol worship again? In any case, "efficiency" is the second justification for empire which Marlow offers. But his account leaves it far from clear that things are very much better now than when the Romans conquered Britain. "And this also," Marlow begins his tale, "has been one of the dark places on the earth." Thus it was when the Romans arrived, conquering, looting, murdering. Now "darkness" seems to be restricted to "the Dark Continent," and more especially to the yellow, blue, and green parts of the map; but the meaning of Kurtz's regression and of Marlow's lie to his "intended" is also to generalize darkness, to show that "this"— England, anywhere—is still "one of the dark places on the earth."

It is obviously harder to see Conrad as an imperialist than to see

Kipling as the poet of empire. What unites them perhaps more than any degree of political agreement are the patterns of social and psychological regression in their stories. Despite their more strident patriotic emphases, many of Kipling's tales—"The Mark of the Beast," "Namgay Doola," "Without Benefit of Clergy," even *Kim*, to name just a few—describe the shedding of civilization by Europeans rather than the civilizing of Indians. It would be difficult to find in Kipling an example of a successfully Europeanized Indian; the movement seems all in the other direction. Even his best moral specimens, like those in "William the Conqueror," seem almost to be pushing duty and work as a way of avoiding the temptations of "going native." Kim cannot make up his mind whether to be white or to go native, but the attractions are clearly on the native side. And a story such as "The Man Who Would Be King" seems almost a parable against imperialism, warning of inevitable downfall to those who invade primitive societies and meddle with their customs. The characters in Conrad's African tales also undergo obvious, self-destructive regressions, similar to the experience of lycanthropy in Kipling's "The Mark of the Beast." In Conrad's oriental tales, the regressions are less severe and often beneficial, even salvations from the frequently false values of civilization, as in Lord Jim's version of going native in Patusan. These regressive patterns involve the perception (quite conscious on Conrad's part, probably less so on Kipling's) of the cold, destructive emptiness at the heart of empires both ancient and modern, and of the secret attractions of decadence and barbarism.

The problems of mass production and of alienated masses were both reflected in the larger patterns of European imperialism. Empire and industry were linked by economic expansion and the competition for cheap labor, new resources, and new markets. Empire and the emergence of the masses were linked by the same forces, together with the population explosion, which seemed to be producing new, mostly internal "barbarian" hordes and creating pressure for *Lebensraum*. The Marxism that accused bourgeois society of decadence argued that modern imperialism is the final stage of "monopoly" or "late" capitalism, the prelude to the ultimate revolutionary upheaval. The height of the decadent movement in *fin de siècle* Europe also saw the zenith of imperialist expansion in the "scramble for Africa" and for large parts of Asia; there followed the Spanish-American War, the Boer War, the Russo-Japanese War, and World War I.

Imperialists from Sir John R. Seeley down to Mussolini and Hitler invoked the glory rather than the decline of Rome. In *The Expansion of England* (1883), Seeley remarks that there is a crucial "difference between the Roman Empire and other Empires founded on conquest, [which] arises from the superiority in civilisation of the conquerors to the conquered."[42] Many empires have been forged by barbarian warlords such as Genghis Khan, but the Roman Empire was the work of a highly civilized society. "The domination of Rome over the western races was the empire of civilization over barbarism. Among the Gauls and Iberians Rome stood as a beacon-light" (192). Seeley believes that the British Empire embodies the same qualities that had distinguished the Roman, for it too is the bearer of light to the dark places of the earth. Nor was the advance in civilization of the subject peoples the only benefit claimed for empire. As late as 1941, Baron Hailey could assert that "the privileges which the Roman Empire held out to its subject peoples were the guarantee of peace, and participation in a system of law," and that along with these boons the British Empire also offered eventual independence to its colonies. This is the same as arguing that subjugation now will mean freedom later— after the subject peoples have been "improved." Hailey thus expressed the reality of the decline and fall of the British Empire, a fact by 1941, in the most positive terms possible.[43]

In contrast to Hailey, those who defended empire in the second half of the nineteenth century often did so in improbable Virgilian terms, as *imperium sine fine dedi* (empire without end). Of course Rome's fall posed difficulties, but these could be offset by arguing that the British (or French or German) Empire had a moral or divine mission that would ensure its survival. According to Lord Curzon, empires fell only when they lost sight of their ideals. If the British maintained their "faithful attachment to the acquisitions of [their] forefathers," and if they kept their "national character . . . high and undefiled," they would never experience the fate of lesser empires.[44] Other imperialists acknowledged the inevitability of decline and fall, often explaining

42. Sir J. R. Seeley, *The Expansion of England* (Chicago: The University of Chicago Press, 1971), p. 188.

43. William Malcolm, Baron Hailey, "Romanes Lecture," 14 May 1941, in George Bennett, ed., *The Concept of Empire: Burke to Attlee, 1774–1947* (London: Adam & Charles Black, 1962), p. 412.

44. Lord Curzon of Kedleston, speech at Birmingham, 11 December 1907, in Bennett, *The Concept of Empire*, p. 356.

this unhappy outcome in Darwinian terms as the death of an organism progressing naturally to the end of its life cycle. From about 1870 down to World War I, social Darwinists like Ernst Haeckel and Karl Pearson defended empire on the "scientific" grounds of racial superiority and "survival of the fittest." Paradoxically, however, racist theories of empire lend themselves more easily to ideas of decadence than of progress, as in Joseph de Gobineau's *Essai sur l'inégalité des races humaines* (1853). Starting from the assumption of a pure race in the past—"the Aryan myth," for example—racist theories arrive easily at the idea of corruption by miscegenation in the present. Unless standards of racial purity can be strictly enforced, the course of history is inevitably downward. Commenting on the relation of this pattern to imperialism, Hannah Arendt quotes Gobineau's first sentence: "The fall of civilization is the most striking and, at the same time, the most obscure of all phenomena of history." Gobineau, Arendt remarks, was "fascinated by the fall and hardly interested in the rise of civilizations."[45]

In what may be the most thorough application of Roman parallels to the British Empire, *Greater Rome and Greater Britain* (1912), Sir Charles P. Lucas writes:

> Manual labour among the Romans was, under the Republic and at the beginning of the Empire, almost exclusively slave labour. . . . The Roman plebs, who demanded *panem et circenses*, did not apparently consist of wage earners. They were rather a privileged class of unemployed, who looked to the State and to the conquests made by the State to keep them fed and amused. This fact, that manual labour was in the main slave labour, accounts for the absence of any definite labour movement or labour problems in the Roman Empire.[46]

That modern mass movements like trade unionism, strikes, and socialism were missing from Roman history, Lucas thinks, makes the British record much preferable—labor is now "free" to express itself—though he does not approve of trade unionism, strikes, and socialism. Perhaps because of his conservative attitudes, Lucas is cited by Lenin

45. Hannah Arendt, *Imperialism*, part 2 of *The Origins of Totalitarianism* (New York: Harcourt, Brace & World, 1968 [1951]), p. 51.

46. Sir Charles P. Lucas, *Greater Rome and Greater Britain* (Oxford: Clarendon, 1912), p. 103.

in *Imperialism, the Highest Stage of Capitalism* (1916) as an example of what is wrong with Roman analogizing: "Disquisitions on imperialism, which ignore, or put into the background, the fundamental difference between social-economic systems, inevitably degenerate into the most vapid banality or bragging, like the comparison: 'Greater Rome and Greater Britain.'"[47] But if Lenin disapproved of pro-empire Roman analogizing, he was nevertheless influenced by the chief British opponent of imperialism, J. A. Hobson, though Hobson also has much to say about Roman parallels: "Whether we regard Imperialism [as a general historical pattern] or as confined to the policy of Great Britain," Hobson writes, "we find much that is closely analogous to the Imperialism of Rome."[48]

Rather than Roman glory, of course, Hobson in *Imperialism* (1902) stresses decline and fall. Referring to the wild celebration after one of the key battles of the Boer War, which he felt had been turned into a series of "spectacular" events by the sensation-mongering press, Hobson declares that *"panem et circenses* interpreted into English means cheap booze and Mafficking" (101). He adds: "Popular education, instead of serving as a defense, is an incitement towards Imperialism; it has opened up a panorama of vulgar pride and crude sensationalism to a great inert mass who see current history and the tangled maze of world movements with dim, bewildered eyes, and are the inevitable dupes of the able organized interests who can lure, or scare, or drive them into any convenient course." Thus through the press and the schools the "glories" of empire and of nationalist warfare were helping to fill in the content of the new, raw, industrialized mass culture, closing the vicious circle that joins the production of alienated masses to the pursuit of expansionist foreign policies.

Though Hobson stops short of Marxism, his analysis does not differ substantially from Lenin's. The two chief economic causes of empire Hobson sees as underconsumption in home markets and a conspiracy of big businessmen, bankers, and financiers in search of foreign markets and resources. A similar pattern of "parasitism" or economic vampirism by a wealthy, nonlaboring class explains the downfall of

47. V. I. Lenin, *Imperialism, The Highest Stage of Capitalism* (Peking: Foreign Languages, 1975), p. 97.
48. J. A. Hobson, *Imperialism: A Study* (Ann Arbor: University of Michigan Press, 1965), p. 365.

Rome. "This is the largest, plainest instance history presents of the social parasitic process by which a moneyed interest within the State, usurping the reins of government, makes for imperial expansion in order to fasten economic suckers into foreign bodies so as to drain them of their wealth in order to support domestic luxury" (367). Hobson adds: "The new Imperialism differs in no vital point from this old example." Applying social Darwinist metaphors in reverse, he concludes: "The laws which, operative throughout nature, doom the parasite to atrophy, decay, and final extinction, are not evaded by nations any more than by individual organisms" (367). Hobson is especially good at demolishing the ideological rationalizations for "parasitism" provided by social Darwinists such as Karl Pearson: "The notion of the world as a cock-pit of nations in which round after round shall eliminate feebler fighters and leave in the end one nation, the most efficient, to lord it on the dung-hill, has no scientific validity. Invoked to support the claims of militant nationalism, it begins by ignoring the very nature and purposes of national life," which are to provide security through cooperation and law and order for individual development (188–89). The surest way for an empire to fall, says Hobson, is to nurture "the habit of economic parasitism" manifest in the bread and circuses syndrome.[49] The inevitable result must be the overwhelming of the parasitic civilization by the barbarians whom it excludes (193–94). Lenin's chief difference from Hobson, whom he considers a shrewd but incomplete "petit bourgeois" theorist, lies in Lenin's belief that it will take much more to stop imperialist expansion than curing "underconsumption" at home. From Lenin's standpoint, imperialism is precisely capitalism in the midst of its death throes, from which there can be no escape.

iv

The controversies over imperialism, socialism, and decadence formed the intellectual context of the arts and crafts movement associated with William Morris, who combined Marxism with elements of a decadent romanticism. As Morris's biographer E. P. Thompson notes,

49. Hobson uses the metaphor of the "arena" of competition or conflict throughout *Imperialism* to describe social Darwinist doctrine, perhaps echoing Thomas Huxley's criticism of the "gladiatorial theory of existence" in *Evolution and Ethics.*

imperialism is what "brought him to Socialism."[50] Morris's definition of imperialism is close to Hobson's and Lenin's: "It is simply the agony of capitalism driven by a force it cannot resist to seek for new and ever new markets at any price and any risk."[51] The rapacity and violence of imperialism destroys more peaceful, "savage" and "barbarian" social and cultural patterns throughout the world. The process of exploitation turns "fairly happy barbarians into very miserable half-civilized people surrounded by a fringe of exploiters and middle-men varied in nation but of one religion—'Take care of Number One'" (384–85). Morris condemns jingoism and the idea of Britain's civilizing mission as sheer hypocrisy. The "barbarians" needing to be "civilized" may be primitive peoples, but Morris is just as ready to turn the former word into a charge against his own countrymen: "Strange that the new Attila, the new Genghis Khan, the modern scourge of God, should be destined to stalk through the world in the gentlemanly broadcloth of a Quaker manufacturer!" (719). Like Marx and Engels before and Lenin after him, Morris sees imperialism as the last phase of capitalism, its final desperate search for new sources of profit and new solutions to its periodic crises. It is a method of imposing "civilization"—that is, exploitation—at the end of a bayonet, and it is sure to end in a worldwide "doom of Blood and Iron" (720).

Morris arrived at his Marxist views by an apparently circuitous path. In common with the romantics and decadents who also deplored bourgeois industrialism, Morris's earliest concerns were esthetic, not political. His intellectual lineage runs back through the Pre-Raphaelite Brotherhood to the Gothic revival in architecture, which especially through the proselytizing of A. W. N. Pugin pointed the way to John Ruskin's theory of Gothic. In his *True Principles of Pointed or Christian Architecture* (1841), Pugin rejects industrial techniques almost wholesale. He cries out against "those inexhaustible mines of bad taste, Birmingham and Sheffield," and he lambastes modern industrial design generally under the sarcastic epithet "Sheffield eternal."[52] Industrialism is the main antithesis in Pugin's thinking to the

50. E. P. Thompson, *William Morris: Romantic to Revolutionary* (New York: Pantheon, 1977), p. 631.

51. Morris quoted by Thompson, *William Morris*, p. 272. The quotations in the rest of this paragraph are also from Thompson.

52. A. W. N. Pugin, *The True Principles of Pointed or Christian Architecture* (London: J. Weale, 1841). See also Pugin's *Contrasts* and Kenneth Clark, *The Gothic Revival: An Essay in the History of Taste* (Baltimore: Penguin, 1964 [1928]).

one true style of art and building: namely, Gothic. For Pugin, Gothic is Christian, and therefore perfect, art and architecture.

Though Ruskin did not follow Pugin to the letter, both Pugin's insistence that Gothic is the one true style and his hatred of industrialism reappear in *Modern Painters* (1843–60), *The Seven Lamps of Architecture* (1849), and *The Stones of Venice* (1851–53). In these works, Ruskin agrees with Pugin that machine production itself is fraudulent or inauthentic, especially when applied to the arts. Here is Pugin on cast-iron ornamentation, foreshadowing Ruskin: "Cast-iron is a deception; it is seldom or never left as iron. It is disguised by paint, either as stone, wood, or marble. This is a mere trick, and the severity of Christian or Pointed Architecture is utterly opposed to all deception" (*True Principles*, p. 30). Similarly, in *Seven Lamps*, Ruskin declaims against what he calls "architectural deceits." There are three kinds of such fraudulence, the last of which is "operative deceit," by which he means "the use of cast or machine-made ornaments of any kind." "There are two reasons, both weighty, against [operative deceit]; one, that all cast and machine work is bad, as work; the other, that it is dishonest."[53]

In this sort of argument, machine production and the devaluation or cheapening and democratizing of symbols go hand in hand, as in Flaubert's tirade against industrialized life. Pugin and Ruskin point directly to two of the principal associations of industrialized mass culture with decadence: handwork is perceived as intrinsically more valuable and "honest" than machine work; and the virtually endless replication and dissemination of objects made possible by machinery seems to destroy their esthetic value by destroying their economic value. The latter is not an argument actually presented by Pugin and Ruskin, though it is implicit in many of their assertions, as also in the attacks on machinery and on mass-produced goods made by Carlyle, Baudelaire, Flaubert, and many other nineteenth-century intellectuals and artists. They are especially disturbed by what they perceive as the misuse of machinery to imitate, and consequently cheapen, the forms of the past. Pugin and Ruskin themselves, however, seek to resuscitate these forms in authentic, nonindustrial ways: not classical,

53. John Ruskin, *The Seven Lamps of Architecture*, in the Library Edition of the *Works*, 39 vols., ed. E. T. Cook and Alexander Wedderburn (New York: Longmans, Green, 1903), VIII, 81.

but Gothic art and architecture and, for Ruskin, the hypothetical conditions of freedom which the Gothic worker enjoyed.

Central to Ruskin's social criticism are his identifications of art with freedom and of industrial techniques with slavery. Ruskin sees in machine production a rebirth of the system of "servile ornament" that characterizes the architecture of the ancient slave civilizations. The very perfection of antique architecture and sculpture reveals their roots in slavery. The classical slave laborer could execute only the finite and therefore perfectible designs imposed upon him by his masters. "But in the medieval, or especially Christian, system of ornament, this slavery is done away with altogether; Christianity having recognized, in small things as well as great, the individual value of every soul."[54] For this reason especially, "Gothic is not only the best, but the *only rational* architecture" (x:212). Unfortunately, history moved on from the Middle Ages to the corruptions of the Renaissance, of which the fate of Venice is emblematic; Ruskin invokes biblical terms in his descriptions of its eclipse: "That ancient curse was upon her, the curse of the Cities of the Plain, 'Pride, fulness of bread, and abundance of idleness.' By the inner burning of her own passions, as fatal as the fiery rain of Gomorrah, she was consumed from her place among the nations; and her ashes are choking the channels of the dead, salt sea" (xi:195). So fell Venice, that focal point of the clash between barbarism and classical civilization which Ruskin views as itself a kind of artistic mausoleum "charged with embayed fragments of the Roman wreck" (ix:38). But the downfall of Venice is, of course, not attributable to mechanization; Ruskin thinks it was due rather to the two apparently opposite corruptions of secularization and Roman Catholicism.

For Ruskin the course of both social and cultural history has declined from the age of Gothic to the nadir of the industrial present, with its new system of slavery and esthetic degradation based on machinery. Ruskin's powers as a prophet of nearly biblical eloquence are greatest when he focuses on machinery and its effects: "Alas! if read rightly, these [mechanical] perfectnesses are signs of a slavery in our England a thousand times more bitter and more degrading than that of the scourged African, or helot Greek" (x:193). He declares that

54. John Ruskin, *The Stones of Venice*, Works, x, 189–90.

to purchase and enjoy machine-made artifacts is to perpetuate a system that degrades "the operative into a machine"; "every young lady, therefore, who buys glass beads is engaged in the slave-trade" (x:197). Once again, what seems to be progress proves to be decadence. Ruskin sees with great clarity and bitterness how the division of labor dehumanizes and creates revolutionary discontent: "The great cry that rises from all our manufacturing cities, louder than their furnace blast, is all in very deed for this,—that we manufacture everything there except men" (x:196). Instead of discovering in modern industrial techniques a new esthetic discipline and a promise of social liberation, Ruskin sees in them at best mere utilitarian expediency and at worst a regression to slavery on the antique model, all the more apparent from the very "perfectness" of mass-produced artifacts. Perfection means the substitution of mechanical for spiritual ends; it is always a symptom of slavery, whether ancient or modern. The exactness of execution of Greek architecture, Ruskin thinks, is a symptom of the "degradation" of the workman: Egyptian or Ninevite work is freer, but medieval work is the only truly free work of the past. Because "there is perpetual change both in design and in execution" in Gothic architecture, "the workman must be altogether set free" (x:204–5).

Of course such a diagnostic method is much too simplistic; Ruskin's claim that the Greek worker was less free than the Egyptian or the Ninevite is nonsense. But Ruskin points ahead to arguments like those in Oswald Spengler's *Man and Technics* (1931) and Friedrich Jünger's *The Failure of Technology* (1949), where the antithesis between art and machinery, genuine culture and anything mass-produced, is maintained just as rigidly as in *The Stones of Venice*.[55] And Roman

---

55. Both Spengler's and Jünger's essays offer versions of negative classicism. Like Volney musing upon the ruins of the past, the prophets of the demise of machine civilization muse upon the ruins of the future. "The earth-spanning power of technology is of an ephemeral kind," writes Jünger. "Everywhere it is threatened by decay, given over to decay, and decay follows upon its heels all the more insistently and closely, the faster it marches on towards new triumphs" (*The Failure of Technology* [Chicago: Henry Regnery, 1956 (1949)], pp. 26–27). Jünger thinks that, though "the technical organization of Imperial Rome cannot be compared to ours, . . . imperialism and the formation of the masses go hand in hand," and he invokes "bread and circuses" to prove his point (pp. 158–60). Similarly, Spengler decries the subversion of spirituality, art, and culture by the utilitarian and industrial partly in these terms: "It is the *panem et circenses* of the giant city of the late periods that is presenting itself" (*Man and Technics*, tr. Charles Atkinson [London: George Allen and Unwin, 1932 (1931)], p. 6).

analogies are never far from his thinking, just as they form an important element in the anti-industrial theories of the esthetic decadents
and of both the right and the left today:

> Now, you are to remember that all these vilenesses had taken pos-
> session of the civilized world under the Roman Empire, just as they
> have done at this present time. The forms of Scorn, Disobedience,
> Cowardice, Lust, and Infidelity correspond in the closest manner, in
> the temper of the Romans in their last decline, with those man-
> ifested among ourselves at this day; what cure may be done on
> ourselves remains for us and our children to feel, and already it is
> becoming sharp. [xx:358]

As a Gothicist rather than a Hellenic classicist, Ruskin, like Thomas
Carlyle before him, sees a possible salvation for corrupt civilization in
a return of the barbarians, for "the cure of the Roman degeneracy was
in the descent upon them of the Northern tribes, some to slay and
some to govern, some to reinhabit; all of them alike gifted with a new
terrific force of will and passion, and a fertility of savage blood which
was again to give Italy suck from the teat of the wolf" (xx:358–59).

In *The House of the Wolfings* (1888), Ruskin's disciple William
Morris portrays a courageous barbarian tribe defending its forest
homeland against the rapacious tyranny of Rome. "Now the name of
this House was the Wolfings, and they bore a Wolf on their banners,
and their warriors were marked on the breast with the image of the
Wolf, that they might be known for what they were if they fell in
battle."[56] Morris perhaps has in mind the triumph of Hermann over
the Roman army in the Battle of Teutoberger Forest, an event dear to
the hearts of German *völkisch* nationalists from Friedrich Jahn
through Richard Wagner down to the Nazis, and celebrated in that
nineteenth-century bestseller Felix Dahn's *Kampf um Rom* (1867).
Certain it is that Morris's version of the Gothic revival often goes
beyond the polite if vaguely decadent re-creations of Dante, Chaucer,
and Arthurian legend associated with the Pre-Raphaelite Brotherhood
and with much of his own artwork. In *Sigurd the Volsung, The House
of the Wolfings, The Roots of the Mountains*, and his Icelandic translations, Morris seeks to re-create barbarian vigor and freedom and to
uphold barbarism at least by analogy as an alternative to "this filth of

56. William Morris, *The House of the Wolfings*, in *Collected Works*, 24 vols., ed.
May Morris (London: Longmans, Green, 1912), xiv, 5.

civilization." And throughout Morris's writings, the Romans "are a most evil folk," as a Wolfing warrior puts it (46).

According to Carl Schorske, "Wagner and Morris both quested for the future in the relics of the past."[57] Though *The House of the Wolfings* and his other Teutonic romances are Wagnerian both in their operatic qualities and in their celebration of antique, mythic virtues, Morris is not inventing or echoing a racist version of history. For him, the analogy is not between barbarism and Aryan racial superiority, but between barbarism and the industrial proletariat. And Rome for Morris is not parallel to a decadent because racially impure Europe as it had been for Gobineau; Rome is instead parallel to the tyranny of industrial capitalism and modern imperialism.[58] Like Ruskin and Carlyle, Morris interprets the overthrow of Rome by the barbarians as a necessary purgation and renewal of a decadent world ("and so Rome fell and Europe rose, and the hope of the world was born again"); it is this interpretation that underlies *The House of the Wolfings*. In contrast to most late nineteenth-century fictional accounts of the triumph of barbarism and religion over the Roman Empire—*Quo Vadis* (1897) and *Ben-Hur* (1899), for example—Morris ignores religion and sentimentalizes barbarism instead. Therefore, "to those that have hearts to understand," the fall of Rome "is a parable of the days to come; of the change in store for us hidden in the breast of the Barbarism of civilisation—the Proletariat."[59]

The great, heroic, bloody war waged by the Wolfings against the Romans, mirroring a dim, precivilized, preimperialized past, is one of Morris's many adumbrations of the longed-for revolution, the eschatological Judgment Day battle or *Ragnarök* of the communist future. All of Morris's art, even when it seems most vapidly escapist, involves a search for what is least civilized, most vigorously primitive, or at any rate most distant from or defiant of modern industrial and imperialist society. His is a utopian primitivism that seeks to transcend the features of both positive and negative classicism, but that in doing so itself acquires the features of decadent escapism.

57. Carl Schorske, "The Quest for the Grail: Wagner and Morris," in Kurt H. Wolff and Barrington Moore, Jr., eds., *The Critical Spirit: Essays in Honor of Herbert Marcuse* (Boston: Beacon, 1967), p. 216.

58. William Morris, "Art and Socialism," in G. D. H. Cole, ed., *William Morris* (New York: Random House, 1934), p. 636.

59. Ibid.

> Forget six counties overhung with smoke,
> Forget the snorting steam and piston stroke,
> Forget the spreading of the hideous town.[60]

In his account of how he became a socialist, Morris writes: "Apart from the desire to produce beautiful things, the leading passion of my life has been and is hatred of modern civilization."[61] Given this twin motivation, Morris's Pre-Raphaelitism, his Icelandic translations, his prose romances and fantasies, and his work in the anti-industrial arts and crafts movement, of which he was a founder and leader, can all be seen as consistent with his esthetic version of Marxism. As does Marx, however, Morris holds an ambivalent attitude toward machinery—an attitude more ambivalent than many of his anti-industrial and anti-bourgeois pronouncements suggest. Machinery for Morris promises freedom and leisure, even though under capitalism it only adds to the oppression of the masses.[62] Machine technology has a shadowy role to play even in the pastoral utopia of *News from Nowhere*, which Morris wrote in conscious opposition to the industrial regimentation idealized by Edward Bellamy in *Looking Backward*. It appeared to Morris that machinery could help people achieve the utopia of popular art by shortening labor time, but he did not see—as do Lewis Mumford and Susan Sontag, for example—an esthetic potential in machinery itself.[63]

The arts and crafts movement, however, was deliberately anti-mechanistic, setting handcrafted artifacts in contrast to machine-made goods. Its ultimate goal was to transform all workers into artists and all labor into esthetically pleasing experience. Like Ruskin, Morris identifies freedom with esthetic fulfillment; the utopia that ought to follow the coming revolution would mean the reign of "popular art," by

60. William Morris, opening lines of *The Earthly Paradise* (1868–70), *Works* III, 3.
61. Cole, *William Morris*, p. 657.
62. Ibid., p. 625.
63. For Lewis Mumford, see, for example, *Interpretations and Forecasts, 1922–1972* (New York: Harcourt Brace Jovanovich, 1979), p. 231: "If the goods of industrialism are still largely evanescent, its aesthetic is a durable contribution," etc. In *Against Interpretation* (New York: Dell, 1969), pp. 297–98, Susan Sontag writes that "the distinction between 'high' and 'low' (or 'mass' or 'popular') culture is based partly on an evaluation of the difference between unique and mass-produced objects," but that "in the light of contemporary practice in the arts, this distinction appears extremely shallow. . . . The exploration of the impersonal (and trans-personal) in contemporary art is the new classicism."

which Morris means something like mass culture humanized or de-reified. To a defender of technical expertise and "the instinct of work-manship" like Thorstein Veblen, the arts and crafts movement looked silly and sentimental. The "visible imperfections" of "handwrought goods" are considered "honorific," Veblen writes, at least according to the "barbarian" scale of values of "the leisure class." Ruskin and Morris have exalted "the defective" and defended "crudity and wasted effort."[64] Veblen detects in the arts and crafts movement ele-ments of snobbery that would hardly seem to fit such a dedicated socialist as Morris, were it not for the fact that Morris himself criticizes his esthetic endeavors on the grounds of their elitist nature. "What business have we to do with art unless all can share it?"[65] Sharing many of the values of the esthetic decadents, Morris stands their antidemocratic attitudes upside down and arrives at the ideal of the complete democratization of the arts. He wanted to be an artist for the masses, but he knew he was an artist only for the few, and he thought this would always be the case under capitalism. Given this theoretical predicament, even his praise of barbarism looks like the last refine-ment of a decadent age, the longing for a rejuvenation that seems both impossibly remote and historically inevitable, close at hand.

In *The Pilgrims of Hope*, like *Germinal* published in 1885, Morris interprets the Paris Commune in Marxist terms as a tragic defeat for the revolution. The crushing of the Commune was the apotheosis of the tyranny of industrial capitalism over the enslaved masses. But the revolution would come, even against the war machine of the bour-geoisie, which in Morris's poem mows down the heroic workers. The sunrise for both Marx and Morris, as also for Etienne Lantier, would be bloodred. After the Wolfings and their Gothic allies have beaten back the Romans in one of their engagements, Morris's noble barbar-ians sing their victory song:

> Now hearken and hear
> Of the day-dawn of fear,
> And how up rose the sun

64. Thorstein Veblen, *Theory of the Leisure Class*, in Max Lerner, ed., *The Porta-ble Veblen* (New York: Viking, 1948), p. 192.

65. William Morris, *Selected Writings and Designs*, ed. Asa Briggs (Baltimore: Penguin, 1962), p. 139.

> On the battle begun.
> All night lay a-hiding,
> Our anger abiding,
> Dark down in the wood
> The sharp seekers of blood.
>
> [XIV:183]

Like the Wolfings' weapons ("sharp seekers of blood"), the machinery of Western civilization, based on capitalist wage slavery and the competition for empire, has produced more than one sort of Gothic revival in the twentieth century.

"In my country there are no gods left," says the Cappodocian in Oscar Wilde's *Salomé*. "The Romans have driven them out." For the decadent writers and artists of the nineteenth century, the imperial powers-that-be had also driven out art, the possibility of the beautiful, and genuine culture, replacing them with the sham goods of industrialized mass culture. For Marxists and radicals like Morris, the charges against "the Romans" went further: their form of civilization meant slavery, their vaunted progress was nothing more than an unmitigated catastrophe. Perhaps it would make sense to speak of "decadence" wherever the longing for "barbarism" arises, and vice versa. In an essay on "barbarism" and "decadence" in the work of three modernist poets (C. P. Cavafy, Valery Bryusov, and W. B. Yeats), Renato Poggioli contends that these concepts have an affinity for each other. He suggests that they are sadomasochistic antonyms which imply the goals of an exhausted civilization, a civilization that yearns for endings, for destruction and peace, for suicide and new life. "Decadence may well be another name for civilization's self-betrayal," says Poggioli, "a truth more or less knowingly reflected in many literary documents of our time."[66] Morris and Wilde would have agreed with this assessment; so would Verlaine, whose self-identification with decadence includes a glowing report on the barbarians:

> Je suis l'Empire à la fin de la décadence,
> Qui regarde passer les grands Barbares blancs.[67]

66. Renato Poggioli, "*Qualis Artifex Pereo!* or Barbarism and Decadence," *Harvard Library Bulletin*, 13 (1959), 135–59.

67. "I am the Empire at the end of the decadence, / Who watches the great white Barbarians pass by."

CHAPTER 5

Crowd Psychology and Freud's Model of Perpetual Decadence

> *We can hardly realize the whirlwinds of brutality and un-chained libido that roared through the streets of Imperial Rome. But we would know that feeling again if ever we understood, clearly and in all its consequences, what is happening under our very eyes. The civilized man of today seems very far from that. He has merely become neurotic.*
>
> —CARL JUNG

i

BECAUSE Nietzsche interprets history from the origins of Christianity down to the present in terms of decadence, he has frequently been seen in relation to the decadent movement in literature and the arts. The other existentialists from Kierkegaard down to Jean-Paul Sartre have sometimes also been treated as theorists of decline and fall, while existentialism as a whole has been viewed, particularly by Marxists, as symptomatic of decay. Thus, Norberto Bobbio's term for existentialism in all its varieties is "decadentism," defined as "the philosophy of a worn-out generation," trapped in an age "of great and ill-comprehended upheavals." He proceeds to compare existentialism, "with its ethic of solitude," to the philosophies that corresponded to the decline and fall of ancient civilization, stoicism and Epicureanism. According to Bobbio:

> As decadent literature is directly bound up with Romanticism, of which it is the direct, if also the degenerate, descendant, so existen-

tialism . . . is unintelligible save in terms of Romantic thought, of which, through Nietzsche, it forms the extreme development. It harps to an excessive degree on the Romantic motif of the human personality, regarded as the centre, the original individuality, the heroic and solitary singularity. . . . This quest [for the "single"] is conducted in the form of revelation and intimate confession. The final result is the triumph of the motif—a permanent characteristic of decadentism—of human singularity cast into the world without security, ensnared in its situation as in a prison, invoking the transcendancy of its own nothingness.[1]

Bobbio's analysis is similar to Paul Bourget's in that both define decadence in terms of the "anarchy of atoms" and the subjectivism produced by extreme individualism. Other theorists have also seen in such apparently narcissistic phenomena as consumerism and the spread of psychoanalytic ideas symptoms of social morbidity. In *Decadence: A Philosophical Inquiry* (1948), Cyril Joad refers to a solipsistic "dropping of the object," evident in the "culture of the many" and the modern "'psychologizing' of morals and thinking," as the main cause of "decadence in our time."[2] Among other sources of decay, modern psychology, Joad argues, with its belief in "instinct" and the "unconscious," makes objective truth secondary to individual, subjective motivation. Reference to external authority, which Joad takes to be the measure of a healthy culture, vanishes through the "psychologizing" of experience. Psychoanalysis is thus a prime culprit in Joad's diagnosis. And with its stress on personality and "intimate confession," psychoanalysis also may be regarded as a version of "decadentism" in Bobbio's sense, a modern stoicism.[3] Like Kierkegaard and Nietzsche, Freud also seeks the redemption of the individual, cast into a hostile social environment. He too views modern society as essentially decadent; he shares with existentialism a fear of the destructive power of the masses and a pessimism about the development of a democratic civilization.

1. Norberto Bobbio, *The Philosophy of Decadentism: A Study in Existentialism*, tr. David Moore (Oxford: Blackwell, 1948), p. 51.

2. Cyril E. M. Joad, *Decadence: A Philosophical Inquiry* (London: Faber and Faber, 1948), pp. 118, 145, 251.

3. For the treatment of psychoanalysis as a form of decadence see, for example, Russell Jacoby, *Social Amnesia: A Critique of Conformist Psychology from Adler to Laing* (Boston: Beacon, 1975). For Marxist attitudes toward existentialism, see George Novack, ed., *Existentialism versus Marxism: Conflicting Views on Humanism* (New York: Dell, 1966), especially pp. 134–72 and 258–76.

While Nietzsche, Paul Bourget, William Morris, Max Nordau, and others were mapping the causes of social decadence between the 1880s and 1900, Freud was beginning his explorations of the causes of psychological decadence or neurosis. Once he could explain individual mental breakdown, moreover, he turned to the question of social breakdown. The decay and final collapse of the Habsburg Empire formed the background of Freud's education and early career, both of which were impeded by anti-Semitism. "The wider context of Freud's professional frustrations was a seething atmosphere of almost continuous political crisis," writes Carl Schorske in *Fin-de-Siècle Vienna*. "During the last five years of the nineteenth century Austria-Hungary seemed to be serving, as one of its poets observed, as 'a little world in which the big one holds its tryouts'—tryouts for Europe's social and political disintegration."[4] The years down to Freud's death in 1939 formed a climate even less conducive to the development of an optimistic social philosophy. Freud's writings are punctuated by asides about the historical crises he was living through. His 1915 essay "Thoughts for the Times on War and Death" points to the theory of the "death instinct" developed in *Beyond the Pleasure Principle* (1920). In the midst of his last completed work, *Moses and Monotheism* (1939), appear the paragraphs describing the disruption of his work and his emigration to England to escape the Nazis, in which he says: "We are living in a specially remarkable period. We find to our astonishment that progress has allied itself with barbarism."[5] Even without his keen interests in archaeology and the classics, Freud might have been driven by the political chaos and violence of his era to try to explain how "progress" or civilization could produce "barbarism."

Freud's approach to the problem of civilization as the source of barbarism is neither directly historical nor political. He psychoanalyzes civilization much as he psychoanalyzes his patients, by tracing it back to its roots, to what he conceives to be mankind's earliest memories in mythology and classical literature. Outside psychology, Freud's first intellectual love was archaeology, and the two are inti-

4. Carl Schorske, *Fin-de-Siècle Vienna: Politics and Culture* (New York: Knopf, 1980), pp. 184–85.

5. Sigmund Freud, *Moses and Monotheism*, tr. James Strachey, *Works*, 24 vols. (London: Hogarth, 1964), XXIII, 54.

mately related in his writings.[6] Far more than a mere analogy, archaeology was Freud's main way of connecting the history of the individual with the history of the species. He declares in *The Interpretation of Dreams* (1900): "Dreaming is on the whole an example of regression to the dreamer's earliest condition, a revival of his childhood, of the instinctual impulses which dominated it and of the methods of expression which were then available to him."[7] What is more, because "ontogeny recapitulates phylogeny," the dreams of the individual recapitulate the dreams or buried memories of the species. "Behind this childhood of the individual we are promised a picture of a phylogenetic childhood—a picture of the development of the human race, of which the individual's development is in fact an abbreviated recapitulation influenced by the chance circumstances of life." Recalling Nietzsche's speculations about dreams as the origin of myths in *The Birth of Tragedy*, Freud quotes him to the effect that in dreams "some primaeval relic of humanity is at work which we can now scarcely reach any longer by a direct path," and he concludes: "We may expect that the analysis of dreams will lead us to a knowledge of man's archaic heritage, of what is psychically innate in him. Dreams and neuroses seem to have preserved more mental antiquities than we could have imagined possible; so that psychoanalysis may claim a high place among the sciences which are concerned with the reconstruction of the earliest and most obscure periods of the beginnings of the human race" (549).

Freud writes to Stefan Zweig that "I have sacrificed a great deal for my collection of Greek, Roman and Egyptian antiquities [and] have actually read more archaeology than psychology." What is more, he tells Zweig, "before the war and once after its end I felt compelled to spend every year at least several days or weeks in Rome."[8] Freud elsewhere speaks of his "Rome neurosis," based on his youthful "long-

---

6. Philip Rieff points out that "dream-interpretation becomes a form of archaeology in which the analyst has the task of recovering 'mental antiquities'" (*Freud: The Mind of the Moralist* [Garden City, N. Y.: Doubleday Anchor, 1961], p. 208). See also Suzanne Cassirer Bernfeld, "Freud and Archaeology," *American Imago*, 8 (1951), pp. 107–28.

7. Sigmund Freud, *The Interpretation of Dreams*, tr. James Strachey, *Works* London: Hogarth, 1958), v, 548. Abbreviated *ID* in the text.

8. Sigmund Freud, letter to Stefan Zweig, 7 February 1931, in *Letters of Sigmund Freud, 1873–1939*, ed. Ernst L. Freud (London: Hogarth, 1961), p. 402.

ing to go to Rome," which expressed itself in several of his fantasies in *The Interpretation of Dreams;* through his fascination with Roman antiquities, Rome emerges in his writings as a complex symbol both for historical permanence and for decay.[9] Toward the beginning of *Civilization and Its Discontents* (1930), Freud points to "the history of the Eternal City" to illustrate his thesis that "in mental life nothing which has once been formed can perish."[10] The actual Eternal City is in fact not eternal; it is instead an architectural graveyard, ruins piled on ruins. But imagine, Freud says, "that Rome is not a human habitation but a psychical entity": by analogy, let the physical history of Rome stand for the mental history of an individual. In this introjected Rome, "nothing that has once come into existence will have passed away. . . . This would mean that . . . the palaces of the Caesars and the Septizonium of Septimius Severus would still be rising to their old height on the Palatine. . . . In the place occupied by the Palazzo Caffarelli would once more stand—without the Palazzo having to be removed—the Temple of Jupiter Capitolinus. . . . Where the Coliseum now stands we could at the same time admire Nero's vanished Golden House" (*CD* 70). And so forth. Freud's Roman fantasy suggests the durability if not exactly the eternality of mental processes. Entire civilizations decline and fall, but everything that happens to an individual remains with him from cradle to grave. The mechanisms of repression and forgetfulness render much unconscious, but they destroy nothing; if the psychoanalytic archaeologist proceeds carefully, he will disinter mental structures that are changeless.

Freud digs into the buried past of the individual to discover the foundations of neuroses. Because of the constancy of human nature, what he unearths in an individual can be applied to outward history, to civilization in its entirety. The individual, again, recapitulates the stages through which the species has developed. Freud makes no sharp distinction between biological and historical stages, so that the regression to infantile stages of a neurotic and the regression to bar-

9. See Schorske, *Fin-de-Siècle Vienna,* pp. 189–93; Ronald W. Clark, *Freud: The Man and the Cause* (New York: Random House, 1980), pp. 200–201; and Erik H Erikson, *Life History and the Historical Moment* (New York: Norton, 1975), pp 72–75.

10. Sigmund Freud, *Civilization and Its Discontents,* tr. James Strachey, *Work* (London: Hogarth, 1961), XXI, 69. Abbreviated *CD* in the text.

barism of a civilized society appear to have the same causal foundation. Development on either the individual or the historical plane involves the repression of infantile instincts. The thesis that Freud advances most fully in *Civilization and Its Discontents* is that development can be carried too far and hence lead to its opposite, to regression. Civilization is "built up upon a renunciation of instinct," which leads to unhappiness and "cultural frustration." Such frustration "dominates the large field of social relationships between human beings" and "is the cause of the hostility against which all civilizations have to struggle" (*CD* 97). "A good part of the struggles of mankind centre round the single task of finding an expedient accommodation— one, that is, that will bring happiness—between this claim of the individual and the cultural claims of the group; and one of the problems that touches the fate of humanity is whether such an accommodation can be reached by means of some particular form of civilization or whether this conflict is irreconcilable" (*CD* 96). If the contest between the "primitive" or "infantile" instincts of too many individuals and the claims of society turns out to be "irreconcilable," then the fate of civilization will be inevitable and probably violent disintegration.[11]

The paradox that "what we call our civilization is largely responsible for our misery, and that we should be much happier if we gave it up and returned to primitive conditions" (*CD* 86) sounds like a modern version of Rousseau, but Freud is not offering a romantic version of primitivism. The utopian form of society that would both maximize happiness and control instinctual aggression would represent an almost inconceivable advance over civilization as presently constituted. In any event, the image of the pent-up individual chafing at the bit because civilization has called upon him to repress or deflect his most powerful drives leads to another: that of the internal or "vertical

---

11. Freud had made similar arguments earlier, in "'Civilized' Sexual Morality and Modern Nervous Illness" (1908) and again in "Thoughts for the Times on War and Death" (1915). "Civilization is the fruit of renunciation of instinctual satisfaction and from each new-comer in turn it exacts the same renunciation," he says in the latter. Thus it appears that civilization can be too civilized: "The resulting strain . . . betrays itself in the most remarkable phenomena of reaction and compensation formation." Among these reactions Freud has in mind not only the symptoms of neurosis in individuals, but mass neurosis or psychosis as well—as evidenced by the World War which he is trying to explain. This essay is in *Collected Papers*, tr. Joan Riviere, 5 vols. New York: Basic, 1959), IV, 299.

barbarian" who, if given the chance, will tear down civilization from the inside. It is here, in the multiplication of individuals whom the thin defenses of civilization barely restrain, that the threat of "the masses" becomes evident in Freud's thought. A minority of individuals—"culture heroes" like Sophocles and Moses, perhaps, or those who through self-will and genius learn to sublimate their instincts into creative paths—do the work of civilization. The great majority undergo instinctual renunciation or acculturation unwillingly, harboring unconscious hostility or Nietzschean *ressentiment* toward their leaders and the institutions that restrain them. The result is a dangerous imbalance; like Nietzsche, Freud argues that the hostility of the masses, breaking its bonds in times of social or political crisis, has repeatedly toppled the edifice of civilization. Citing the barbarian "atrocities committed during the racial migrations or the invasions of the Huns, or by the people known as Mongols under Jenghiz Khan and Tamerlane, or at the capture of Jerusalem by the pious Crusaders, or even, indeed, the horrors of the recent World War," Freud declares that "the original nature of man" harbors an "inclination to aggression" that in most people is only barely held in check by the dictates of society. "In consequence of this primary mutual hostility of human beings, civilized society is perpetually threatened with disintegration" (*CD* 112). Here is the basis of Freud's negative classicism, his model of perpetual decadence. The pattern of history, as it did to the classical philosophers, appears to be cyclic, because at its peak civilization demands too much renunciation and thus, through a "return of the repressed," commits suicide by internal barbarism.

When Freud asks what mechanisms of repression civilization exercises, he gives several related answers, all based on the "sublimation" of the instincts. These mechanisms include law, morality, culture and the arts, and—perhaps most important—religion. But in naming religion one of the key builders of civilization, Freud is caught up in the logic that also sees religion and civilization as antithetical. On the one hand, following his scientific and Enlightenment inclinations, he wants to identify civilization with reason, and more specifically with the critical rationality embodied in psychoanalysis. On the other, he understands how great a role unreason plays in the civilizing process particularly through religion. *Civilization and Its Discontents* can be read partly as a continuation of the demolition of religion which Freud begins in *The Future of an Illusion* (1927). He mentions that in the earlier essay he was less concerned "with the deepest sources of the religious feeling than with what the common man understands by his religion" (*CD* 74)—that is, with religion as a kind of mass culture, which is also religion at its most irrational. Whereas art as a form of sublimation leads us away "from the pressures of vital needs" temporarily, "it is not strong enough to make us forget real misery" (*CD* 81). Religion, on the other hand, offers a more potent "narcosis" (*CD* 81), just as Marx contended—a system of illusions that functions like a mass psychosis. Religion works by "depressing the value of life and distorting the picture of the real world in a delusional manner—which presupposes an intimidation of the intelligence. At this price, by forcibly fixing them in a state of psychical infantilism and by drawing them into a mass delusion, religion succeeds in sparing many people an individual neurosis. But hardly anything more" (*CD* 84–85).

Though also treating religion as "mass delusion," Freud sounds much more pessimistic than Marx or than the *philosophes* about the prospect of making enlightenment general (which would mean, in part, the prospect of creating a rational, liberated culture on a mass basis). The early bourgeois liberals who constructed the theory of public opinion as the foundation of a democratic culture thought that the voice of reason could be heard by everyone. Freud finds that voice much less audible, although it is still the most important one to listen for. "There is no appeal to a court above that of reason," Freud writes in rejecting Tertullian's *credo quia absurdum*.[12] Psychoanalysis is obviously grounded upon the ideal of reason and upon the conviction that education has the power to make people conform to its findings. Sometimes Freud suggests that the course of history will be increasingly shaped by reason and that "the great majority of mortals" may one day live by the light of science: "The voice of the intellect is a soft one, but it does not rest until it has gained a hearing. Finally, after a countless succession of rebuffs, it succeeds. This is one of the few points on which one may be optimistic about the future of mankind" (*FI* 53). Ultimately, then, the illusion of religion will probably be

---

12. Sigmund Freud, *The Future of an Illusion*, tr. James Strachey, *Works* (London: Hogarth, 1961), XXI, 28. Abbreviated *FI* in the text.

displaced by science. Infantilism—Freud's scientific version of original sin—wreaks havoc upon individuals and also upon entire civilizations, "but surely infantilism is destined to be surmounted" (FI 49).

Freud nevertheless answers negatively the question of whether
reason can be much exercised by "the great majority of mortals" in the
present. The only culture now possible on a mass basis seems to be
"mass delusion." The cyclic revolutions of civilization and barbarism
suggest an even more pessimistic conclusion: an ultimate stalemate in
the conflict between reason and instinct. This is the conclusion to
which Freud's other, more archaeological writings about religion and
culture point. In Darwin and several early anthropologists (J. J. Atkinson, Robertson Smith, Sir James Frazer), Freud believed that he
found the keys to unlock the childhood of mankind. With their aid, he
constructs the oedipal theory of "the primal horde," "a scientific
myth," as Freud himself calls it, that he first expounds in Totem and
Taboo and that he repeats, with variations, in Civilization and Its
Discontents, Group Psychology and the Analysis of the Ego, Moses
and Monotheism, and elsewhere.[13] The theory postulates that civilization derives from the murder of "the primal father" by his sons. There
follow the formation of the clan brotherhood upon the basis of mutual
guilt; the enactment of "the totem feast" as ritual expiation of that
guilt; and the inventions of exogamy and division of labor to solve the
problem of competition among the clan brothers. The guilt of the
patricidal brothers gives rise to all later social institutions, law and
order arising from lawlessness, culture from anarchy—a process like
symptom formation in the neurotic individual. Civilization stands
upon a foundation of coercion, rebellion, murder, and guilt. The foundation is permanent enough; but the superstructure threatens at
every moment to fall back into ruins, to rejoin the foundation.

To this gloomy idea Freud adds a still gloomier one, that of the
death instinct. Early in his career, he assumed that regressive behavior was an abnormal interruption of the course of normal psychic
development, but he gradually expanded the role that he assigned to

13. Freud calls the theory of the "primal horde" a "scientific myth" in Group
Psychology and the Analysis of the Ego, tr. James Strachey, Works (London: Hogarth,
1955), XVIII, 135, abbreviated as GP in the text. He also calls it a "conjecture," a
"hypothesis," and almost—accepting a criticism which he attributes to Alfred Kroe-
ber—a "Just-So" story.

it. His theory that a "compulsion to repeat" is built into all organisms derives from the idea that regression is not abnormal at all, but necessary—the inevitable, cyclic reverse of development. Because death is the most obvious way in which all organisms regress, Freud gives Thanatos equal power with Eros: the death instinct takes its place beside the instinct to create, to construct, to make new life. In *Beyond the Pleasure Principle*, Freud writes: "If we are to take it as a truth that knows no exception that everything living dies for *internal* reasons—becomes inorganic once again—then we shall be compelled to say that 'the aim of all life is death.'"[14] As civilization is no more than the mature individual writ large, the death instinct points directly to the cyclic nature of history and the ultimate failure of all progressive social developments. The constructive powers of human nature cannot claim any final victory over the aggressive and destructive powers. Thinking of World War I, Freud quotes Plautus: "*Homo homini lupus*—man is a wolf to man," and adds: "Who, in the face of all his experience of life and history, will have the courage to dispute this assertion?" (*CD* 111).

Freud's speculations about prehistory work to some extent tautologically: by personification, he identifies the negative or antisocial attributes of infancy with primitive social life; he then discovers at the back of primitive social life the most basic of all infantile attributes, the Oedipus complex, enacted as a presumably real (though also merely hypothetical or mythic—Freud will have it both ways) historical event. Then he is able to suggest that the more civilized the abstract person of society grows, the more it is likely to regress, to fall prey to neurosis or barbarism, to turn suicidal. In the development from prehistory to modern civilization, religion functions as little more than a screen, a system of fantasy rationalizations evolving out of the guilt shared by the clan brothers for the murder of the primal father. The "totem feast" (originally the cannibalization of the murdered ur-father) is the first liturgy, and totemism is the first religion. As Freud makes clear in *The Future of an Illusion* and *Moses and Monotheism*, all subsequent religions are totemism in disguise, reformed and mystified to suit apparently less primitive times. If the first religion was a

14. Sigmund Freud, *Beyond the Pleasure Principle*, tr. James Strachey, *Works* London: Hogarth, 1955), XVIII, 38.

shared paranoid delusion, based on fear and guilt, later ones are also forms of collective paranoia. And though these religions only distantly remember the murder in the primal horde, they all reenact that oedipal crime in their mythologies, in their rituals, and too often—as in the practice of human sacrifice or the exorcism of scapegoats—in reality as well.

Freud's primal horde theory can be contrasted to another "scientific myth" about prehistory, that of "primitive communism." Some forty years before Freud began his "metapsychological" speculations, Marx and Engels found in the researches of Johann Bachofen and Lewis H. Morgan the ideas that the earliest social organization was matriarchal instead of patriarchal and that (rather than being tyrannized over by an ur-father who monopolized all the females, as in Freud) the members of this first organization shared sex as they shared everything else. Against Freud's "scientific" discovery of primal murder and guilt, Marxist anthropology, as first elaborated by Marx in *Pre-Capitalist Economic Formations* (1858) and by Engels in *The Origin of the Family, Private Property and the State* (1884), offers a "scientific" reinvention of the Golden Age. Despite their optimism about human nature, however, Marx and Engels present a theory of history in which progress—the development of monogamy, private property, class relations, slavery, serfdom, the state, mechanization, and wage slavery—resembles a process of steadily intensifying tyranny and alienation. It is at any rate a progress away from primitive communism through stages of increasing unfreedom to the advanced communism of the future, though because Marx and Engels abstain from utopian speculation it is not clear how the two communisms, of prehistory and of the future, will ultimately differ. But in *Ancient Society* (1877), Morgan writes of the future that "it will be a revival, in a higher form, of the liberty, equality, and fraternity of the ancient gentes," an idea clearly attractive to both Marx and Engels. Progress from primitive communism to the communism of the future begins to look cyclic. The chief difference between the hints of cyclism in Marx and Freud's version of negative classicism may be that the beginnings and endings of Freud's cycles entail barbarisms, declines and falls, while the beginning and end of Marx's apparent cycle are utopian, the apotheosis of freedom and equality, the primitive communism of the past succeeded by the civilized communism of the future. Freud, of course, wants to preserve the higher elements of civilization or of what lies in the present, in the midst of the current cycle; Marx wants to revolutionize at least those higher elements that are based on class domination. Out of nineteenth-century anthropology and archaeology, then, it was possible to construct two antithetical visions of the origins of culture, and two seemingly opposite visions of the future. Entering the major currents of contemporary thought through Marxism and psychoanalysis, these visions (with many variations, of course) shape the two main ways in which we conceive of the distant past and the future. The primitivist and Marxist streaks in Claude Lévi-Strauss, for example, underlie his belief in the possibility of breaking through the repressive limits of civilization to a primitivelike utopian future, whereas most versions of negative classicism, even when not directly influenced by Freud, view the future in terms of a destructive "return of the repressed."[15]

The pessimism that Freud expresses about the infantilism of "the great majority" who "will never be able to rise above [the religious] view of life" (*CD* 74) suggests that, in his view, the construction of a rational scientific culture on a mass basis may be impossible. It will at least require the guidance by enlightened minorities of the many who are prone to unreason. Freud's social and political assertions are usually grounded upon one of two elitist dichotomies: the division of

15. For the Morgan quotation, see Melvin Rader, *Marx's Interpretation of History* (New York: Oxford University Press, 1979), pp. 121–22. See also the introduction by E. J. Hobsbawm to Karl Marx, *Pre-Capitalist Economic Formations* (London: Lawrence and Wishart, 1964). Marx argues that empire enslaves "the member of the primitive community founded upon landed property," when he "happens to have lost his ownership of land without as yet having advanced to property [in the instrument of labor], as in the case of the Roman plebs at the time of 'bread and circuses'" (p. 102). For Claude Lévi-Strauss, besides the primitivist inclinations of *Tristes Tropiques*, see *The Scope of Anthropology*, tr. S. D. and R. A. Paul (London: Jonathan Cape, 1967), pp. 46–50. Much recent anthropology follows what Stanley Diamond calls "the Rousseauan and Marxist tradition" and at least covertly celebrates the virtues of primitive life against the corruptions of modern civilization. Diamond himself declares that "civilization originates in conquest abroad and repression at home." "As civilization spreads and deepens, it is ultimately man's self, his species being, which is imperialized" (*In Search of the Primitive* [New Brunswick, N.J.: Transaction, 1974], pp. 111, 1, and 10). As Herbert Marcuse recognizes in *Eros and Civilization*, the Freudian tradition coincides with the Rousseauist-Marxist one at least in viewing civilization as based on repression, a kind of internal imperialization of the self if not of the "species being."

mankind either into leaders and led ("heroes" and "hordes") or into rational minorities who ought to rule and irrational majorities who rule too often in the present and in the foreseeable future. Both dichotomies appear in *Group Psychology and the Analysis of the Ego*, written partly to answer criticisms lodged against *Totem and Taboo*. In *Group Psychology*, Freud draws much of his thinking about collective behavior from the "crowd psychologists," particularly Gustave Le Bon, Gabriel Tarde, William McDougall, William Trotter, and—not the least of them, although unacknowledged—Friedrich Nietzsche.[16] Through criticizing but also adopting many of their ideas, Freud constructs a social psychology similar in several ways to Nietzsche's, whose influence may be apparent in the idea that "social feeling is based upon the reversal of what was first a hostile feeling into a positively-toned tie in the nature of an identification" (*GP* 121). Here is the genealogy of morals from their opposites, love out of hatred, law out of lawlessness, a transvaluation of values that corresponds to the emergence of civilization from a prehistory that was bloody and violent in the extreme. For Freud as for Nietzsche, moreover, socialism is an avatar of religion, and both are equally irrational and perhaps destructive: "If another group tie takes the place of the religious one—and the socialistic tie seems to be succeeding in doing so—then there will be the same intolerance towards outsiders as in the age of the Wars of Religion" (*GP* 99).

Freud bases much of his social psychology on Gustave Le Bon's *Psychologie des foules* (*The Crowd*, 1895), which offers a diluted version of Nietzsche's cultural politics. (Le Bon's essay in turn offers many of the leading ideas to be found thirty-five years later in Ortega's *The Revolt of the Masses*.) Le Bon's work appealed to Freud partly because of its stress upon the unconscious, whose preponderance in modern times is a sign of social decadence. "The substitution of the unconscious action of crowds for the conscious action of individuals,"

16. Although Freud mentions Nietzsche on page 123 of *Group Psychology*, it is in an ironic context that fails to suggest the impact of Nietzsche's thinking on his social psychology. Discussing the ideas and values that Freud may have adapted from Nietzsche, Philip Rieff observes that they both "proclaimed the master science of the future to be not history but psychology. History becomes *mass* psychology." It is as a "mass psychologist" that Nietzsche writes in many of his essays (*Freud: The Mind of the Moralist*, pp. 230–31).

Le Bon declares, "is one of the principal characteristics of the present age."17 Though agreeing with this statement, Freud must surely have wanted to qualify it, because the behavior of individuals is also largely determined by the unconscious. The antithesis of individual and society is less sharply drawn by Freud than by Le Bon, or rather it is drawn in a different manner. Le Bon's underlying concern is to show how the rational individual can protect himself against the encroachments of the irrational "crowd." Freud's underlying concern is the contrary one of explaining how civilization can continue to grow and survive in the face of the hostility of the irrational individuals who are its members, and who bear the destructive oedipal seeds of the primal murder and guilt. Despite this difference, often in Freud as in Le Bon the antagonism between civilization and "the masses" seems total:

> It is just as impossible to do without control of the mass by a minority as it is to dispense with coercion in the work of civilization. For masses are lazy and unintelligent; they have no love for instinctual renunciation, and they are not to be convinced by argument of its inevitability; and the individuals composing them support one another in giving free reign to their indiscipline. It is only through the influence of individuals who can set an example and whom masses recognize as their leaders that they can be induced to perform the work and undergo the renunciations on which the existence of civilization depends.   [*FI* 7–8]

The masses for Freud stand outside or beneath civilization, like Ortega's "barbarians" or Arnold Toynbee's "proletarians," and would do away with it if they could. Indeed, civilization seems mainly the work of charismatic leaders who can control the masses, like the Egyptian Moses, who, Freud believes, imposed his monotheism on the Jews.

Much as Ortega applies the idea of a rebellion by the masses to all aspects of collective behavior in the modern world, Le Bon applies "crowd psychology" to all groups and to modern society as a whole.

17. Gustave Le Bon, *The Crowd: A Study of the Popular Mind*, intro. Robert K. Merton (New York: Viking, 1960). See also Paul Reiwald, *Vom Geist der Massen: Handbuch der Massenpsychologie* (Zurich: Pan-Verlag Zurich, 1946); Robert A. Nye, *The Origins of Crowd Psychology: Gustave Le Bon and the Crisis of Mass Democracy in the Third Republic* (Beverly Hills, Calif.: SAGE, 1975); and Susanna Barrows, *Distorting Mirrors: Visions of the Crowd in Late Nineteenth-Century France* (New Haven: Yale University Press, 1981).

Indeed, "the crowd mind" is universal, forming wherever social groups form, and is the same in all ages. Le Bon's essay is therefore characterized by negative classicism: "Crowds being only capable of thinking in images are only to be impressed by images. . . . For this reason theatrical representations . . . always have an enormous influence on crowds. Bread and spectacular shows constituted for the plebeians of ancient Rome the ideal of happiness, and they asked for nothing more. Throughout the successive ages this ideal has scarcely varied" (68). Le Bon's attempt to construct a typology of groups is overshadowed by his thesis that all "crowds" behave alike—that is, irrationally, from unconscious impulse. Whereas Freud distinguishes between unstable groups based on temporary impulses and stable ones based on tradition, on law and order, and sometimes on reason, Le Bon sees little difference between a revolutionary party and a rioting mob, between a "criminal crowd" and a "criminal jury," and between an ignorant and irrational "electoral crowd" and the "parliamentary crowd" that it elects. All are "crowds" or "mobs" (*foule* suggests riotous street gatherings) and all form that larger collective monstrosity, the great "crowd" of society. As do the masses for Nietzsche and Orgeta, the crowd for Le Bon stands for the opposite of culture, for the decline and fall of civilization. "The crowd state and the domination of crowds is equivalent to the barbarian state, or a return to it" (158).

In one of the passages from *The Crowd* that Freud quotes with apparent approval, Le Bon writes: "By the mere fact that he forms part of an organized group, a man descends several rungs in the ladder of civilization. Isolated, he may be a cultivated individual; in a crowd, he is a barbarian—that is, a creature acting by instinct" (9). That Freud quotes this passage without criticizing it is surprising; one of his main themes, in *Group Psychology* as elsewhere, concerns the socialization of the individual, obviously through the family but through other institutions as well, and no individual is cultivated in isolation as Le Bon suggests. But Freud wants to stress the ease with which the individual can regress in a "crowd" situation. In situations of panic or riot, at least, civilization proves to be only skin-deep. Le Bon himself here betrays the reactionary individualism that led him on an ironically circular path from enmity toward the "crowd" to support of Mussolini's "classical revival," a development that must have been anathema to Freud. Any liberal ideas that can be found in Freud's own work, however, must be qualified by his pessimistic view of human nature and by his conviction that all social bonds bear the traces of the "primal horde." If historic Romes decline and fall, they do so because psychic Romes are everlasting—prehistory stands invisibly but indestructibly on the same foundation as history.

Freud devotes a chapter of *Group Psychology* to William Trotter's *The Instincts of the Herd in Peace and War*, and decides to "correct Trotter's pronouncement that man is a herd animal and assert that he is rather a horde animal, an individual creature in a horde led by a chief" (*GP* 121). But this modification, which still situates the essence of all social groups in a primitive prototype, does not advance beyond the idea of "instinct" to consider what is specifically human and potentially if not actually rational in modern social formations. Freud is for the moment content to explain all groups in terms of "primitive" or "infantile" "libidinal ties" that are created through a process of group bonding akin to hypnosis. Trotter's thoughtful study of animal in relation to human behavior, however, expresses a fact overlooked by Freud in his own "primal horde" thesis: social organization is not specifically human. The search for the "primal horde" or for any original of human society must be pushed impossibly far back—to the birds, let us suppose. Birds flock together, mate, form temporary families. Is it necessary to imagine a rebellion of bird sons against their ur-father to explain the establishment of the first flock or the building of the first nest? This question is not facetious: "Sociobiologists" from Darwin through Trotter down to Edward O. Wilson have discovered many highly "human" traits among birds (Konrad Lorenz's greylag goose, for instance) as well as among other animals. And the notion that "man is a wolf to man," though perhaps an accurate assessment of human behavior, does less than justice to wolves. Human nature seems to be both more "bestial" and more "human" than animal nature. Perhaps it would help to argue, as does the psychoanalytic anthropologist Geza Roheim, that culture is the defensive response of humans to their long period of childhood dependency—something they do not share with most animals.[18] Just as culture can be seen as a

18. Geza Roheim, *The Origin and Function of Culture* (Garden City, N. Y.: Doubleday Anchor, 1971 [1943]).

derivative of childhood dependency, so can the worst aspects of human behavior: "infantilism" is not a charge likely to be made against any animal other than man (for the same reason, it would make no sense to search for analogues to the Oedipus complex among animals).

Though Freud's "scientific myth" of the primal horde may be finally implausible, the general paradox on which it rests is obviously true: civilization grows out of savagery just as the adult grows from the child or as mankind evolves from the apes. But in skipping over the long stages of cultural evolution to delve into prehistory, Freud runs the risk of turning the paradox of progress (or the apparent historical pattern of something out of nothing) into a covert identity, so that the differences between civilization and "primal horde," complex institutions and "herds," are understated or even erased as they are in Le Bon. This is a central fallacy not just in "crowd psychology," but also in all versions of social Darwinism that substitute competition, war, and "the law of the jungle" for civilized law and ideals of peace and cooperation. For many of the social Darwinists, even the possibility of social rationality vanishes behind the irrational and instinctual; "the survival of the fittest," "the white man's burden," "the purification of the Aryan race," and other irrational and irrationalist slogans emerge to dominate political discourse. The same biological terminology used between the 1870s and World War I "scientifically" to condemn the masses and the emergence of labor as a factor in politics, as in Le Bon, was also used, often by the same writers, to justify imperialist expansion at the expense of "inferior breeds." Whether or not the increasing political importance of "the herd" was a cause of World War I, there can be no doubt of the proimperialist and prowar influence of "the gladiatorial conception of the struggle for existence" promoted by many intellectuals—a conception according to which society seemed not much different from "a Coliseum where human beasts strive with one another in moral darkness."[19]

Freud avoids identifying barbarism with civilization and the irrational with the rational because he keeps sight of reason as the ultimate court of appeal. Though the grounds for optimism are few, and

19. Jacques Barzun, *Darwin, Marx, Wagner: Critique of a Heritage* (Garden City, N.Y.: Doubleday, 1958 [1941]), pp. 104 and 109. Barzun is recollecting Thomas Henry Huxley's condemnation of "the gladiatorial conception of existence" in *Evolution and Ethics.*

though the conflict between instinct and society may prove irreconcilable in the long run, he believes that on both the individual and the historical scale hope lies in reason. Psychoanalysis shows how difficult it is to fulfill the Socratic injunction "Know thyself," but it remains possible to fulfill it. This hope is implicit in Freud's treatment of classical culture, including classical mythology—a treatment far more reverential than that which he accords to religion. *Oedipus Rex* reveals to Freud the primitive ground of all culture—indeed, the very roots of civilization in the Oedipus complex, with its "memory trace" of the murder in the primal horde. But it also reveals Oedipus struggling to self-knowledge, tragic recognition. Freud compares Sophocles' drama to psychoanalysis: "The action of the play consists in nothing other than the process of revealing, with cunning delays and ever-mounting excitement—a process that can be likened to the work of a psychoanalysis—that Oedipus himself is the murderer of Laius, but further that he is the son of the murdered man and of Jocasta" (*ID* 261–62). Freud sees in *Oedipus Rex* a mirror of the most primitive instincts; he also sees in it how the greatest cultural achievements can act to master those instincts through self-knowledge.

ii

According to the crowd psychologists, the instruments that have evolved since 1789 to shape and express public opinion—the press, the schools, universal suffrage, the mass media—are failures; at best they merely lend the appearance of reason to irrational proceedings, like the imagery of dreams. Although Freud has little to say about mass culture in the narrow sense of the productions of the mass media, his social thinking focuses upon the antithesis between "the masses" and "civilization." In showing human nature to be mostly determined by the unconscious, and in adapting crowd psychology to his versions of archaeological and sociological explanation, Freud created a powerful fusion of ideas that has influenced all subsequent social theory. Even theorists who reject psychoanalysis have to come to terms with it. Many critiques of mass society and culture—Karen Horney's *The Neurotic Personality of Our Time* (1937), David Riesman's *The Lonely Crowd* (1950), Alexander Mitscherlich's *Society without the Father* (1963), Christopher Lasch's *The Culture of Nar-*

cissism (1978), to name just a few—are Freudian to greater or lesser extent. Many others seek to combine psychoanalysis with its apparent opposite, Marxism; works in this category include Wilhelm Reich's *The Mass Psychology of Fascism* (1933), Erich Fromm's *Escape from Freedom* (1942), Theodor Adorno and Max Horkheimer's *The Dialectic of Enlightenment* (1944), Herbert Marcuse's *One-Dimensional Man* (1964), and Lasch again. And if critics of mass society and culture have been influenced by psychoanalytic thinking, so have the artists and managers who run the mass media. According to the dictum of Leo Löwenthal, "Mass culture is psychoanalysis in reverse."[20] This is true in the sense that many of the products of mass culture—advertising, for example—function by stimulating wishful thinking, illusions, the irrational; it is also true in the sense that ad makers, movie directors, television producers, and public relations "image makers" all think in Freudian terms and shape their products accordingly.[21] An aspect of contemporary mass culture which is obviously psychoanalytic in orientation, furthermore, consists of the hundreds of therapeutic techniques, associations, and cults for personality shaping and adjustment that take their inspiration at least distantly from Freud. Another name for what Cyril Joad, in his investigation of decadence, describes as "the 'psychologizing' of morals and thinking" is "the psychological society."[22]

As recently as the middle of this century, theories of mass communications and mass audiences were still being framed by references to "crowd psychology," "instincts," and animal behavior, as in Robert MacIver and Charles Page's chapter "Herd, Crowd, and Mass Communications" in their *Society: An Introductory Analysis* (1949). In an even more reductive fashion, overlaying the modern with the primitive, Elias Canetti in *Crowds and Power* (1960) ransacks anthropology and psychology to demonstrate the paranoid nature of the social bond itself. Having investigated group behavior and the general irrationality of politics among both primitive and civilized peoples, Canet-

20. Leo Löwenthal quoted by Martin Jay, *The Dialectical Imagination* (Boston: Little, Brown, 1973), p. 173.

21. The psychology used by advertisers is often a mix of Freudianism with behaviorism, both in diluted forms that even more than their original sources emphasize the irrationality of the public or the masses.

22. Joad, *Decadence*, p. 195.

ti turns to Freud's study of paranoia, the case of Daniel Paul Schreber, for his final model of the psychology of power, and hence for his final model of political organization.[23] More recently still, in *Charisma: A Psychoanalytic Look at Mass Society* (1973), Irvine Schiffer relies on Freud to explain "the need of the masses to be dominated by the great man," which is in turn the source of the general irrationality of politics and the mass media.[24] Schiffer argues that "large numbers of people, though they may be relatively realistic in their personal lives, do in fact still select their public leaders predominantly on the basis of imagery." By "imagery" Schiffer pretty clearly means mass culture; he adds that the people who "image" rather than reason "have the capacity to reject or to glamorize—even to deify—a political leader, while having about the same level of comprehension about the leader as they might have for a popular entertainer" (10). Even in the most up-to-date, technologically advanced democracies, Schiffer detects "a rescue-hungry people, prepared in their distress to invest a leader with charisma" (11). Like Freud's own archaeological social psychology, such analyses tend to bypass actual politics for questions and solutions that express the despair of negative classicism, or the belief that the changeless irrationality of human nature dooms all progressive movements to fail, to follow the pattern of classical tragedy, to fall backward on the wheel of history.

Among the more orthodox psychoanalytic critiques of mass society and culture, Alexander Mitscherlich's *Society without the Father* is instructive for its attempt to transcend the more pessimistic aspects of Freud's metapsychology. The patriarchal societies of the past, Mitscherlich believes, had recourse to mythology or religion in order to justify patterns of domination and repression. "In a less repressive society, less subject to magical modes of thought, better integrated, and with a more fully developed conscious, the authority of the code of behaviour will have a form and function different from any that we can yet imagine."[25] Clearly modern societies have not yet escaped

23. Robert M. MacIver and Charles H. Page, *Society: An Introductory Analysis* (New York: Rinehart, 1949), pp. 417–36; Elias Canetti, *Crowds and Power* (London: Gollancz, 1962 [1960]).

24. Irvine Schiffer, *Charisma: A Psychoanalytic Look at Mass Society* (Toronto: University of Toronto Press, 1973), p. 93.

25. Alexander Mitscherlich, *Society without the Father*, tr. Eric Mosbacher (New York: Schocken, 1970 [1963]), p. 39.

from at least the psychological kinds of bondage that Mitscherlich identifies with patriarchy. His "fatherless society" is a Freudian utopia, liberated from the false authority of "a mythical father and his terrestrial representatives" (39). On another level, however, the "fatherless society" is already with us, in the form of modern mass society. The work of casting off false authority through secularization and modernization has led to a situation where a few rational or sane individuals are surrounded by masses irrationally motivated, like the brothers of the primal horde, to seek to restore authority. On the one hand, "the authority of the mythical traditions is no longer sufficient to bring about a social integration of mass society"; mass culture, which has taken their place, cannot do so. On the other hand, the "ultimate outcome" of mass society "is always dictatorship" (39). As Mitscherlich puts it toward the conclusion of his study, "The collapse of paternal authority automatically sets in train a search for a new father on whom to rely" (300–301).

But if mass society leads inevitably to a restoration of the murdered father in the guise of the dictator, it is difficult to understand how Mitscherlich envisages the achievement of the utopian version of a "society without the father." The process he advocates for converting irrational "mass man" into the rational, free citizen of utopia he calls "ego-strengthening," which is the concept of education dressed in Freudian garb. "Development of the ego forces has always been a greater necessity for the ruling group than for the masses; it took place at the expense of the masses" (131). So much for the cultural elitism of the past. "Today mass man," Mitscherlich continues, "needs a capacity for self-orientation instead of blind or fatalistic loyalty to the imagos of paternal figures who in the present structure of society can no longer possess the overriding authority attributed to them by conservative fantasy" (131). But what is to do the work of "ego-strengthening" for the masses? The media of mass communication would seem to be logical candidates, but Mitscherlich sees them only as fostering the irrationality of the masses.

> There can be no doubt that the sum-total of the traditional and presently effective stereotypes of our society perform the task of education in strengthening the ego very feebly indeed. That is not contradicted by the cult of popular idols who are taken to represent

the maximum achievable human happiness. These idols have too many marks of autocracy, eccentricity, or sheer rebelliousness to be regarded as successful examples of ego maturity achieved in co-operation with the instinctual trends. Too much unresolved infantilism attaches to them. [135]

The work of the mass media—the production of "stereotypes" and "popular idols"—Mitscherlich sees only as contributing to the development of a mindless "factory and management culture" (115).

> The lavish provision of means of entertainment that is so characteristic of our age serves two functions of a very different type, one open and the other masked. The propaganda of the pleasure providers is based with apparent *naïveté* on the promise that they will relieve our burden of unpleasure, but the concealed dynamics that makes them so successful is of quite different origin. It arises from the anxiety produced by the frustrations of mass living. The individual must be very ill armed against them, or the violence with which the anxiety has to be warded off would be inexplicable. The morbid plunge into surrogate pleasures can be explained only as a reaction-formation against an anxiety with which the ego cannot cope. [170].

Despite his belief that mass culture is debilitating rather than "ego-strengthening," Mitscherlich seeks to dissociate his own ideas from the kind of "cultural criticism" that impedes "critical examination" of the modern technical environment, "populated by the masses." "In their hostility to the masses" the cultural critics themselves succumb "to regressive, anxious withdrawal" (274). Mitscherlich wishes to avoid "the disastrous distinction between civilization (for the uneducated masses) and culture (for the educated few)" (114), but his theories are based on that very distinction which, in more familiar language, is nothing other than the dichotomy between mass and high culture. With the important qualifications that liberation must come through modernization and entail the freeing of the masses from "magical modes of thought" as well as from dictators, Mitscherlich's social psychology is rooted in the same assumptions about the irrationality and destructive tendencies of "the masses," "mass man," and "mass culture" as Le Bon's or Freud's.

Mitscherlich almost recognizes that the Freudian definition of masses is a form of the same sort of culture criticism that he condemns as regressive, but he seems unable to distance himself from his own psychoanalytic categories sufficiently to understand the political assumptions underlying them. Similar difficulties emerge in most of the attempts to synthesize Marx and Freud. In *The Mass Psychology of Fascism*, Wilhelm Reich, one of the first theorists to try to put Freud and Marx together, goes one step beyond Freud when he claims that man has "three different layers of . . . biopsychic structure." The first is the surface layer, where the average man shows himself to be "reserved, polite, compassionate, responsible, conscientious." All would be well if it were not that the next, buried or unconscious layer "consists exclusively of cruel, sadistic, lascivious, rapacious, and envious impulses." This is the layer that "represents the Freudian 'unconscious' or 'what is repressed,'" and it is the source of "social tragedy." But there is still another level, Reich believes, one that is overlooked by Freud. This is mankind's true nature, primitive treasure, the "biologic core" of our being. "In this core, under favorable social conditions, man is an essentially honest, industrious, cooperative, loving, and, if motivated, rationally hating animal."[26] Here is Reich's version of Rousseau's noble savage, buried beneath layers of civilized repression. To tap this "biologic core," he believes, would lead to the victory over fascism of liberated workers who would then establish the "natural work-democracy" of the future. Of course Reich has done little more than give the Freudian version of human nature a substratum based on the Marxist version of human nature. It therefore seems possible to dismiss his theory of the biologic core of mankind and his subsequent researches into "orgone energy" as an evasion of the hard issues raised by Freud about the persistence of infantilism into adulthood.

Later attempts to combine Marx and Freud have been more complex and influential; notable among these is Herbert Marcuse's politicization of Freud in *Eros and Civilization*. Freud's ambivalence about the repressiveness of civilization allows Marcuse to draw from psychoanalysis a program of political liberation. Marcuse adopts the theory of the primal horde, recognizing at the same time that Freud's idea of history is cyclic and that the original crime against the ur-father is

26. Wilhelm Reich, *The Mass Psychology of Fascism*, tr. Vincent R. Carfagno (New York: Farrar, Straus, and Giroux, 1970), p. xi.

reenacted endlessly. The latent cyclism in Marx and Engels also stands forth clearly as Marcuse aligns it with the cyclism in Freud:

> We have seen that Freud's theory is focused on the recurrent cycle "domination-rebellion-domination." But the second domination is not simply a repetition of the first one; the cyclical movement is *progress* in domination. From the primal father via the brother clan to the system of institutional authority characteristic of mature civilization, domination becomes increasingly impersonal, objective, universal, and also increasingly rational, effective, productive. At the end, under the rule of the fully developed performance principle [the social equivalent of Freud's "reality principle"], subordination appears as implemented through the social division of labor itself. . . . Society emerges as a . . . system of useful performances; the hierarchy of functions . . . assumes the form of objective reason: law and order are identical with the life of society itself.[27]

At the end of so-called progress, "domination" will be complete—the repressiveness of civilization will reach its limit in the total alienation of labor, the total administration of life, and the worldwide appearance of concentration camps as the ultimate factories of death.

Such, at least, is the pessimistic side of Marcuse's vision. But revolution and the turn to the primitive that will occur when civilization has reached the limits of its oppressiveness show the hopeful side of the cycle. The Freudian concept of "surplus repression" is related in Marcuse's thought to the Marxist concept of alienated labor. Heretofore "progress" has led in a "vicious circle," civilizations reaching peaks of repression and then disintegrating. But, given the technological capabilities of modern society, present-day civilization may break the cycle. As Marcuse says in his 1968 lecture "Progress and Freud's Theory of Instincts," "The achievements of repressive progress herald the abolition of the repressive principle of progress itself. It becomes possible to envisage a state in which there is no productivity resulting from and conditioning renunciation and no alienated labor: a state in which the growing mechanization of labor enables an ever larger part of the instinctual energy that had to be withdrawn for alienated labor to return to its original form, in other words, to be

27. Herbert Marcuse, *Eros and Civilization: A Philosophical Inquiry into Freud* (New York: Vintage, 1962 [1955]), p. 81.

changed back into energy of the life instincts."[28] Drawing on Friedrich Schiller's *On the Aesthetic Education of Man*, Marcuse adumbrates the utopian prospect of the metamorphosis of labor into play or art: "The crucial thought is that of the transformation of labor into the free play of human faculties as the authentic goal of existence, the only mode of existence worthy of man" (42). Marcuse imagines a de-reified or totally liberated democratic culture of the future, mass culture transformed by abolishing "surplus repression." This utopian culture will come into being only through revolution (if at all), because the managers of the new technological capabilities are not about to relinquish power by abolishing "surplus repression" themselves. Presumably the instincts liberated by revolution will prove to be not destructive, as Freud feared, but closer to Wilhelm Reich's biologic core.

Marcuse gives the psychoanalytic terminology of "repression" and "the return of the repressed," "sublimation" and "regression," the political meanings of injustice and liberation. Those meanings are implicit in Freud but without any positive valuation (rather, a negative one) attached to "the return of the repressed." Freudian theory, however, has had a "liberating" influence—one unintended by Freud and not viewed as liberating by Marxists—in the development of "the psychological society." At the end of *Freud: The Mind of the Moralist*, Philip Rieff announces the advent of "psychological man," product of an age of mass culture "in which technics is invading and conquering the last enemy—man's inner life, the psyche itself" (391). There have been three previous "character ideals" that have dominated Western civilization. These are the classical ideal of "political man," the Judeo-Christian ideal of "religious man," and the bourgeois-industrial ideal of "economic man." For Rieff, the emergence of "psychological man" does not represent progress, but something perhaps closer to the disintegration of the central ideals of Western civilization. Unlike political man, psychological man "is not committed to the public life," and of course he has no faith in anything transcendent. "We will recognize in the case history of psychological man the nervous habits of his father, economic man: he is anti-heroic, shrewd, carefully

---

28. Herbert Marcuse, *Five Lectures: Psychoanalysis, Politics, and Utopia* (Boston: Beacon, 1970), p. 39.

counting his satisfactions and dissatisfactions, studying unprofitable commitments as the sins most to be avoided" (391). In terms which point even more definitely to decadence, Christopher Lasch writes that "the contemporary climate is therapeutic, not religious. People today hunger not for personal salvation, let alone for the restoration of an earlier golden age, but for the feeling, the momentary illusion, of personal well-being."[29] Hence, the culture of narcissism. Lasch's version of psychological man is the "narcissist," the most recent avatar of mass man, forever searching for reassuring images of himself in the mirrors of the mass media and in psychiatrists' offices. "Bureaucracy, the proliferation of images, therapeutic ideologies, the rationalization of the inner life, the cult of consumption"—all contribute to narcissism on a mass scale.

The spawning of dozens of new therapies and therapeutic societies is one of the clearest symptoms of mass narcissism for Lasch, as it is also for Martin Gross, author of *The Psychological Society* (1978). Like Lasch, Gross sees the turning inward that he is diagnosing as decadent, a danger to democracy and perhaps to civilization. Stimulated in the first place by democracy, "our desperate search for psychic understanding and repair" has destabilized modern culture, "accelerated man's tendency toward anxiety and insecurity," and is "shaking the very underpinnings of Western civilization. It is now apparent that the Judeo-Christian society in which psychology began its ascendancy is atrophying under the massive impact of several forces, particularly that of modern psychology. In its place stands a new culture of a troubled and confused citizenry, the Psychological Society."[30] So, it appears, the psychological society is also a sick society. This is all the more true because of the similarities that Gross sees between new psychotherapies and the old religions. "When educated man lost faith in formal religion, he required a substitute belief that would be as reputable in the last half of the twentieth century as Christianity was in the first. Psychology and psychiatry have now assumed that special role. They offer mass belief, a promise of a better future, opportunity for confession, unseen mystical workings and a trained priesthood of

29. Christopher Lasch, *The Culture of Narcissism: American Life in an Age of Diminishing Expectations* (New York: Norton, 1978), p. 7.

30. Martin L. Gross, *The Psychological Society* (New York: Simon & Schuster, 1978), p. 9.

helping professionals devoted to servicing the paying-by-the-hour communicants" (9). Freud is the new Messiah; inventors of new therapies like Arthur Janov, Fritz Perls, and Werner Erhard are seers or prophets; sickness is the new equivalent for sin; psychoanalytic sessions are the new Eucharist.

It is ironic, of course, given Freud's attempts to demystify religion, that Gross debunks the new psychotherapies by comparing them to religious cults. As with Marxism, here is another case of a secular ideology taking on the appearance of a substitute religion even as it aims at the demystification of religion. Recognizing this irony, Philip Rieff argues that the faith in reason of the master, Freud, has given way to the faith in the irrational of his heretical disciples.

> In Jung, Adler, Reich, and in many others among his major followers as well as opponents, Freud's analytic patience ran out. Only the minor followers remained orthodox; the others wanted something more than a middle way between emergency treatment and the illusion of a permanent cure. Each sought to combine analysis with a therapy of commitment, complete with symbolic, or a real return to some saving community—Christian, Marxist, or merely Reichian, for example. The schismatics have a certain analytic power, although far inferior to Freud's; more importantly, all have the authority of experience on their side, for it is probably the community that cures.[31]

As Engels found in early Christianity an analogy for the communist party, despite the fact that it was Marx's intention to demolish religion, so Rieff finds in early Christianity an analogy for the psychoanalytic movement and its offshoots, despite the fact that it was Freud's intention to lead men to live by the light of science. Psychoanalysis is one aspect of the kind of "cultural revolution" which "occurs when the releasing or remissive symbolic grows more compelling than the controlling one; then it is that the inherent tensions [in society] reach a breaking point." Rieff adds: "Roman culture may have been moving toward such a breaking point when Christianity appeared, as a new symbolic order of controls and remissions" (233–34). So once again the future veers toward the past, toward a new Middle

31. Philip Rieff, *The Triumph of the Therapeutic: Uses of Faith After Freud* (London: Chatto and Windus, 1966), pp. 46–47.

Ages if not clearly a new Golden Age. "At the breaking point, a culture can no longer maintain itself as an established span of moral demands. Its jurisdiction contracts; it demands less, permits more. Bread and circuses become confused with right and duty. Spectacle becomes a functional substitute for sacrament. Massive regressions occur, with large sections of tbe population returning to levels of destructive aggression" (234). Such is Rieff's account, via negative classicism, of our contemporary crisis, in which psychoanalysis appears as a new faith, a new instrument of salvation. In Freud, this instrument is reason; in Freud's disciples, it is either faith in Freud or one heresy or another.

Paradoxically, like that other "opium of the intellectuals," Marxism, Freud's efforts to undo the illusions of religion have spawned new faiths, new myths, and even, with Carl Jung, an attempt to resurrect all faiths and myths. Largely through the influence of psychoanalysis, a vast new culture industry has arisen, catering to the needs and tastes of the masses for symbols, therapy, salvation, transcendence, peace of mind. The immensely difficult Socratic task of self-knowing, the aim of all Freud's work, vanishes in the contemporary welter of charms, spectacles, cults, all of them influenced by psychoanalysis itself. In "the psychological society," all self-knowledge threatens to dissolve into one form or another of narcissism. Given Freud's vision of the importance and permanence of infantile factors in human nature, such a result may have been inevitable: reason is rare; it perhaps can never penetrate the masses. Freud's political pessimism approaches the dismal assessment of the masses made by Sir Clifford in *Lady Chatterley's Lover*:

> The masses were always the same, and will always be the same. Nero's slaves were extremely little different from our colliers or the Ford motorcar workmen. I mean Nero's mine slaves and his field slaves. It is the masses: they are unchangeable. An individual may emerge from the masses. But the emergence doesn't alter the mass. The masses are unalterable. It is one of the most momentous facts of social science. *Panem et circenses!* Only today education is one of the bad substitutes for a circus. What is wrong today is that we've made a profound hash of the circuses part of the program, and poisoned our masses with a little education.[32]

32. D. H. Lawrence, *Lady Chatterley's Lover* (New York: Grove, 1957), p. 239.

Of course Freud would not have agreed with Sir Clifford about the futility of education. D. H. Lawrence, one of Freud's most interesting schismatic disciples, himself agrees only in part with this statement. Lawrence sees in the masses a permanent, unalterable architecture, but it is a vital, potentially beautiful one—the "religion of the blood," the "life of the instincts," the "dark," creative side of human nature that Freud believes to be mainly destructive and that is invisible to Sir Clifford.

Lawrence is, of course, only one of many theorists who have accepted Freud's categories while reversing his valuations. Jung, the most theological of Freud's immediate disciples (and therefore also the greatest apostate), would have agreed with much of Rieff's assessment of "the triumph of the therapeutic." Jung also believes that we are undergoing social breakdown, on the verge of discovering a new "symbolic," a new faith, a new world order. True, "in this age of Americanization we are still far from anything of the sort," Jung thinks; "we are only at the threshold."[33] But we *are* at the threshold, Jung claims, and he does not hesitate to speak as a prophet of "the new spiritual epoch." Nothing could seem more unlikely than the great spiritual transformation Jung believes is about to occur; but that is only because the scales of consciousness on our eyes prevent us from seeing the future. "To me the crux of the spiritual problem of today is to be found in the fascination which psychic life exerts upon modern man. If we are pessimists, we shall call it a sign of decadence; if we are optimistically inclined, we shall see in it the promise of a far-reaching spiritual change in the Western World"—a change that, Jung believes, will bring from the depths of human nature the tools for the salvation of human nature (217). Repeatedly in his essays Jung describes the future in terms of negative classicism—the breakdown of the Roman Empire, the rise of the City of God. In the modern world, too, religion will prove to be the antidote to materialistic "mass-mindedness" and "Caesarism." "Along the great highroads of the world everything seems desolate and outworn. Instinctively the modern man leaves the trodden ways to explore the by-paths and lanes, just as the man of the Graeco-Roman world cast off his defunct Olym-

33. Carl G. Jung, *Modern Man in Search of a Soul* (New York: Harcourt, Brace, 1933), p. 217.

pian gods and turned to the mystery-cults of Asia" (218). As in Lawrence, so in Jung: it is from man's buried "psychic life" that the "new
spiritual forms will arise" (217). Jung charts the site upon which the
religious archaeologists of the future will dig.

The Freudian tradition underlies Jung's optimistic version of negative classicism; it also underlies the insistence on at least the possibility of achieving a rational secular society which we see in
Mitscherlich and Marcuse. Though the "psychologizing" of society
may be decadent or narcissistic, it also holds forth the promise of the
achievement of individual self-knowledge and freedom from illusion,
the only conceivable basis for the evolution of what another psychoanalytic Marxist, Erich Fromm, has called "the sane society." The
misapplication of Freud's ideas in much political propaganda and commercial mass culture has obscured the liberating goal of psychoanalysis. But through the noise, the disappointments, and the frustrations of the "psychological society," Freud's own insistence on both
the difficulty and the necessity of rationality remains clear.

CHAPTER 6

Three Versions of
Modern Classicism:
Ortega, Eliot, Camus

*A classical revival is taking place. The soulless, drab
egalitarianism of democracy, which had taken the colour out
of life and crushed all personality, is on its death-bed. New
kinds of aristocracy are arising, now that we have proof that
the masses cannot be the protagonists but only the tools of
history.*

—BENITO MUSSOLINI

INSOFAR as analyses of mass culture have gone beyond mere repetitions of the neoclassical contest between the ancients and the
moderns, they have usually involved questions about the impact
of egalitarian leveling on the creative elites or minorities thought to be
necessary to the development of art and ideas. Many of the optimistic
analyses have come from American liberals such as John Dewey, who
believe that genuine culture can and does flourish in democratic conditions.[1] The pessimistic analyses have come from both the right and
the left, and frequently also from liberals who might be characterized
as cautious or disillusioned. According to the pessimists, mass culture

1. Examples include Walt Whitman, *Democratic Vistas;* John Dewey, *Art as Experience* (New York: Minton Balch, 1934), *Freedom and Culture* (New York: Putnam,
1939), etc.; Carl J. Friedrich, *The New Belief in the Common Man* (Boston: Little,
Brown, 1942); Herbert Gans, *Popular Culture and High Culture* (New York: Basic,
1974). See also the writings on mass culture by Lyman Bryson, Reuel Denney, Russell
Lynes, Paul Meadows, David Riesman, Gilbert Seldes, and Edward Shils.

is either a travesty of high culture or else an impossibility, a meaningless phrase. The Marxist position (with many variants, of course) is that because the ruling ideas of any society are those of its ruling class, the mass culture of the bourgeois era is by definition a "mystification" or "false consciousness."[2] For the left, religion, "the opium of the people," is an obvious example of false consciousness, but conservatives often identify religion with genuine culture and claim that both are threatened by the masses or by bourgeois materialism or by both. In the view of cautious or disillusioned liberals, if a satisfactory culture for a democratic society has not yet developed, it may do so through education and through the creation of institutions that safeguard creative minorities against "the tyranny of the majority." According to both the conservative and the Marxist viewpoints, mass culture tends to be totalitarian rather than democratic; it is flawed by the worst effects of bourgeois ideology and industrialism. Conservative theorists also tend to see mass culture as mechanical rather than organic, secular rather than sacred, commercial rather than free or unconditioned, plebeian or bourgeois and vulgar rather than aristocratic and "noble," based on self-interest rather than on high ideals (or, appealing to the worse instincts in people rather than to the best), cheap and shoddy rather than enduring, imitative rather than original, and urban, bureaucratic, and centralized rather than close to nature, communal, and individualized. The first two figures discussed in this chapter, José Ortega y Gasset and T. S. Eliot, both view mass culture in these terms. While Ortega can be characterized either as a disillusioned liberal or as a conservative and Eliot is clearly conservative, both offer versions of negative classicism based on condemnations of the masses and mass culture. Albert Camus, in contrast, though very much a positive classicist, affirms the creative potential of the ordinary individual and, hence, the possibility of a democratic culture of the masses at least in the future. The theories of these three writers exhibit many of the themes in modern responses to mass culture, democratization,

2. For Marxism and mass culture, see Martin Jay, *The Dialectical Imagination: A History of the Frankfurt School and the Institute of Social Research 1923–1950* (Boston: Little, Brown, 1973), chap. 6; Bruce Brown, *Marx, Freud, and the Critique of Everyday Life* (New York: Monthly Review, 1973); and Adolfo Sanchez Vasques, *Art and Society: Essays in Marxist Aesthetics* (New York: Monthly Review, 1973).

and the mass media; they express a range of ideas distinct from both the psychoanalytic ones discussed in Chapter 5 and Marxist ones, which will be dealt with more fully in Chapter 7.

i

The most extreme answer to the question of whether genuine culture can flourish on a mass basis is a simple negative, and that is the answer given by José Ortega y Gasset in his influential essay *The Revolt of the Masses* (1930).[3] Ortega's tract for the times stands at the opening of a decade marked by political and economic crisis in Europe and America. He writes from the standpoint of a cautious liberalism that was failing to make much headway either against the Church and aristocratic reaction or against the deeply rooted problems of poverty and illiteracy in Spain: in 1931, when Ortega was beginning his two-year term as a representative in the legislature of the Second Republic, the forces were gathering that would lead to the Spanish Civil War and to nearly forty years of military dictatorship under Franco. Fascism in Italy, Nazism in Germany, and Stalinism in the Soviet Union all pointed in the same direction: to the breakup of democratic hopes and institutions, and perhaps to the breakup of European civilization.[4]

Everywhere in modern Europe Ortega sees the incompetent majority usurping the place of the competent minority. "The characteristic of the hour is that the commonplace mind, knowing itself to be commonplace, has the assurance to proclaim the rights of the commonplace and to impose them wherever it will" (18). That new Caliban without qualities, "the average man," has thrown off the yoke of traditional authority and gone hunting for new masters, and he is finding them in Mussolini, Hitler, and Stalin. The modern condition is one of instability and decadence, brought on by industrialization, secularization, the population explosion, the immense parasitic

---

3. José Ortega y Gasset, *The Revolt of the Masses* (New York: Norton, 1957 [1930]). Page numbers are given in parentheses.
4. For a list of works that reflect the political and economic crises of the 1930s in terms of a "revolt of the masses," see the bibliography appended to the second edition of Sigmund Neumann, *Permanent Revolution: Totalitarianism in the Age of the International Civil War* (London: Pall Mall, 1965).

growth of governmental and corporate bureaucracies, and a new, nearly universal literacy that does not seem to increase the level of social intelligence among ordinary people but only to make them more vulnerable to propaganda. Ortega thinks that the new dictatorship of the commonplace, far from generating a new culture, is only throttling the old one. Average or "mass man" does not "represent a new civilization struggling with a previous one, but a mere negation" (190). Ideas, standards, and principles, the bases of traditional culture, could be created and maintained only by educated elites. "When all these things are lacking, there is no culture; there is in the strictest sense of the word, barbarism" (72). The uprising of the masses involves a "vertical invasion" of barbarism from the middle and lower classes, something that had happened before in history, most notably in the case of Rome. Thus, we have again become subject to "the brutal empire of the masses" (19).

Ortega's essay is an important expression of negative classicism. We are literally living in an interregnum, Ortega believes, "an empty space between two organisations of historical rule" (182) like the period of chaos that began in the fourth century; we are reliving the deaththroes of the Roman Empire before the longer interregnum of the Dark Ages. Like Mikhail Rostovtzeff, Ortega interprets the downfall of Rome in terms of the rise of the Roman masses. "The history of the Roman Empire is also the history of the uprising of the Empire of the Masses, who absorb and annul the directing minorities and put themselves in their place. Then, also, is produced the phenomenon of agglomeration, of 'the full'" (19)—a reference to the quasi-Malthusian horror of "masses" which suffuses Ortega's essay.

The Revolt of the Masses is a sort of *Communist Manifesto* in reverse. Although Ortega sees tyranny where Marx and Engels see liberation, he accepts and even exaggerates the main premise of Marxism: the idea of a revolution carried out by the masses against the ruling and owning classes. Marx and Engels were predicting a future "revolution," of course, whereas Ortega describes a "revolt" that is occurring now. Ortega's "revolt" is a metaphor for a degenerative process or disease that is attacking society at all levels—it is almost a metaphor for modernity. But perhaps the greatest difference between Ortega and Marx lies in the fact that Ortega does not think in terms of economic causation. He believes that, in the conflict of democratic ideals, equality has vanquished liberty, but he does not primarily mean economic equality. "Average man" is not a factory operative or a longshoreman. He has not even the distinction of belonging to a definite social class, and hence of sharing strong group loyalties and hatreds. He is just "average," with no more individuality than a brass tack. His only characteristics are ignorance, contented vulgarity, and lack of identity. It is easy to see how Marx could expect a numerous, injured, angry, and sometimes organized proletariat to rebel against its oppressors. Class warfare manifested itself in strikes, riots, mass movements, radical organizations, and failed revolutions throughout the nineteenth century. The uprising of Ortega's mass nobodies, in contrast, spells the demise of Marxist hopes for a proletarian revolution. "The revolt of the masses" above all means fascism, a victory for Nietzschean *ressentiment* over authority which is itself destructively authoritarian.

Ortega's mass man is thus similar to the alienated individual who figures in modern Marxist analyses of fascism and monopoly capitalism. He is the same empty shell of a human being as Herbert Marcuse's "one-dimensional man" or as the "authoritarian personality" diagnosed by Max Horkheimer and Theodor Adorno. But the Marxist mass man is above all the exploited victim of the elite groups responsible for fascism and monopoly capitalism; he is less history's agent than its dupe. In the late 1920s and early 1930s, before it was clear that capitalism would survive the crises in the Western democracies, a Marxist such as Christopher Caudwell could project essentially the same vision of a "dying culture" that Ortega projects, only with the hopeful conclusion that a new and just social order would rise phoenix-like from the ashes of "bourgeois culture":

> [World War I] at last survived, there come new horrors. The eating disintegration of the slump. Nazism outpouring a flood of barbarism and horror. And what next? Armaments piling up like an accumulating catastrophe, mass neurosis, nations like mad dogs. . . . How can the bourgeois still pretend to be free, to find salvation individually? Only by sinking himself in still cruder illusions, by denying art, science, emotion, even ultimately life itself. Humanism, the creation of bourgeois culture, finally separates from it. Against the sky stands Capitalism without a rag to cover it, naked in its terror. And

humanism, leaving it, or rather, forcibly thrust aside, must either pass into the ranks of the proletariat or, going quietly into a corner, cut its throat.[5]

Ortega does not accept these extreme alternatives for humanism; it is above all the threat to a humane or liberal culture which he fears. But his analysis still points to the emergence from powerlessness of the very proletariat that Caudwell expects to lead the way to a new era of cultural greatness based on egalitarianism.

Ortega's chief authority on the masses was of course not Marx, much less Christopher Caudwell. He was instead influenced by an even more conservative prophet of doom than himself, Oswald Spengler, whose *The Decline of the West* had been making a great stir since 1918. Along with such concepts as "agglomeration" and the "barbarism" of technical specialization, Spengler offered Ortega one explanation for what seemed to be the inevitable metamorphosis of democracy into mass tyranny, or of the apparently suicidal tendencies of progress and civilization. At the end of the life cycles of all cultures comes "Caesarism," Spengler claims, following shortly upon the sere and yellow leaf of "Megapolitanism." A great "world-city" stands at the summit of every civilization, containing the vertical barbarians who mine its foundations from within. These are the "dregs, *canaille*, mob, *Pöbel* . . . a mass of rootless fragments of population [standing] outside all social linkages . . . ready for anything, devoid of all respect for orderliness."[6] Spengler's depiction of the residents of the "world-city" is close to Ortega's of "average man": "In place of a type-true people, born of and grown on the soil, there is a new sort of nomad, cohering unstably in fluid masses, the parasitical city dweller, traditionless, utterly matter-of-fact, religionless, clever, unfruitful, deeply contemptuous of the countryman and especially that highest form of countryman, the country gentleman" (I, 32). Materialistic and scientific skepticism filtering down to the "fluid masses" of the "world-city" breeds trouble. In such "parasitical" and "unfruitful" hands, the high

5. Christopher Caudwell, *Studies and Further Studies in a Dying Culture* (New York: Monthly Review, 1971), p. 72.

6. Oswald Spengler, *The Decline of the West*, tr. Charles Francis Atkinson, 2 vols. (New York: Knopf, 1980 [1926–28]), II, 399–400. Volume and page numbers hereafter are given in parentheses.

culture of the past, no longer lovingly tended by "country gentle-men," perishes like an uprooted flower:

> To the world-city belongs not a folk but a mass. Its uncomprehend-ing hostility to all the traditions representative of the Culture (no-bility, church, privileges, dynasties, convention in art and limits of knowledge in science), the keen and cold intelligence that confounds the wisdom of the peasant, the new-fashioned naturalism that in relation to all matters of sex and society goes back far beyond Rou-sseau and Socrates to quite primitive instincts and conditions, the reappearance of the *panem et circenses* in the form of wage-disputes and football-grounds—all these things betoken the definite closing-down of the Culture and the opening of a quite new phase of human existence—anti-provincial, late, futureless, but quite inevita-ble. [1, 32–33]

Ortega apparently rejects Spengler's fatalistic organicism, perhaps finding some of it too optimistic (after all, Spengler postpones the death of Western Civilization to the twenty-second century), but he applies his decline and fall mythology to modern society anyway, refashioning Spengler's negative classicism to suit his own purposes.

Ortega's echoes of Spengler's "Caesarism" are ironic in light of his praise of Caesar at the end of *The Revolt of the Masses*. On the one hand, Ortega calls "the state" the greatest danger to civilization, seeing in its rise and influence the shadow of Roman oppression and "the lamentable fate of ancient civilisation. . . . Already in the times of the Antonines . . . the State overbears society with its anti-vital supremacy. Society begins to be enslaved, to be unable to live except *in the service of the State*. The whole of life is bureaucratised. What results? The bureaucratisation of life brings about its absolute decay in all orders" (121). On the other hand, it is precisely to a rebirth or rejuvenation of something like state organization on a European scale that Ortega looks for an escape from "the brutal empire of the masses," and hence he turns to Caesar as one of the two "clear heads" in the ancient world (the other was Themistocles). As Caesar pointed the way to the modern state, so some new charismatic figure must point the way to the unification of Europe. "Only the determination to construct a great nation from the group of peoples of the Continent would give new life to the pulses of Europe" (183). Only the project of unifying Europe, in short, can counteract "the decadence of Europe" (145). For this reason, we must return to the experience of Caesar, paying not too much attention to his overriding of the democratic procedures of the Republic, which had grown corrupt through expansion and massification: "As genuine elections were impossible, it was necessary to falsify them, and the candidates organised gangs of bravoes from army veterans or circus athletes, whose business was to intimidate the voters. Without the support of a genuine suffrage democratic institutions are in the air. Words are things of air, and 'the Republic is nothing more than a word.' The expression is Caesar's" (158–59). Caesar, the man of imagination, looks beyond the limits of the classical city-state to the new international state of the growing Empire (155–56). Thus the Empire itself serves as an image of the future unification of Europe, even while it also serves as an image of oppression, decadence, and the barbarism of the masses. Ortega does nothing to straighten out this contradiction beyond declaring in a footnote that "it is well known that the Empire of Augustus is the *opposite* of what his adoptive father Caesar aspired to create" (165). What Caesar looked forward to, however, was apparently just that nightmare of antivital statism that Ortega calls "the greatest danger."

It is difficult to see how the positive sort of statism supposedly envisaged by Caesar can save us from the negative sort supposedly established by Augustus, especially when the central problem of "the masses" has to do with certain deficiencies in average human nature. Both Ortega and Spengler owe a great deal to yet another enemy of the commonplace, Friedrich Nietzsche, who, although he did not have Mussolini, Hitler, and Stalin to point to as proofs of the incompetence of "average man," still had much to say about nationalism and socialism as manifestations of the "herd instinct":

> The overall degeneration of man down to what today appears to the socialist dolts and flatheads as their "man of the future"—as their ideal—this degeneration and diminution of man into the perfect herd animal (or, as they say, to the man of the "free society"), this animalization of man into the dwarf animal of equal rights and claims, is *possible*, there is no doubt of it. Anyone who has once thought through this possibility to the end knows one kind of nausea that other men don't know—

though it is less Nietzsche's "nausea" that Ortega expresses than the bewilderment of a frustrated liberal, confronting the terrible paradox that liberalism seems to defeat itself in its moment of triumph.[7] And whereas Nietzsche's herd animal is motivated by *ressentiment* to tear down whatever is fine and "noble," Ortega's mass man" seems to be more self-satisfied than vindictive, a Babbitt who looks into the mirror in the morning, sees nothing looking back, and believes that he is the Supreme Being. "He is satisfied with himself exactly as he is" (62).

As already noted, Nietzsche's voice was only one of many in the last decades of the nineteenth century which helped to solidify the pessimistic view of human nature which underlies Spengler's urban mob and Ortega's average man. The naturalist movement in literature—for Spengler a symptom of decadence, as it had been for Max Nordau— portrayed the average man as the pawn of environment and heredity, and often as the victim of vast collective forces: economic depression and unemployment, riots, revolutions, and wars. The symbolist and decadent movements offered the other side of this picture: average man could have no share in the arts, which were sublime mysteries beyond the grasp of all but the initiated.[8] Reinforcing the literary naturalists, the social Darwinists offered their "gladiatorial theory of existence," while the crowd psychologists projected the elements of mob action onto all forms of collective behavior.[9] These sources of social pessimism were reinforced by many other explorers of the irrational: Freud, of course, but also Emile Durkheim, Max Weber, Henri Bergson, Georges Sorel. Viewed as a cultural trend, their explorations have an ambiguous quality: on the one hand, especially with Freud, Durkheim, and Weber, "the social thinkers of the 1890s were concerned with the irrational only to exorcise it"; on the other, the irrational was worshiped by neo-romantics and nihilists, while violence and warfare received "scientific" approval along with imperialist expansion.[10] Thus, the heritage of high culture itself seemed ambigu-

7. Friedrich Nietzsche, *Beyond Good and Evil*, tr. Walter Kaufmann (New York: Vintage, 1966), p. 118.

8. See, for example, Edmund Wilson, *Axel's Castle* (New York: Scribner, 1931), pp. 257–98.

9. Huxley speaks of the "gladiatorial theory of existence" in *Evolution and Ethics*.

10. H. Stuart Hughes, *Consciousness and Society: The Reorientation of European Social Thought, 1890–1930* (New York: Vintage, 1958), pp. 35–36.

ous: by the turn of the century, it almost appeared that culture was in alliance with anarchy—that it had patched up its differences with barbarism and gone looking for fights elsewhere: in the latest imperialist land grabs, but also in the parlors and boudoirs of the bourgeoisie, whose complacent respectability so many artists and intellectuals wanted to explode. There may be some exaggeration in Karl Löwith's assessment of the opinions of educated Europeans before World War I, but he differs from Ortega chiefly in emphasizing the disillusionment of the cultured rather than the ignorance of the masses: "Nihilism as the disavowal of existing civilization was the only real belief of all truly educated people at the beginning of the twentieth century. Nihilism is not a result of the Great War, but on the contrary, its cause."[11]

Matthew Arnold's antithesis proves thus to be also an affinity, anarchy as a product of culture, if only because the most powerful currents in recent intellectual history have flowed with rather than against the rising tides of democracy and the masses. Although Ortega does not offer an extended analysis of the "treason of the intellectuals"[12] or of the more complicated paradox of culture producing anarchy, he gives it general expression:

> It will not do, then, to dignify the actual crisis by presenting it as the conflict between two moralities, two civilisations, one in decay, the other at its dawn. The mass-man is simply without morality. . . . How has it been possible to believe in the amorality of life? Doubtless, because all modern culture and civilisation tend to that conviction. Europe is now reaping the painful results of her spiritual conduct. She has adopted blindly a culture which is magnificent, but has no roots. [189]

Much of what Ortega means by Europe's "spiritual conduct" is summed up in his chapter on "the barbarism of 'specialisation.'" There he argues that mass man is the direct product of "nineteenth-century civilisation," which in turn was based on the progress of

11. Karl Löwith, "The Historical Background of European Nihilism," in *Nature, History and Existentialism* (Evanston, Ill.: Northwestern University Press, 1966), p. 10.

12. Julien Benda, *The Treason of the Intellectuals*, tr. Richard Aldington (New York: Norton, 1969 [1928]).

science and technology.[13] It then appears that "the prototype of the mass-man" is not an illiterate thug, but "the actual scientific man." Through specialization, "science itself—the root of our civilisation—automatically converts him into mass-man, makes of him a primitive, a modern barbarian" (109). The worst, most typical sort of mass man is thus a "learned ignoramus," convinced of his general knowledge because of his narrow expertise in one very specialized line. In short, the progress of civilization fabricates the materials for its own disintegration.

> That state of "not listening," of not submitting to higher courts of appeal which I have repeatedly put forward as characteristic of the mass-man, reaches its height precisely in these partially qualified men. They symbolise, and to a great extent constitute, the actual domination of the masses, and their barbarism is the most immediate cause of European demoralisation. Furthermore, they afford the clearest, most striking example of how the civilisation of the last century, abandoned to its own devices, has brought about this rebirth of primitivism and barbarism. [113]

Whereas "the Roman Empire came to an end for lack of technique" (90), the problem with modern society is nearly the opposite. Technical progress is real enough and valued by Ortega; "but to-day it is man who is the failure, because he is unable to keep pace with the progress of his own civilisation" (91). Put in somewhat different terms, the barbarian specialist has only his own interest and that of his special field in view, to the detriment of a general culture; "the direction of society has been taken over by a type of man who is not interested in the principles of civilisation" (81).

Even though he has in mind the scientific and technical division of labor, Ortega is not criticizing a particular category of culture that might be labeled "mass," but modern culture in general. The argument for high against mass culture thus recedes beyond two horizons. First, there is the rejection of mass culture itself, or rather of the "barbarism" of the masses. Second, there is the rejection of the progressive, scientific, and "anarchic" elements in high culture as well,

13. Here is another place where Ortega finds Spengler "far too optimistic," because Spengler "believes that 'technicism' can go on living when interest in the principles underlying culture are dead" (*Revolt of the Masses*, p. 83).

until there remain only a set of reactionary political attitudes and a call for a religious revival. Ortega does not follow his argument to this reactionary conclusion (instead of calling for religion, he calls for a united Europe). But similar arguments have frequently been difficult to distinguish from fascism, so that attempts at classical and religious revivals often blur into the "revolt of the masses" that they are meant to counteract.

Ortega's essay involves a theory of history based on the concepts of the illegitimacy of any large state machinery and of inevitable, cyclic social regression. Although Ortega claims that he is not a determinist and that "everything is possible in history" (79), his argument still follows the pattern of negative classicism. In his critique of Arnold Toynbee, *An Interpretation of Universal History*, Ortega asks:

> Is it an accident, or a law of history, that every civilization reaches a point in which it must set up an Empire, a universal state which means power among all nations, and that this universal state is inundated from the subsoil (at a certain period literally inundated by subterranean peoples coming from the catacombs), by a religious principle which originates among the internal proletariat of that civilization; and that while this religion is swelling and filling the spaces of that universal state, the barbarians—that is, the inferior peoples which surround the frontiers of that civilization—burst into the state and destroy it?[14]

Although Ortega thinks that in Toynbee's *Study of History* "there is not a single sharp, perspicacious idea" (230), his own answer to this question seems to be affirmative. Ortega criticizes Toynbee for carrying the "exemplary character of Roman history to the extreme" (127), but Roman decline and fall is also Ortega's most frequent model for the modern experience. "The pure truth is that the Roman Empire has never disappeared from the Western world" (96). This fact, says Ortega, would be "a first-rate theme for any young historian who has the wit to see it—the history of the Roman Empire after its official disappearance, that is to say, the history of how this proud historic figure survived after it ceased to live" (96).

In essence, this "first-rate theme" is Ortega's own in all his writings

14. José Ortega y Gasset, *An Interpretation of Universal History*, tr. Mildred Adams (New York: Norton, 1975 [1948]), p. 55. Abbreviated in the text as *IUH*.

about history. At the start of *An Interpretation of Universal History*, he draws from classical political theory three principles that he believes to be of universal significance, visible in Roman as well as in modern history. Ortega finds in Plato and Aristotle the idea that every government has "its own congenital vice, and therefore it inevitably degenerates." Democracy in particular "quickly becomes pure disorder and anarchy, swayed by demagogues, and ending by being the brutal oppression of the masses which were then called . . . the rabble, *okhlos*, and thence okhlocracy." This is the classical model of the "revolt of the masses." It is also one basis for a cyclic view of history and for "despair of the political" (*IUH* 33). But, says Ortega, in order to escape from the cycle, Plato and Aristotle recommend a "mixed constitution," made up of the best features of monarchy, aristocracy, and democracy. And this is the second universal principle. The third one, drawn from classical experience rather than philosophy, is the *translatio imperii* or the apparent movement of empire from east to west, following the stars. Empire, says Ortega, seems to "follow a sidereal course" (*IUH* 35–36).

Although Ortega calls forth these three principles in order to question them, and although he appears to be questioning Toynbee's laws of "universal history" in the same manner, he does not reject them. They are the groundwork for his later argument about the illegitimacy of all large state organizations and, hence, of empire. Ortega analyzes the evolution of Roman imperialism to show that "the state, the exercise of public power, begins by being illegitimate and ends by being illegitimate" (*IUH* 198). This leads to a question that might serve as a summary of *The Revolt of the Masses* and, indeed, of all Ortega's writings about modern society: "what should we do when the life of a whole civilization enters the stage of constitutive illegitimacy?" (*IUH* 199).

Ortega's question is clearer than his solutions. What is most evident in his work is his belief in the decadence of modern society, the main symptom of which is the new "barbarism" of the masses. The revolt of the masses is in fact a cyclic occurrence in history to which Ortega attaches the label "rebarbarization." As he says in *Man and Crisis*, "It is not easy to doubt that the phenomenon of rebarbarization has repeatedly recurred throughout history."[15] As in Rome, so in more

15. José Ortega y Gasset, *Man and Crisis*, tr. Mildred Adams (New York: Norton, 1958), pp. 95–96. Abbreviated in the text as *MC*.

recent times: "An excess of sudden dread, a period of many changes, plunges man back into nature, makes him an animal, that is, a barbarian. This was a very serious feature of the greatest crisis in history, at the end of the ancient world" (*MC* 95–96). Barbarism destroyed ancient civilization from within as well as from without. Its internal symptoms included a withdrawal from politics into self, represented by stoicism; the increasing predominance of the urban "rabble," which (Ortega quotes Polybius) was "dedicated to festivals and spectacles, to luxury and to [sexual] disorders"; and the substitution of mechanical and bureaucratic techniques for tradition, religion, and community. All of these symptoms are apparent again in the modern "rebarbarization" of society. Of the last symptom, for example, Ortega says that the very faith in progress through technology is itself a source of decay: "The belief in progress, the conviction that on this level of history a major setback can no longer happen and the world will mechanically go the full length of prosperity, has loosened the rivets of human caution and flung open the gates for a new invasion of barbarism."[16]

What Ortega offers as an antidote to modern "rebarbarization" is much less specific and vivid than his diagnosis. Ultimately, however, he places his faith in reason, although as with Freud this faith seems more tenuous than his belief in the cyclic recurrence of decline and fall. Our need to rely on reason is in any case tragic. Perhaps echoing Albert Camus's *The Myth of Sisyphus* (1942), Ortega writes: "Man is condemned to reason; therefore to a task which is always incomplete, always fragile, always having to be commenced anew, as Sisyphus had always to go back to pushing to the top of the mountain the rock that was eternally bent on rolling down to the valley" (*IUH* 172).

Ortega's political philosophy, based on a sharp but also abstract dichotomy between elites and masses (compare Gaetano Mosca and Vilfredo Pareto in Italy), is vague enough to be considered fascist by the left and perhaps too liberal by the right. According to Franz Niedermayer, an admiring critic, "*The Revolt of the Masses* remained a best seller in Germany . . . regardless of political regime because all factions found in its pages something of value to them" (a typical formula for mass market success).[17] Niedermayer quotes the editor of

16. José Ortega y Gasset, *History as a System*, tr. Mildred Adams (New York: Norton, 1961), p. 104–105.
17. Franz Niedermayer, *José Ortega y Gasset* (New York: Ungar, 1973), p. 65.

Europäische Revue, Joachim Moras, who says that during the Third Reich "we could read T. S. Eliot, Paul Valéry, and André Gide, but not W. H. Auden or André Malraux. We did have Pío Baroja y Nessi and Gomez de la Serna, and again and again Ortega, but no García Lorca" (65–66). And Niedermayer says that though in 1933 Ortega rejected the proposals of the founder of the Falangist party (his pupil José Antonio Primo de Rivera, son of the former dictator) that he become its intellectual leader, that party itself "was an expression of Ortega's spirit" (68). Ortega's version of negative classicism, mingling the themes of disappointed liberalism with more conservative ones, provides a vivid diagnosis of some of the problems of modern society. It also fails to transcend ideas and attitudes—nostalgia for lost authority, a loathing for the vulgar and the common man, distrust of science and of democratic procedures—compatible with the fascism that he sees as one of the most tragic consequences of the revolt of the masses.

While Ortega is loftily obscure enough to have become a popular author for readers of various political persuasions, his diagnosis of "the revolt of the masses" was made many times over by other writers in the 1930s.[18] In a decade when republics were being crushed under the iron heels of imperialistic dictatorships, what seemed most evident was the weakness of democracy. The rise of mass or totalitarian societies, the transformation of older cultural forms—partly through the use of the new mass media for propaganda purposes—into "barbarism," the erection of racist concepts into ideologies accepted by "the masses"—these seemed indeed to involve a "classical revival," but of the Roman imperial rather than of the Athenian kind.

ii

Like Ortega, the great Dutch historian Johan Huizinga worried about "the masses" in the 1930s. His *In the Shadow of Tomorrow* (1935), in which he analyzes the parallels between *panem et circenses* and modern totalitarian movements, laid the groundwork for his study of the relationship between play and culture, *Homo Ludens* (1944). In

18. Besides the works listed in Neumann, *Permanent Revolution*, see Leonard Woolf, *Barbarians Within and Without* (New York: Harcourt, Brace, 1939), and Simone Weil, "The Great Beast, Some Reflections on the Origins of Hitlerism, 1939–40," *Selected Essays, 1934–43* (London: Oxford University Press, 1962).

the latter, Huizinga writes: "Roman society could not live without games. They were as necessary to its existence as bread—for they were holy games and the people's right to them was a holy right."[19] But the religious quality of the Roman games had shriveled to almost nothing by the time that Juvenal wrote. Huizinga declares: "Few of the brutalized mob of spectators [during imperial times] felt anything of the religious quality inherent in these performances, and the Emperor's liberality on such occasions had sunk to mere alms-giving on a gigantic scale to a miserable proletariat." Huizinga sees the same analogy to modern conditions that Le Bon, Spengler, Ortega, and many others have seen: the Roman "cry for *panem et circenses*" is not much different from "the demand of the unemployed proletariat for the dole and free cinema tickets"—except that it was perhaps a little more sacred or less worldly (or perhaps just more classical?). Huizinga goes on to diagnose modern decadence in terms like those of Ortega and Spengler, calling much of what he sees about him "Puerilism"— "the most appropriate appellation for that blend of adolescence and barbarity which has been rampant all over the world for the last two or three decades" (205). Puerilism involves a "world-wide bastardization of culture" and "the entry of half-educated masses into the international traffic of the mind," accompanied by a "relaxation of morals" and a "hypertrophy of technics" (205). These symptoms Huizinga links to totalitarianism, or "the spectacle of a society rapidly goose-stepping into helotry" (206).

Huizinga is especially concerned with the processes of secularization which he believes undermine the legitimacy and energy of the play element in culture. The erosion of the sacred in modern society is also one of the central themes in T. S. Eliot's essays against the "new paganism." At the end of the 1930s, Eliot published his attack on liberalism and fascism, *The Idea of a Christian Society*. On one level, his argument is little more than a call for a religious revival (despite the fact that Eliot thinks religion is eternal and therefore can neither die nor revive). Eliot's dismal picture of a "revolt of the masses" is much the same as Ortega's. He is more specific in assessing blame than Ortega, however, perhaps because his version of "rebarbariza-

19. Johan Huizinga, *In the Shadow of Tomorrow* (New York: Norton, 1936); *Homo Ludens: A Study of the Play Element in Culture* (Boston: Beacon, 1955 [1944]), p. 177.

tion" is based on avowed conservatism rather than on disappointed liberalism. Eliot thinks that liberalism itself is the main culprit, paving the way for fascism. Both are versions of paganism, the true antithesis of the Christian society.

One symptom of modern paganism is secularized mass culture. Like Ortega, Eliot thinks of culture and the masses as opposites, so that he rejects the idea of civilizing the masses through education, the press, radio, and cinema in favor of a return to religious orthodoxy and to the authoritarian security of class hierarchy. "A 'mass-culture' will always be a substitute-culture," Eliot says in his *Notes towards the Definition of Culture* (1948), "and sooner or later the deception will become apparent to the more intelligent of those upon whom the culture has been palmed off."[20] Eliot's notion of "mass culture" here echoes Dwight Macdonald's 1944 essay "A Theory of Popular Culture," which Eliot duly acknowledges. Eliot shares with Macdonald the idea of the conspiratorial nature of mass culture: it is a deception that has been palmed off on the unwitting. But Macdonald states this theme more forthrightly than Eliot: "Mass Culture is imposed from above. It is fabricated by technicians hired by businessmen; its audiences are passive consumers, their participation limited to the choice between buying and not buying. The Lords of kitsch, in short, exploit the cultural needs of the masses in order to make a profit and/or to maintain their class rule."[21] One reason why Eliot is not so forthright as Macdonald in presenting mass culture as a conspiracy from above is that he thinks the masses are as much the agents as the victims of the conspiracy. The same ambiguity characterizes Ortega's essay. From one viewpoint (held constantly by Macdonald but only part of the time by Eliot), the masses can only be the dupes of the clever entrepreneurs, the P. T. Barnums of the entertainment business, who know how to squeeze hard cash out of them by appealing to their lowest instincts. From another viewpoint, however, the masses

20. T. S. Eliot, *Notes towards the Definition of Culture*, published with *The Idea of a Christian Society* as *Christianity and Culture* (New York: Harcourt, Brace, 1968), p. 184. Abbreviated in the text as *CC*.
21. Dwight Macdonald, "A Theory of Popular Culture," *Politics*, 1 (February 1944), pp. 20 ff. In revised versions, Macdonald uses "mass" instead of "popular" culture. I have quoted from "A Theory of Mass Culture," *Diogenes*, 3 (Summer 1953), reprinted in Bernard Rosenberg and David Manning White, eds., *Mass Culture: The Popular Arts in America* (Glencoe, Ill., The Free Press, 1957), p. 60.

are the enemies of the established order, and hence of all culture and civilization. Either way, the masses are seen in strictly negative terms. Whether Eliot treats them as the passive victims of a fraudulent commercial culture or as the barbarian ravagers of a genuine high culture, he asserts that they play only a nocuous role in history.

Like Macdonald, Eliot believes that there are distinct levels of culture which are associated with economic classes. Macdonald identifies three levels roughly with the proletariat, the bourgeoisie, and the aristocracy. These he names "masscult," "midcult," and "high culture," a division also apparent in Russell Lynes's "lowbrow," "middlebrow," and "highbrow" (to which might be added G. M. Young's amusing "sniffbrow," in his 1922 essay "The New Cortegiano").[22] Macdonald's schema also includes "folk culture," except that it is now largely extinct, driven out of existence by the new industrial-commercial categories of "masscult" and "midcult." Aristocratic "high culture" for Macdonald is genuine; "masscult" and "midcult," however, are shoddy imitations of the real thing. And "midcult" is especially insidious, Macdonald believes, because of its proximity to the real thing.

Though Eliot insists on the importance of qualitative distinctions based on class, what he means by mass culture is not so much the lowest of Macdonald's levels as the abolition of all levels. It is the specter of a "uniform culture" in a "classless society" which leads Eliot to define a sound culture as dependent on a "healthily stratified" and a "healthily regional" society—in other words, British society as it is, or perhaps as it was before the turn of the century. Whereas Macdonald is chiefly concerned with the deleterious effects of industrialism and commercialism on culture, Eliot is chiefly concerned with the threats of democratic leveling and socialism. It is in the context of "the disintegration of class" that Eliot makes his argument about the dependence of culture on class hierarchy. And it is in the context of the disintegration of religious faith that he asserts the absolute mutual dependence—even identity—of culture and religion: "No culture has appeared or developed except together with a religion" (*CC* 87).

22. Though he did not invent these terms, Russell Lynes's "Lowbrow, Middlebrow, and Highbrow" was first published in *Harper's Magazine* in 1949 and reprinted in *The Tastemakers* (New York: Harper, 1953). G. M. Young's "The New Cortegiano" is in *Daylight and Champaign* (London: Jonathan Cape, 1937).

In defending, partly by identifying, high culture, class hierarchy, and religious orthodoxy, Eliot seeks to refute Karl Mannheim's thesis in *Man and Society in an Age of Reconstruction* (1935) that classes are being supplanted in modern society by meritocratic elites. But Eliot confuses Mannheim's diagnosis with a prescription; no more than Eliot is Mannheim an apologist for "the disintegrated mass society" (*CC* 97) or for the "proletarianization of the intelligentsia" (*CC* 99). This misreading suggests Eliot's distance to the right of Mannheim's liberalism. Mannheim's advocacy of centralized social planning and of mass education, perhaps, tempted Eliot to see him as an apostle of classlessness and cultural uniformity. Against Mannheim's thesis that elites are replacing classes, Eliot argues the necessity for both, and adds that another kind of elite—"*the* elite"—must be drawn from both to lead all the subgroups of society (*CC* 114). This is social stratification with a vengeance. "*The* elite" would seem to mean "the best," in the sense of the most cultured members of society, who in turn should be born and bred aristocrats. Eliot thus trebly seeks to fortify his position against the "nightmare" of "cultural uniformity" in the "classless society": by defending aristocracy, by defending elites, and by defending "*the* elite."

Whereas Macdonald worries about the historical emergence of "low" kinds of culture or "kitsch," Eliot worries about "the causes of a total decline of culture," leaving little to choose between the terms "barbarism" and "decadence": "Excess of unity may be due to barbarism and may lead to tyranny; excess of division may be due to decadence and may also lead to tyranny; either excess will prevent further development in culture" (*CC* 123). Eliot is unsure whether there is any permanent standard by which to judge cultures, but he is quite sure that cultural disintegration is occurring all around us. "We can assert with some confidence that our own period is one of decline; that the standards of culture are lower than they were fifty years ago; and that the evidences of this decline are visible in every department of human activity." And he goes on to imagine, at the end of the chute down which everything valuable is plummeting, a condition in which there may be "*no* culture" (*CC* 91).

This categorical decline and fall, caused by the leveling of classes and the erosion of faith, is not reversible by the "liberal nostrum" of education—certainly it cannot be reversed, Eliot believes, through the nostrum of *mass* education as planned and provided by a secular, centralized government. For mass education itself is a primary cause of the breakup, and is leading not toward a new culture on an egalitarian basis, but toward a new barbarism:

> We know, that whether education can foster and improve culture or not, it can surely adulterate and degrade it. For there is no doubt that in our headlong rush to educate everybody, we are lowering our standards, and more and more abandoning the study of those subjects by which the essentials of our culture—of that part of it which is transmissible by education—are transmitted; destroying our ancient edifices to make ready the ground upon which the barbarian nomads of the future will encamp in their mechanised caravans. [*CC* 185]

In such remarks on education, Eliot comes close to Macdonald's "midcult." For just as Macdonald finds something especially insidious about "middlebrow" dilutions and apings of "highbrow" art, so Eliot finds something dangerous about "half education" (*CC* 182). He would rather see most people contentedly ignorant and rooted to the land than restless, envious, too much moving about like Attilas on wheels. "A high average of general education is perhaps less necessary for a civil society than is a respect for learning" (*CC* 177).[23]

Mass culture for Macdonald connotes a category of debased or shoddy artifacts and amusements that appeal to the poorly educated. Clearly, more schooling and not less is one way to deal with it. He is not talking about "proletarian culture," however, an idea that involves still another meaning of mass culture—that of a working class actively engaged in producing as well as consuming its own art, knowledge, and entertainment. Against Macdonald's commercial "masscult" and "midcult" and also against Eliot's cultural catastrophe must be ranged the ideal of liberated culture expressed by William Morris, Herbert Marcuse, and other Marxists, or in other words the shapes that culture might take in a future classless society. But the utopian adumbrations of the transformation of labor into play in Morris and Marcuse are themselves quite different from the usual understanding of "pro-

---

23. I cannot resist saying that, if G. M. Young's "sniffbrow" was ever applicable to an opinion, it is to this one of Eliot's. See Young's "The New Cortegiano" for an able defense of the middle ranges of the cultural spectrum, in *Daylight and Champaign*, pp. 140–59.

letarian culture," which can be defined in at least two ways. One can define it as that which the working class already produces for its own consumption (existing forms of "popular" and "folk" culture); or one can identify it with the various movements—*Proletkult* and Zhdanovite socialist realism, for example—in the development of Soviet literature and art. Eliot, of course, rejects both the utopian Marxist and the Soviet versions of proletarian culture, although there is an important way in which he is sympathetic toward working-class culture in England.

Eliot is quite willing to look favorably upon manifestations of culture that might be called "proletarian," but only if they appear within the confines of a "healthily stratified" and a "healthily regional" society, presided over by religious orthodoxy. With the "nightmare" of "cultural uniformity" as his backdrop, Eliot names a variety of ingredients, including working-class games and amusements, which compose "that which makes life worth living" (*CC* 100):

> Taking now the point of view of identification, the reader must remind himself, as the author has constantly to do, of how much is here embraced by the term *culture*. It includes all the characteristic activities and interests of a people: Derby Day, Henley Regatta, Cowes, the twelfth of August, a cup final, the dog races, the pin table, the dart board, Wensleydale cheese, boiled cabbage cut into sections, beetroot in vinegar, nineteenth-century Gothic churches and the music of Elgar. [*CC* 104]

Eliot adds, no doubt as a gesture toward making his list complete, "the reader can make his own list." Whatever the ingredients, they must include items that might be defined as folk customs (beetroot in vinegar) as well as items that might be defined as popular amusements (the dog races). In this sense, Eliot's idea of culture embraces working-class experience. But Eliot's assertion that the reader can make his own list is deceptive, because far from being wide-ranging, his list is quite narrow, as remarkable for what it excludes as for what it includes. As Raymond Williams observes, "This pleasant miscellany is evidently narrower in kind than the general description which precedes it. The 'characteristic activities and interests' would also include steelmaking, touring in motor-cars, mixed farming, the Stock Exchange, coal-mining and London Transport."[24] One might as well add: trade unions, the Labour party, the IRA, the *Times*, and BBC. "Any list would be incomplete," Williams says, "but Eliot's categories are sport, food and a little art—a characteristic observation on English leisure." I am tempted to add that Eliot gives us a portrait of English leisure before the advent of cinema, radio, and television, which would mean at least before World War I. On the basis of this and a few other rather narrow "observations" that Eliot makes, Williams concludes that Eliot "recommends . . . substantially what now exists, socially." But his generous assessment of Eliot's cultural recipe is difficult to square with his earlier remark that "Eliot seems always to have in mind, as the normal scheme of his thinking, a society which is at once more stable and more simple than any to which his discussion is likely to be relevant" (236).

Here is a key to understanding Eliot's cultural politics, and perhaps to understanding negative classicism in general. Instead of portraying British society as it was in 1948, Eliot invokes a utopia from the right to counter the utopia of the left, which he perceives as a totalitarian "nightmare." His list of cultural ingredients reads like a Dickens Christmas story: against the cold outer dark of the future classless society—a sort of technological necropolis for Eliot—the list has the feel of the fire on the hearth. This result may derive partly from Eliot's expatriate status: in thinking of such "characteristic" trivia as boiled cabbage cut into sections, he is, as E. M. Forster puts it, "more British than the British." Eliot's Britishness is part of his reactionary utopianism: the search for origins, stability, orthodoxy, leads him ambiguously to praise a sinking England, an England just before the deluge (or perhaps just after it). He opposes not only the classless society of the future, but also the complicated, industrial, semi-democratic, semi-aristocratic, quarrelsome, half-educated, not very satisfactory, and not very religious England of the present, while also viewing it as preferable to America. "Totalitarianism appeals to the desire to return to the womb" (*CC* 142). But it is not altogether clear that Eliot's own brand of retrospective politics does not appeal to the same desire, the wish to find "the still point of the turning world."

24. Raymond Williams, *Culture and Society, 1780–1950* (New York: Harper and Row, 1966 [1958]), p. 234.

In saying so, I do not mean to dismiss Eliot's cultural politics as insignificant. As Williams suggests, his treatment of mass culture is an important contribution to a long tradition of social theory extending back to Burke and Coleridge, although Williams rightly finds Eliot's "new conservatism" "very different from, and much inferior to" theirs. This inferiority stems from Eliot's need to root his opposition to "an 'atomized,' individualist [or mass; they are synonymous here] society" in "the principles of an economic system which is based on just this 'atomized,' individualist society" (242). That is, Eliot is unable to follow the thread of conservative theory away from liberal economics even to the kinds of "conservative socialism" suggested by Coleridge's "clerisy" and by Robert Southey's Owenism. As part of their inferiority to earlier conservatisms, Eliot's politics are not clearly distinguishable from a variant of the arguments used to support the same sort of mass, totalitarian society that Eliot believes he is combatting. This is so even though Eliot attacks liberalism for leading to fascism, and declares: "The fundamental objection to fascist doctrine, the one which we conceal from ourselves because it might condemn ourselves as well, is that it is pagan" (*CC* 15).

Whether Eliot was or was not ever an anti-Semite or an admirer of Mussolini is not important here (there have been numerous treatments of what William Chace calls his "flirtation with fascism," with varying results). But the classicist form of Eliot's social thinking involves contrasting modern democratic-industrial society to an ideal society that, though rooted in the past, is also in several respects like the "corporate state" advocated by fascism. Thus, Eliot's triple defense of elitism (classes, elites, and "*the* elite") might be taken for a simplified version of the theory of elites developed by Gaetano Mosca and Vilfredo Pareto—a theory that, especially through Pareto, became a staple of fascist thought.[25] And like Charles Maurras, whose influence he acknowledged, Eliot is both antidemocratic and anti-

25. William M. Chace, *The Political Identities of Ezra Pound and T. S. Eliot* (Stanford: Stanford University Press, 1973). See also John R. Harrison, *The Reactionaries* (New York: Schocken, 1966). There is a good account of "elite" theories in T. B. Bottomore, *Elites and Society* (Baltimore: Penguin, 1966), especially pp. 7–20. Pareto, whom Mussolini treated "with great respect" and made a senator in 1923, is anthologized in Adrian Lyttelton, ed., *Italian Fascisms: From Pareto to Gentile* (New York: Harper and Row, 1973).

socialistic, both classicist and religiously authoritarian. "[My] general point of view," he could write in 1928, "may be described as classicist in literature, royalist in politics, and anglo-catholic in religion."[26]

Eliot shed the royalist label not long after adopting it, but he remained deeply committed to his conservative brands of classicism and Christianity. He is a Christian first, a classicist second, although the two are inseparable: "Those of us who find ourselves supporting . . . Classicism believe that men cannot get on without giving allegiance to something outside themselves."[27] That "something outside" is ultimately religious. Like T. E. Hulme, whose political and cultural theories he admired, Eliot defines romanticism in terms of emotional solipsism and relativity and classicism in terms of its reference to an external absolute. For both Hulme and Eliot, romanticism equals modern culture decadence—an argument similar to Norberto Bobbio's analysis of "decadentism" or to Cyril Joad's of the subjectivist "dropping of the object" in modern culture. Against the breakdown of external authority which is the modern "wasteland," Eliot looks to literary tradition, "the clerisy," and the Church—at some point in the past themselves forming an organic whole—to restore organic unity to society. It is too easy, he thinks, to see history only in pieces and to make of experience only what one wishes. Eliot believes that there must be something higher to guide us than individual reason in a secularized context. What he says of the writer in "Tradition and the Individual Talent" extends to history in its entirety:

> No poet, no artist of any art, has his complete meaning alone. His significance, his appreciation is the appreciation of his relation to the dead poets and artists . . . . The existing monuments [of an art] form an ideal order among themselves, which is modified by the introduction of the new (the really new) work of art among them. The existing order is complete before the new work arrives; for order to persist after the supervention of novelty, the *whole* existing order must be, if ever so slightly, altered; and so the relations, proportions, values of each work of art toward the whole are readjusted. [*SE* 4–5]

As in most other versions of theoretical conservatism, not only the arts

26. T. S. Eliot, *For Lancelot Andrewes* (London: Faber and Gwyer, 1928), p. ix.

27. T. S. Eliot, *Selected Essays* (New York: Harcourt, Brace and World, 1960), p. 15. Abbreviated later in the text as *SE*.

but society and history form an organic whole. The "pagan" politics of liberalism, fascism, and socialism are what fracture the whole; Christianity is what holds it together.

Christianity is not just the true and absolute religion for Eliot; it is also the preserver of the spirit of the Roman Empire and the transmitter of classicism to modern civilization. The importance of Rome in Eliot's thinking is partly obscured by its evident cultural inferiority to Greece. "The Rome of the imperial era was coarse and beastly enough," says Eliot; "in important respects far less civilized than Athens at its greatest."[28] For example, in contrast to the Greeks, the Romans lacked the "gift" of theater, "which has not been vouchsafed to every race" (*SE* 55). True, the Romans had the wooden tragedies of Seneca and they also had "some success in low comedy, itself an adaptation of Greek models, but their instinct turned to shows and circuses, as does that of the later race which created the Commedia del l'Arte" (*SE* 56). Eliot does not think that too much should be made of "the 'decadence' of the age of Nero" as an explanation for the cultural failings of the Romans; his terminology suggests that cultural endowments come from on high and are bestowed on chosen "races." This logic allows him to insist on the need for every society to pursue its "destiny" and to make the most of whatever cultural endowments it is "vouchsafed." In turn, the importance of "classics" as "gifts" is reinforced; "we must maintain the classic ideal before our eyes" (*OP* 60).

Despite its cultural thinness in comparison to Greece, Rome—especially imperial Rome—is the society most nearly "classic" and it gave birth to the poet closest to the "classic ideal," namely Virgil. As "a classic can only occur when a civilization is mature" (*OP* 54), so "Virgil's maturity of mind, and the maturity of his age" are expressed in *The Aeneid* (*OP* 63). Aeneas points to the "destiny" of Rome which is also our destiny. When Virgil asserts the eternality of the *imperium romanum*, Eliot claims that he is close to prophetic rightness, for Virgil is also of all classical authors "uniquely near to Christianity" (*OP* 146–47). And while the worldly version of the Roman Empire de-

---

28. T. S. Eliot, *On Poetry and Poets* (New York: Noonday, 1961), p. 139. Abbreviated in the text as *OP*.

clined and fell, it did so only to make room for the Holy Roman Empire. Therefore, Eliot says, "we are all, so far as we inherit the civilization of Europe, still citizens of the Roman Empire, and time has not yet proved Virgil wrong when he wrote *nec tempora pono: imperium sine fine dedi*" (I, Jupiter, impose no limits: I have granted empire without end) (*OP* 146).

Not only the pattern of our salvation, but—what is almost the same thing—the pattern of our cultural perfection was "set in Rome" (*OP* 73). Eliot concludes his essay "What Is a Classic?" with a magnificent peroration on Virgil, who produced what is perhaps the one genuine classic by Eliot's standard and who therefore showed the way for the destiny of all European culture. To define and defend what is "classic"—the task of Eliot's sort of criticism—becomes in this peroration the task of defending nothing less than civilization:

> It is sufficient that this standard [for a classic] should have been established once for all; the task does not have to be done again. But the maintenance of the standard is the price of our freedom, the defense of freedom against chaos. We may remind ourselves of this obligation, by our annual observance of piety towards the great ghost who guided Dante's pilgrimage: who, as it was his function to lead Dante towards a vision he could never himself enjoy, led Europe towards the Christian culture which he could never know.   [*OP* 74]

Today, however, under the impact of the new paganisms of secular politics, that Christian culture is in danger. In making his case for Christianity, Eliot at times sounds like Kierkegaard, as when he asserts that "without religion the whole human race would die . . . solely of boredom" (*SE* 326). At others, he sounds more like another Arnold Toynbee or Nicholas Berdyaev, envisaging a new Dark Age:

> The Universal Church is today, it seems to me, more definitely set against the World than at any time since pagan Rome. I do not mean that our times are particularly corrupt; all times are corrupt. I mean that Christianity, in spite of certain local appearances, is not, and cannot be within measurable time, "official." The World is trying the experiment of attempting to form a civilized but non-Christian mentality. The experiment will fail; but we must be very patient in

awaiting its collapse; meanwhile redeeming the time: so that the
Faith may be preserved alive through the dark ages before us; to
renew and rebuild civilization, and save the World from suicide. [*SE* 342]

In terms of Eliot's negative classicism, the new Dark Age is now.

iii

Ortega's vision is rooted in a present in which the highest ideals,
associated with the "generosity" of liberalism and also with the classics, are threatened by progress and its corollary, the ascendancy of
the "masses." *The Revolt of the Masses* is an essay in social tragedy,
with no strong sense that the solutions Ortega suggests either can or
will work. But he understands that these solutions must be political
and must start from the present rather than from the past. Unlike
Ortega, Eliot retreats into the past, into both Christianity and positive
classicism, and in constructing an ideal union between them seeks
salvation from the nihilism that he identifies with modern mass civilization. A third writer who rejects both systems of history and absolu-
tist retreats into the past, and yet who claims to transcend nihilism in
the name of an ardent classicism, is Albert Camus. In some respects
Camus is the antithesis of Ortega. His optimism in the face of catastrophe and his insistence on the dignity of ordinary human nature set
him apart from the aristocratic distrust of the ordinary to be found in
The Revolt of the Masses. "Revolt" is in any case for Camus the
beginning of freedom, as it is also potentially the beginning of despo-
tism. And Camus does not blame the disasters of this century on
falsely aspiring masses, but on intellectual nihilism and on the totalitarian Caesarism of both the right and the left, of both Nazism and
Stalinism.

It is therefore surprising to find Camus calling Ortega "the greatest
of European writers after Nietzsche."[29] What Camus values in Ortega, however, is his rejection of provincial "statism" and his affirmation of European culture and historical continuity as a solution to

29. Albert Camus, *Resistance, Rebellion and Death*, tr. Justin O'Brien (New York:
Knopf, 1969), p. 243. Abbreviated in the text as *R*.

nationalist conflict. Ortega can be a devoted Spaniard and yet speak for all Europe. And Camus can be both Algerian and French, loyal to both heritages, and yet also speak for all Europe—indeed, for mankind. In a 1937 lecture on the possibility of "a new Mediterranean civilization," Camus might almost have been summarizing some of the better aspects of Ortega when he declared: "Nationalisms always make their appearance in history as signs of decadence. When the vast edifice of the Roman empire collapsed, when its spiritual unity, from which so many different regions drew their justification, fell apart, then and only then, at a time of decadence, did nationalisms appear. Since then, the West has never rediscovered its unity."[30] As also for Ortega, internationalism is the solution to the decadence of nationalist conflict. What once gave and still promises to give unity to Mediterranean culture, however, was not the Roman Empire, but the spirit of Greece. Camus asserts that the realization of a new civilization will involve a classical revival antithetical to Mussolini's, a positive instead of a negative classicism. Because the Romans were "imitative and unimaginative," it was "not life which Rome took from Greece, but puerile and over-intellectualized abstractions." The new Mediterranean culture will involve "the very denial of Rome and of the Latin Genius." The true Mediterranean "is alive, and wants no truck with abstractions. And it is quite easy to acknowledge Mussolini as the worthy descendant of the Caesar and Augustus of Imperial Rome, if we mean by this that he, like them, sacrifices truth and greatness to a soulless violence" (*LC* 191).

What permits Camus to speak for a new Mediterranean culture and, indeed, for all Europe, he believes, is a classicism that looks back through the philosophical systems that kill (including both fascism and Marxism) and through the Christianity that too often also kills, to what the Greeks stood for: tragic freedom, human dignity, rational lucidity, and beauty. "For the past two thousand years the Greek value has been constantly and persistently slandered. In this regard Marxism took over from Christianity. And for two thousand years the Greek value has resisted to such a degree that, under its ideologies, the

30. Albert Camus, *Lyrical and Critical Essays*, tr. Philip Thody (London: Hamish Hamilton, 1967), pp. 188–89. Abbreviated in the text as *LC*.

twentieth century is more Greek and pagan than Christian and Russian."[31] At least Camus's own thinking is "more Greek and pagan" than anything else. In another entry in his *Notebooks*, Camus writes: "For Christians, Revelation stands at the beginning of history. For Marxists, it stands at the end. Two religions" (*N* 188). And Camus rejects religion of any sort as falsification, a projection of wishful thinking onto an "absurd" universe. But absurdity does not lead to despair. Not only against Christianity, Marxism, and fascism, but also against existentialism and philosophical systematizing of any sort Camus asserts "the Greek value." German philosophy has substituted the idea of "human situation" for that of human nature, placing history on the throne of God and also, more important, placing it on the pedestal of "ancient equilibrium." Like Matthew Arnold, Camus praises the classical ability to see life steadily and see it whole, to see with the eyes of tragic vision. Existentialism, moreover, which he rejects as a label for his own viewpoint, merely carries the implications of German metaphysical system building to the extreme, Camus thinks, by relativizing even the idea of "human situation." After the process of disintegration has been carried out by modern philosophy, "nothing remains but a motion," meaningless and impossible to pin down. But, Camus says, "like the Greeks, I believe in nature" (*N* 136).

In his 1948 essay "Helen's Exile," Camus declares that we have violated our Greek heritage by rejecting beauty as the first of values and by overstepping the reasonable limits even of reason, transforming it into fanaticism. "We have exiled beauty; the Greeks took up arms for her."[32] Camus distills the essence of both his positive and his negative classicism in these five pages. The very title sums up what he finds most intolerable about the modern condition. The Greek ideal of beauty involved limits, passion tempered by moderation, creative energy but also harmony, proportion. "Our Europe, on the other hand, off in the pursuit of totality, is the child of disproportion" (*MS* 134). Camus turns to the oldest of philosophers for a diagnosis of the modern ailment: "At the dawn of Greek thought Heraclitus was already imagining that justice sets limits for the physical universe itself:

31. Albert Camus, *Notebooks 1942–1951*, tr. Justin O'Brien (New York: Knopf, 1966), p. 263. Abbreviated in the text as *N*.
32. Albert Camus, "Helen's Exile," in *The Myth of Sisyphus and Other Essays*, tr. Justin O'Brien (New York: Knopf, 1969), p. 134. Abbreviated in the text as *MS*.

'The sun will not overstep his measures; if he does, the Erinyes, the handmaids of justice, will find him out' " (*MS* 135). We (the European society of World War II) have overstepped our measures by violating both Greek principles of beauty and reason, and the Erinyes have found us out. According to another Heraclitean fragment that Camus quotes: "Presumption, regression of progress" (*MS* 135).

Camus believes that we are imitating Caesar, not Socrates. Throughout his *Notebooks* are scattered references to a "play on the government of women" which he did not write, in which one of the characters was to have been Socrates, whom Camus makes say: "It's all going to begin over again. . . . They are preparing everything. Big ideas and interpretations of history. In ten years the slaughterhouses" (*N* 135). Camus does not think that history moves in inevitable cycles—he is not a believer in either progress or regression as our inescapable destiny—but he does believe that we have ignored our classical roots to our great cost. "This is why it is improper to proclaim today that we are the sons of Greece. Or else we are renegade sons. Placing history on the throne of God, we are progressing toward theocracy like those whom the Greeks called Barbarians" (*MS* 135).

As that which encompasses nature, beauty, freedom, and human dignity, Camus's primary value is "culture," which he identifies with "the Greek value." It is culture in this Hellenic sense that points beyond modern nihilism to new, creative values. The way forward is also the way back into the past: "If, to outgrow nihilism, one must turn to Christianity, one may well follow the impulse and outgrow Christianity in Hellenism" (*N* 183). The philosopher of the absurd offers a vision of culture largely antithetical to Eliot's authoritarianism, a vision akin to the classicist paganism of Nietzsche but without his anti-democratic tendencies. "Our faith is that throughout the world, beside the impulse toward coercion and death that is darkening history, there is a growing impulse toward persuasion and life, a vast emancipatory movement called culture that is made up both of free creation and of free work" (*R* 164). Camus's rhetoric here may seem vague to the point of cliché, but in the context of the Hungarian rebellion in 1956 it perhaps seemed more specific. Camus means a culture that is both proletarian and intelligent, in this instance the culture of the Hungarian workers and intellectuals, forged from their union in opposition to Soviet domination. Any version of intellectual elitism—the

failure of intellectuals to make common cause with the workers—
Camus rejects out of hand. Both a journalist and a resistance fighter
himself, he places great importance on freedom of the press: it is the
source of a common intelligence that he expects ultimately to defeat
the forces of empire and slavery. Viewed from such a perspective, a
genuine culture of the masses is not only possible, it is the guarantee
of our future life and freedom, a perpetual resistance movement or
rebellion against the forces of oppression, prison camps, elitist art-for-
art's-sake, and the abstract, imperialistic system building of the
philosophers.

Besides the worker and the intellectual, common life and communal intelligence, Camus's classicism unites a number of other apparent
opposites. First among these are restraint and freedom, the Heraclitean doctrine of limits combined with Promethean rebellion. On the
one hand, "classicism is domination of passions" (*N* 99). On the other
hand, "the freest art and the most rebellious will . . . be the most
classical" (*R* 268–69). Camus's originality derives largely from his ability to put the two parts of this contradiction together. Revolt, resistance, rebellion: these become synonyms for freedom through
restraint.

At the end of his remarks on Sisyphus, Ortega, following Nietzsche,
points out, "Sisyphus is the oldest Greek word that means 'the authentic wise man,' or as we would say, 'the genuine intellectual'"
(*IUH* 172). The "genuine intellectual" who has made the most of the
Sisyphus legend is of course Camus, for whom the story of the authentic wise man condemned by the gods "to ceaselessly rolling a rock to
the top of a mountain, whence the stone would fall back of its own
weight," serves as an analogy for the plight of the individual in an
absurd universe and also for the seemingly unending frustrations of
history (*MS* 88). Camus's treatment of Sisyphus is only one of many
invocations of classical mythology in his work. "The world in which I
am most at ease," he says in his *Notebooks*, is the world of "the Greek
myth" (*N* 249). Like Freud with his treatment of Oedipus, Camus
does not mean to retreat to some version of transcendental illusion but
to reclaim the wisdom expressed in the oldest forms of storytelling.
Myth, Camus believes, can be a form of enlightenment after the
classical Greek model; it need not be superstition. The most impor-

tant Greek myths to Camus—Sisyphus, Oedipus, Helen—are stories of mortals, not gods. "There are . . . gods of light and idols of mud. But it is essential to find the middle path leading to the faces of man" (*MS* 76). Camus celebrates the mythology of this world and of humanity rather than of some other time and place. The story of Sisyphus is in this way more significant than that of any god could be.

> Outside of that single fatality of death, everything, joy or happiness, is liberty. A world remains of which man is the sole master. What bound him was the illusion of another world. The outcome of his thought, ceasing to be renunciatory, flowers in images. It frolics—in myths, to be sure, but myths with no other depth than that of human suffering and, like it, inexhaustible. Not the divine fable that amuses and blinds, but the terrestrial face, gesture, and drama in which are summed up a different wisdom and an ephemeral passion.   [*MS* 87]

Camus's "existentialist" novels, *The Stranger*, *The Plague*, and *The Fall*, may be considered myths with no other depth than that of human suffering; they are also all informed by "the Greek value" as Camus understands it. Of *The Plague*, he writes, "from the point of view of a new classicism [it] ought to be the first attempt at shaping a collective passion" (*N* 137)—that is, a political passion—which he considers the first task of culture in modern times.

In his insistence on the values of lucidity and artistic creation in the face of a meaningless universe, Camus comes as close to the spirit of one branch of classical philosophy—stoicism—as any modern writer. If he is an "existentialist" (which he repeatedly denies), then he is one completely antagonistic to the version of absurdity expounded by Kierkegaard and based on Tertullian's *credo quia absurdum*. Kierkegaard's "leap" from reason into faith is, Camus thinks, "philosophical suicide" (*MS* 31), and his examination of the Sisyphus legend convinces him that suicide of any kind is not "legitimate." One must imagine Sisyphus forever shouldering his burden again and, if Camus means his legend to stand for something more than the experience of the individual, mankind forever shouldering its burden again at the bottom of the mountain of history. It is never topped, but it is always there to be topped. The act of "futile and hopeless labor" (*MS* 88) is the only authentic affirmation of life, and therefore we "must imagine

Sisyphus happy" (*MS* 91). Camus's essay affirms that "even within the limits of nihilism it is possible to find the means to proceed beyond nihilism" (*MS* v).

In his Nobel Prize address (1957), Camus defines art—culture, beauty, "the Greek value"—in terms of freedom. Art is the antithesis, indeed, the nemesis, of all forms of oppression. "Tyrants know there is in the work of art an emancipatory force, which is mysterious only to those who do not revere it. Every great work makes the human face more admirable and richer, and this is its whole secret. And thousands of concentration camps and barred cells are not enough to hide this staggering testimony of dignity" (*R* 269). Eliot, too, suggests that the defense of "the Greek value" is somehow identical with the "defense of freedom against chaos," but rather than "emancipatory force" he has in mind the upholding of an antique standard of authority, exemplified by Virgil's *Aeneid*, against everything that he associates with chaos—that is to say, against "paganism." Nothing could seem farther from Camus's pagan classicism, according to which art is a form of the eternal Promethean rebellion against whatever distorts or threatens to blot out "the human face." And insofar as "the human face" is that of ordinary people rather than of geniuses and elites, Camus's classicism is also quite different from Ortega's. Camus's version of the Greek value might be viewed as a kind of positive "revolt of the masses" through which whatever massifies is broken down and replaced by the individual human face. The end of Camus's Nobel Prize address expresses a hope for the future which depends not on a nation or on a single person, but on "millions of solitary individuals whose deeds and works every day negate frontiers and the crudest implications of history. As a result, there shines forth fleetingly the ever-threatened truth that each and every man, on the foundation of his own sufferings and joys, builds for all" (*R* 272).

From the start of his career, Camus delighted in turning Ortega's kind of negative classicism around, identifying "barbarism" with creativity and Roman ruins with a paradoxical hopefulness in new life and the indifference of the universe. In "Summer in Algiers," for example, writing just before the outbreak of World War II, Camus contemplates his countrymen at the seashore and writes: "The opposite of a civilized people is a creative one. These barbarians lounging on the beaches give me the unreasoned hope that, perhaps without knowing it, they are modelling the face of a culture where man's greatness will finally discover its true visage" (*LC* 69). And in his essay meditations on the Roman ruins at Djemila and Tipasa, Camus expresses a similar paradoxical hopefulness in the creativity of ordinary people in the face of death and the indifferent constancy of nature. These pieces belong to the genre of essays on the vanity of empire that runs from Gibbon and Volney down to the present. But the ruins of empire do not represent anything that Camus wants to cling to, to rebuild, or even to mourn; they are only the signs that nature makes grow along the highroads of history to impress upon us that, like Sisyphus, we must always start over again.

Camus's Nobel Prize address continues the theme of the political commitment of the artist which runs through his work and Jean-Paul Sartre's as well. Art does not automatically liberate; the artist must work at being a rebel. Though diverging from Sartre on the issue of Marxism, Camus agrees that art should be politically committed and that any version of elitist art or of art-for-art's-sake is contemptible. Of course it is possible that "on occasion art may be a deceptive luxury" rather than the chief weapon in the fight for freedom and for the dignity and beauty of "the human face." This possibility leads Camus to spin out a Roman analogy: "On the poop deck of slave galleys it is possible, at any time and place, as we know, to sing of the constellations while the convicts bend over the oars and exhaust themselves in the hold; it is always possible to record the social conversation that takes place on the benches of the amphitheater while the lion is crunching its victim" (*R* 253). Camus believes that, for the artist, "remaining aloof has always been possible in history" until the present moment. Now, however, an uncommitted art is unthinkable; "even silence has dangerous implications." Society itself has become an enormous slave galley, and the choice of whether or not to be "committed" is hardly available to the artist, since like everyone else he has been pressed into service and must bend to the oars. The slavedrivers are numerous and "the steering is badly handled." Whether we like it or not, "we are on the high seas" (*R* 250). Camus understands why "artists regret their former comfort." Continuing the second half of his Roman analogy, he suggests that once artists were safe among the spectators at the arena of history, whereas now they have been thrust in among the victims: "history's amphitheater has always contained the martyr and the lion. The former relied on eternal consolations and the latter on raw historical meat. But until now the artist was on the sidelines. He used to sing purposely, for his own sake, or at best to encourage the martyr and make the lion forget his appetite. But now the artist is in the amphitheater" (R 250).

In contrast to Greece, Rome here and elsewhere serves Camus as an image of oppression. In *The Rebel*, both Marxism and fascism are condemned as forms of "Caesarian revolution" leading to "empire and slavery." Their opposite is not liberalism or conservatism, but "rebellion," associated by Camus with another Greek myth, that of Prometheus, whose story begins well but ends tragically when Prometheus is transformed into Caesar (the fate of Marxism, for example) and, hence, when "the real, the eternal Prometheus"—the rebel rather than the too-principled revolutionary—has "assumed the aspect of one of his victims."[33] The moment the rebel becomes an executioner in the name of some cause other than present freedom and beauty, he ceases to be a rebel and joins the forces of Caesar. Like Spengler and Ortega, Camus develops a dystopian vision of mass society that he names "empire" and "Caesarism," but in Camus's view massification grows from the designs of the empire-builders rather than from the aspirations of ordinary men and women.

> The revolution based on principles kills God in the person of His representative on earth. The revolution of the twentieth century kills what remains of God in the principles themselves and consecrates historical nihilism. Whatever paths nihilism may proceed to take, from the moment that it decides to be the creative force of its period and ignores every moral precept, it begins to build the temple of Caesar.　[*RB* 246]

If it succeeds in keeping this side of the threshold of Caesarism, rebellion means freedom, reason, and the return of Helen from exile through the art that celebrates life and "the human face." In the boundary that Camus seeks to define between rebellion and revolution can be seen another version of the Heraclitean doctrine of limits which, if violated, bring retribution. "Moderation is not the opposite of rebellion. Rebellion in itself is moderation, and it demands, de-

33. Albert Camus, *The Rebel*, tr. Anthony Bower (New York: Vintage, 1956), pp. 244–45. Abbreviated in the text as *RB*.

fends, and re-creates it throughout history and its eternal distur-
bances. . . . Moderation, born of rebellion, can only live by rebellion"
(*RB* 301).

Camus's ideas lead to the paradox of a revolutionary classicism that
rejects both revolution in the name of an abstract principle and the
authority of the past as overruling the claims of the present. It is the
seemingly endless violations of moderation, often in the name of justice (again, as with Marxism as Camus interprets it), that bring about
the need for perpetual rebellion and, hence, also create something
like cyclic patterns in history. Through rebellion, empires will always
fall back into ruins. And insofar as rebellion is not the work of van-
guards and elites, but of common men and women asserting their
common dignity against whatever would blot it out, Camus finds a
hopefulness in the modern "revolt of the masses" that Ortega cannot
see, for Camus thinks of the lives of ordinary men and women as a
mute protest against and contradiction of the very conditions of their
massification.

Camus's cultural politics are summed up in his treatment of two
Roman figures who exemplify the tragic course too often followed by
rebellion. The first is Spartacus the gladiator, whose uprising, like all
slave rebellions, was a protest against bondage and an assertion of
equality with the masters. Beyond equality, there was no positive
vision that inspired or justified the rebellion of the gladiators. They
sought only to trade places with their masters: "The slave army liber-
ates slaves and immediately hands over their former masters to them
in bondage. According to one tradition, of doubtful veracity it is true,
gladiatorial combats were even organized between several hundred
Roman citizens, while the slaves sat in the grandstands delirious with
joy and excitement. But to kill men leads to nothing but killing more
men" (*RB* 109). Because they were inspired by no higher aim than to
become masters themselves, Spartacus's army stalled before Rome.
"The city of light of which Spartacus dreamed could only have been
built on the ruins of eternal Rome. . . . At the descisive moment,
however, within sight of the sacred walls, the army halts and wavers,
as if it were retreating before the principles, the institutions, the city
of the gods" (*RB* 109). Spartacus's rebellion embodied no new principles, nothing that had not already been shaped by Roman laws and
customs. Camus's treatment of Spartacus and of the crucifixion of his

followers by Crassus leads to a paragraph on Christ, but his gladiator-martyr does not look beyond the confines of the Roman Empire to Christianity and Marxism. Though exemplary of all other slave rebellions including Christianity and Marxism, the Spartacus uprising, Camus thinks, was self-contained and self-defeating, a tragic heroism that did not find its way out of the labyrinth of empire and eternal injustice.

Camus's second Roman figure is the seeming antithesis of Spartacus, that most cruel and capricious of emperors, Caligula. Camus's play of that title, written in 1938 but not performed until 1945, with the Nazi nightmare as background, makes its protagonist out to be, by Caligula's own assertion, "the one free man in the whole Roman Empire."[34] But it is a false freedom, that of the totalitarian dictator who acknowledges no authority higher than his own whim, and in such a condition one can only be "free at someone else's expense" (*C* 28). Camus presents Caligula as a philosophical emperor who lives this false principle out to the end through tyranny and murder. Caligula's ideal is an empire of silence, a necropolis in which death—by his command—levels all distinctions, everything living. If he is the opposite of Spartacus in being a master instead of a slave, Caligula shares with the gladiator-rebel the goal of a murderous equality. Against Caesonia's assertion that "there's good and bad, high and low, justice and injustice" which will never change, Caligula says: "And I'm resolved to change them. . . . I shall make this age of ours a kingly gift—the gift of equality. And when all is levelled out, when the impossible has come to earth and the moon is in my hands—then, perhaps, I shall be transfigured and the world renewed; then men will die no more and at last be happy" (*C* 17). But the path to this utopian goal—the elimination of death—lies through death, just as Spartacus's city of the sun cannot be reached except across a river of blood choked with the remains of history's victims. Spartacus's rebellion was justified—rendered inevitable, in fact—by exactly the sort of homicidal domination that Caligula represents. The two figures exemplify the two aspects of totalitarianism: Caligula's fanatical pursuit of the "impossible" as cause and Spartacus's rebellion as result, an inevitable

---

34. Albert Camus, *Caligula and Three Other Plays*, tr. Stuart Gilbert (New York: Knopf, 1972), p. 14. Abbreviated in the text as *C*.

and tragic cycle of domination, slavery, and revolution that makes Rome, for Camus as for many other writers of his generation, an appropriate analogy for fascism, Nazism, and Stalinism.

Despite the historical nightmares that Camus witnessed, he remained optimistic because of his faith in ordinary human nature, and also because of his faith in "the Greek value." He touches often upon the themes and images of negative classicism, but usually to stand them on their heads or reject them outright, as he does in the ruins of Djemila and Tipasa. "I am not one of those who proclaim that the world is rushing to its doom," Camus said in an interview in 1951. "I do not believe in the final collapse of our civilization. I believe . . . that a renaissance is possible." Negative classicism, indeed, is part of the problem rather than its solution. "If the world were rushing to its doom, we should have to lay the blame for this on apocalyptic modes of thought" (*LC* 263). In contrast, Camus is much more insistent on the continuity of the traditions represented by positive classicism. Against the deadly spirit of Rome, he asserts the living spirit of Greece: "We shall choose Ithaca, the faithful land, frugal and audacious thought, lucid action, and the generosity of the man who understands. In the light, the earth remains our first and last love" (*RB* 306).

CHAPTER 7

The Dialectic
of Enlightenment

Judging by the meaning of Christianity and the rules of a few monastic orders, things as they are afford no reason for joy. They are marked by injustice and terrible suffering. To be conscious of this day and night was a matter of course, and the sleeping in coffins a symbol, similar to the Jewish custom of wearing the shroud on the highest holy day. The thought of happiness was identical with that of eternal salvation, it referred to something other than the world as it is. National customs have always been the opposite of such belief. In the late Rome, the circenses served pleasure as the goal of life, and the people of modern history have always put a premium on healthy good spirits. In a different form, those decent folk that are celebrated in the paintings of the peasant Brueghel are still the goal and purpose of today's mass media.

—MAX HORKHEIMER

"IF the fall of antiquity were dictated by the autonomous necessity of life and by the expression of its 'soul,'" writes Theodor Adorno in a 1941 essay on Spengler's *The Decline of the West*, "then indeed it takes on the aspect of fatality and by . . . analogy . . . carries over to the present situation."[1] As a Marxist, Adorno rejects Spengler's historical fatalism and the Roman analogizing on which it is largely based. He does so, however, not because he believes that the dialectical processes of history are progressive, leading ultimately and inevitably to liberation. If Adorno cannot subscribe to the pessimistic

1. Theodor W. Adorno, "Spengler Today," *Studies in Philosophy and Social Science*, 9 (1941), 305–25.

and organicist fatalism of Spengler, neither can he subscribe to the optimistic, dialectical or Hegelian teleology present in Marx. Although the ultimate liberation of mankind from all forms of social oppression always remained possible for Adorno, that possibility, viewed from the historical dead ends of Weimar and Nazi Germany, was far from inevitable. "If . . . the fall of antiquity can be understood by its unproductive system of latifundia and the slave economy related to it, the fatality can be mastered if men succeed in overcoming such and similar structures of domination. In such a case, Spengler's universal structure reveals itself as a false analogy drawn from a bad solitary happening—solitary in spite of its threatening recurrence." Adorno hopes that this is the case; as the two "ifs" in the first sentence suggest, however, he is far from certain.

Instead of the proletarian revolution predicted by Marx, capitalism in its monopolistic and imperialistic stage had produced the fascist and Nazi nightmares. Some Marxists interpreted these movements as a sign of the final crisis of capitalism and hence as the prelude to genuine revolution.[2] But Adorno and his colleagues in the Frankfurt Institute for Social Research—Max Horkheimer, Herbert Marcuse, Walter Benjamin, Leo Löwenthal, Erich Fromm—witnessed the near-extinction of left-wing opposition politics in Germany, the seduction of the masses into the camp of reaction, and the totalitarian and genocidal aftermath. At its zenith, civilization produced its opposite, barbarism. As Marcuse says, "the historical fact that civilization has progressed as organized *domination*" means that "the very progress of civilization leads to the release of increasingly destructive forces."[3]

With the prospect for liberation hinging on possibilities that seemed increasingly remote and utopian, history was perhaps congealing into exactly the shapes that Spengler predicted. At the same time that Adorno denounces *The Decline of the West* as "gigantic and destructive soothsaying" in which "the petty bourgeois celebrates his intellectual triumph," he also praises it for the accuracy of many of its

2. See, for example, the quotation on p. 188 from Christopher Caudwell, *Studies and Further Studies in a Dying Culture* (New York: Monthly Review, 1971).

3. Herbert Marcuse, *Eros and Civilization* (New York: Vintage, 1962 [1955]), pp. 32, 41. Abbreviated in the text as *EC*. On the Frankfurt School in general see Martin Jay, *The Dialectical Imagination: A History of the Frankfurt School and the Institute of Social Research, 1923–1950* (Boston: Little, Brown, 1973).

predictions and for its trenchant critique of liberalism: "The forgotten
Spengler takes his revenge by threatening to be right." In a very real
sense, Spengler will be right if the chance for liberation is missed—
and that is a chance wholly contingent upon the future actions and
consciousness of very weak, capricious, fallible human beings. In
Negative Dialectics (1966), Adorno writes:

> In this age of universal social repression, the picture of freedom
> against society lives in the crushed, abused individual's features
> alone. Where that freedom will hide out at any moment in history
> cannot be decreed once for all. Freedom turns concrete in the
> changing forms of repression, as resistance to repression. There has
> been as much free will as there were men with the will to be free.[4]

In such a passage, Adorno sounds almost like Albert Camus praising
rebellion and the classical beauty of "the human face." But true rebels
are much harder for Adorno to identify, to pick out of the swarms of
those deluded by mass culture and the blandishments of fascist propaganda. It is also evident that Adorno, unlike Camus, is not a classicist
in the straightforward sense of believing that past culture can help
cure present social injustice. Past culture is instead the source of
present injustice.

Whatever else he has done, Adorno thinks, Spengler has shown
once and for all that culture cannot be the solution to the crisis of
culture. "More strikingly than almost anyone else, [Spengler] has
demonstrated how [the] rawness of culture again and again drives it to
decay and how, as form and order, culture is affiliated with that blind
domination which, through permanent crises, is always prone to anni-
hilate itself and its victims." As Freud had declared, "the essence of
culture bears the mark of Death" ("Spengler Today"). The end product of every culture is "Caesarism," followed by decline and fall. This
idea brings Adorno close to validating Spengler's entire historical system: "There is no chance of evading the magic circle of Spengler's
morphology by defaming barbarism and relying upon the healthiness
of culture. Any such straightforward optimism is proscribed by the
present situation. Instead, we should become aware of the element of

---

4. Theodor W. Adorno, *Negative Dialectics*, tr. E. B. Ashton (New York: Seabury,
1973 [1966]), p. 265. Abbreviated in the text as *ND*.

barbarism inherent in culture itself." The mechanism of liberation must come from some source other than culture, which Spengler shows well enough to be doomed to the cycles of negative classicism. Unless something disrupts it, history moves forever within the closed orbits of violence and domination. But what mechanism can disrupt it?

Unlike most Marxists, Adorno has little faith in the proletariat as the agent of revolution, for, much like Ortega, he sees the masses as having been bought off by the mass media and by the forces of reaction. Adorno appears to place his faith in the historical efficacy of "negativity," but without a clear historical agent such negativity seems to be little more than the capacity for radical criticism inherent in the philosophical tradition. Besides, what is philosophy except a version of culture (albeit the highest version, the one most removed from the contaminations and misunderstandings of "mass culture"—a Heraclitean position almost matching Heraclitus's animosity to "the mass")? Stripped of its idealist illusions, philosophy itself appears to collaborate with barbarism, as in this demolition, by way of negative classicism, of Hegel's theory of history:

> The world spirit's Hegelian migration from one popular spirit to the next is the Migration of Nations blown up into metaphysics; the human steamroller of that migration is of course a prototype of world history itself, whose Augustinian conception coincided with the era of the Great Migration. The unity of world history which animates the philosopher to trace it as the path of the world spirit is the unity of terror rolling over mankind. [*ND* 341]

At his most negative, which may also be his logically most consistent, Adorno appears to have no faith in any prospective liberation or redemption through culture, even philosophy: "All post-Auschwitz culture, including its urgent critique, is garbage. . . . Not even silence gets us out of the circle" (*ND* 367).

In his essay on Spengler, however, Adorno is more optimistic than mere "negativity" suggests. Hope lies in what Spengler overlooks, "the forces set free by decay." At present, these forces radiate unconsciously from the oppressed and deluded masses themselves, still the agent of liberation no matter how monstrously distorted their faces have grown. The victims of history "personify negatively within the

negativity of this culture that which promises, however weakly, to
break the spell of culture and to make an end to the horror of prehistory." This is not to say that the culture itself is not fated to decline;
self-destruction is built directly into its system of domination. But
against the decadent culture of the present arises "the Utopia that is
silently embodied in the image of decline" and also in the minds, even
if unconscious, of the oppressed.

Here we see Adorno at his most hopeful, champion of the masses
and of all the victims of history, as are the other theorists of the
Frankfurt Institute. But it is not apparent to any of them that their
championship will count for much—not even apparent that anything
will necessarily happen to realize the utopia implicit in bondage and
decadence, and wholly unapparent that many of the oppressed will
ever know themselves to be oppressed. The reified false consciousness of industrialized mass culture has settled like a pall over history,
masking the facts of violence and exploitation so completely that the
majority of victims (that is, the majority of mankind) move through life
like anesthetized zombies, believing themselves to be free individuals
(success stories, even) instead of victims. Rarely has a thinker,
Spengler not excepted, taken a more dismal view of those he is championing, or of the prospects for the liberation to which he is devoted,
than has Adorno.

Only the faint vision of an admittedly utopian freedom keeps Adorno from accepting Spengler's organic historical cycles as fate. At the
same time, the improbability of liberation renders Adorno's social
thinking both apocalyptic and dependent upon the very culture, especially philosophy and art, which he declares to be a non-solution.
His thinking becomes apocalyptic to the degree that he conceives of
all history as domination, to be broken only by a future revolution
that, because of its uniqueness and improbability, acquires the character of a miracle, a Judgment Day that will bring history itself to a
close. This millenarian strain is apparent in the other Frankfurt theorists, particularly Walter Benjamin, for whom Judaic eschatology is
the source of the idea of "messianic time" that, he thinks, characterizes Marxism: "A historical materialist cannot do without the notion of
a present which is not a transition, but in which time stands still and

5. Walter Benjamin, *Illuminations*, ed. Hannah Arendt (New York: Schocken,
1969), p. 262. Abbreviated in the text as *IL*.

has come to a stop."[5] This messianic "present" is identical to the revolutionary utopia of the oppressed, seen as the goal of history by Adorno, Benjamin, and the other Frankfurt intellectuals.

Adorno's thinking also depends upon high culture—art, music, philosophy—despite the fact that he agrees with Spengler in viewing culture as domination and as inevitably spiraling back into death. High culture is the antithesis of mass culture, as authentic experience is the antithesis of reified consciousness. Only in the forms of high culture can the idea of utopia be protected from the all-pervasive false consciousness produced by the mass media. As Max Horkheimer puts it in his 1941 essay "Art and Mass Culture," "Art, since it became autonomous, has preserved the utopia that evaporated from religion."[6] For Adorno, genuine art is negativity, the critique of that which exists. "The authentic cultural object must retain and preserve whatever goes by the wayside in that process of increasing domination over nature which is reflected by expanding rationality and ever more rational forms of domination. Culture is the perennial protestation of the particular against the general, as long as the latter remains irreconcilable with the particular."[7] "Particularity" here denotes the opposite of "mass-ness," or of those processes of social rationalization which produce mass culture.

Just as the masses are everything and nothing, the solution and yet also the problem of history, so culture is identical both with its antithesis, the barbarism of domination, and with the chief place where the vision of freedom is nurtured. These seemingly contradictory attitudes are present in all the Frankfurt theorists. Seeking to combine Marxism with the insights into mass behavior and regression of Freud, Nietzsche, and even Ortega and Spengler, they all arrive at a richly ambiguous combination of ideas which leads one recent critic to declare "it is far more useful and evocative to regard the members of the Frankfurt School as men of the Right than of the Left."[8] However that may be (and it is ultimately not very important to place them at one

6. Max Horkheimer, "Art and Mass Culture," in *Critical Theory: Selected Essays* (New York: Herder and Herder), p. 275. Abbreviated in the text as *CT*.

7. Theodor W. Adorno, "The Culture Industry Reconsidered," *New German Critique*, 6 (Fall 1975), p. 6.

8. George Friedman, *The Political Philosophy of the Frankfurt School* (Ithaca: Cornell University Press, 1981), p. 32. I have followed several of Friedman's suggestions about the indebtedness of the Frankfurt theorists to conservative thinkers, including Spengler.

end or the other of the political spectrum), their general project is best
described by the label Max Horkheimer gave it, "Critical Theory,"
which has as its first goal the creation and defense of a radical philosophical consciousness against several opponents: positivism, pragma-
tism, and "instrumental reason" on the plane of philosophy; reification, commercialization, mass culture and the mass media on the
plane of art and culture; and all forms of domination and enslavement
on the plane of politics. "The critical theory of society . . . has for its
object men as producers of their own historical way of life in its
totality," says Horkheimer; he then proceeds to give this Marxist
definition a classicist content: "Its goal is man's emancipation from
slavery. In this it resembles Greek philosophy, not so much in the
Hellenistic age of resignation as in the golden age of Plato and Aristotle" (CT 244, 246).

Like classical Greek philosophy (at least as Horkheimer interprets
it), Critical Theory aims at liberation from all forms of domination. In
The Eclipse of Reason, Horkheimer expresses his positive classicism
when he invokes Socrates both as the model of the critical theorist and
also as a martyr: "Socrates died because he subjected the most sacred
and most familiar ideas of his community and his country to the critique of the daimonion, or dialectical thought, as Plato called it."[9] In
the martyrdom of Socrates, Horkheimer perceives one possible and
not unlikely outcome of Critical Theory, which shares with high culture the task of bearing the ark of liberation through the fire and the
flood of contemporary history. Horkheimer may be writing the history
of the Frankfurt School when he declares, "Under the conditions of
later capitalism and the impotence of the workers before the authoritarian state's apparatus of oppression, truth has sought refuge
among small groups of admirable men. But these have been deci-
mated by terrorism and have little time for refining the theory. Char-
latans profit by this situation and the general intellectual level of the
masses is rapidly declining" (CT 237). Like Socrates, the proponents
of Critical Theory also lived in the shadow of exile and death; most of
them survived the Nazi period, although one of the most brilliant—
Walter Benjamin—did not. Critical Theory launches its project in a

9. Max Horkheimer, The Eclipse of Reason (New York: Oxford University Press,
1947), p. 10.

hostile world where the central problem, both to explain and to over-come, is the terrible and dangerous resistance of that world to its own liberation.

All the Frankfurt intellectuals are painfully aware that Critical The-ory and high culture cannot by themselves lead to emancipation; they can only preserve the idea of it against the forces that threaten to overwhelm even these vestiges of the possible. Their predicament is evident in their remarks on culture in the jointly authored volume *Aspects of Sociology*, where they warn: "It is not proper to invoke culture against [mass] civilization. The gesture of invocation itself, the exalting of culture at the expense of mass society, the devoted con-sumption of cultural values as a confirmation of one's elevated internal spiritual equipment, these are inseparable from the decadent charac-ter of the civilization. The invocation of culture is powerless."[10] But with the shrinking of hope in the revolutionary potential of the pro-letariat, art and Critical Theory seem all that remain to set against the totality of mass society and its fraudulent mass culture. Even while declaring culture to be part of the problem instead of the solution, each of the Frankfurt theorists falls back on some version of high culture—art, literature, or the philosophic tradition—as the last line of defense against "barbarism" and the ultimate self-destruction of civilization.

Like Critical Theory itself, art gains importance as society is more and more dominated by mass culture. This is perhaps most apparent in Herbert Marcuse's treatment of "the aesthetic dimension" as the antithesis to the "one-dimensionality" of mass society. For Marcuse, however, art is something more than mere negativity; it is also the positive category of liberation itself, the shape of human life freed from all domination. Beauty, in other words, is another name for utopia, life as a work of art, as it had been for John Ruskin and William Morris. This esthetic utopia is to be achieved above all by the transfor-mation of labor into play, or into esthetically pleasing experience, which in turn involves the dissolution of the category of art as some-thing separate from life. As Marcuse writes in *The Aesthetic Dimen-sion*, "The autonomy of art reflects the unfreedom of individuals in the unfree society. If people were free, then art would be the form and

10. *Aspects of Sociology*, tr. John Viertel (Boston: Beacon, 1972 [1956]), p. 94.

expression of their freedom."[11] Art is not just *une promesse de bonheur* as in Stendhal, but "the promise of liberation" (*AD* 46). Similarly, in his *Essay on Liberation,* Marcuse writes: "The aesthetic as the possible Form of a free society appears at that stage of development where the intellectual and material resources for the conquest of scarcity are available."[12] In this his most optimistic essay (perhaps the most optimistic by any member of the Frankfurt Institute), he asserts that the stage has been reached where society can produce all the requisites for freedom. For Marcuse, the May 1968 rebellion in France and the New Left and the flower children in America heralded a new, free social structure based on the esthetic dimension. For a while he was even their prophet.

Freedom is promised by the enormous productive capacity of technology, which, at least in the *Essay on Liberation,* Marcuse treats more hopefully than do his colleagues. "Utopian possibilities are inherent in the technical and technological forces of advanced capitalism and socialism: the rational utilization of these forces on a global scale would terminate poverty and scarcity within a very foreseeable future" (*EL* 4). Ordinarily a vexed subject for all the Frankfurt theorists including Marcuse, machinery here appears in its most constructive guise. Everything seems ripe for the liberation that, according to all Marxisms, is or at least should be the goal of history.

What, then, prevents this outcome? Marcuse believes that there are three primary barriers to the realization of utopia. The first is the irrationality of the power structure ("the Establishment" or "the military-industrial complex") which governs technological and productive capacity. The second is the mass media and mass culture, which justify the status quo or divert attention from the oppressions and failures of the power structure. And the third is the psychological makeup of most people, which is shaped by scarcity economics and social class through "the performance principle" and "surplus repression," terms central to Marcuse's political transvaluation of Freud in *Eros and Civilization.* The result of these three obstacles to freedom is

11. Herbert Marcuse, *The Aesthetic Dimension* (Boston: Beacon, 1978), pp. 72–73. Abbreviated in the text as *AD.*

12. Herbert Marcuse, *An Essay on Liberation* (Boston: Beacon, 1969), p. 25. Abbreviated in the text as *EL.*

the supremely irrational phenomenon of a society that desperately and violently resists the very goals that through most of its history it has been bent on achieving.

> Civilization has to defend itself against the specter of a world which could be free. If society cannot use its growing productivity for reducing repression (because such usage would upset the hierarchy of the *status quo*), productivity must be turned *against* the individuals; it becomes itself an instrument of universal control. Totalitarianism spreads over late industrial civilization wherever the interests of domination prevail upon productivity, arresting and diverting its potentialities. [*EC* 85]

The very ferocity and desperation of totalitarianism, operating like defense mechanisms in a neurotic patient, suggest to Marcuse our proximity to freedom. For Freud as for Spengler, civilization was bound inevitably to double back on itself, to regress, perhaps to commit suicide. But Marcuse finds in the student revolutionaries, hippies, and black militants of the 1960s a "new sensibility," the promise of a transformed human nature, which at least for a time he believed might break the cycles of domination.

Those whom Marcuse recognized in 1969 as exemplars of the new sensibility, harbingers of the esthetic dimension, had broken away from the masses and from mass culture into the New Left and the counterculture celebrated by Theodore Roszak. What prevents others from making the same break is above all mass culture, the chief enemy of the esthetic dimension. Mass culture is an especially important category for Marcuse, because, at least in America and Western Europe, domination is largely psychological, the project of the mass media working through the internalization of false needs and false consciousness. What the mass media work upon—their raw material—is the contrary of the flower children and student revolutionaries; this raw material is another version of "mass man," whom Marcuse had seen in 1964 as forming the vast majority of people, much as Ortega had seen massified human beings everywhere in 1930. In *One-Dimensional Man*, even the esthetic dimension is being squeezed out of existence by the mass media, through which "the alien and alienating oeuvres of intellectual culture become familiar goods and services."[13] Not only do the mass media produce their spurious mass culture, they also "co-opt" the great works of "high culture." Through the process of "repressive desublimation" (which basically means making everything except radical thought and practice permissible) the great and invaluable "sublimations of higher culture" are being "obliterated." "This liquidation of *two-dimensional* culture takes place not through the denial and rejection of the cultural values, but through their wholesale incorporation into the established order, through their reproduction and display on a massive scale" (*ODM* 57). Marcuse recognizes that mass culture does not replace high culture, but instead includes it; this "wholesale incorporation" is not an advance over the past, however, but an unmitigated disaster: the mass engulfs the higher culture, rendering it harmless by adulterating and making it ubiquitous.

In the conclusion of *One-Dimensional Man* (1964), Marcuse writes: "Nothing indicates that it will be a good end. . . . The facile historical parallel with the barbarians threatening the empire of civilization prejudges the issue; the second period of barbarism may well be the continued empire of civilization itself" (*ODM* 257). Marcuse sounds more optimistic in his *Essay on Liberation* (1969) but by the time of *The Aesthetic Dimension* (1978) he has returned to something like the negative classicism expressed at the end of *One-Dimensional Man*. Rejecting the false initiatives of the 1960s he writes: "A real counter-culture would have to insist on the autonomy of art, on its *own* autonomous art. Consequently, would not an art which rebels against integration into the market necessarily appear as 'elitist'?" (*AD* 52–53). No longer does Marcuse see a union between the promise of liberation in the arts and any existing group of rebels.

> If it is at all meaningful to speak of a mass base for art in capitalist society, this would refer only to pop art and best sellers. In the present, the subject to which authentic art appeals is socially anonymous; it does not coincide with the potential subject of revolutionary practice. And the more the exploited classes, "the people," succumb to the powers that be, the more will art be estranged from "the people." [*AD* 32]

13. Herbert Marcuse, *One-Dimensional Man* (Boston: Beacon, 1964), p. 61. Abbreviated in the text as *ODM*.

Having almost come together in "the new sensibility" of the 1960s, the revolutionary consciousness embedded in genuine art and the practice of rebellion by student groups, black militants, and others have parted company by 1978. Art retreats to its lofty perch, outside and above practice.

Marcuse is well aware that his position may seem like the cultural elitism of the conservatives, of a Nietzsche or an Ortega. " 'Elitism' today," however, "may well have a radical content" (*AD* 35), and so may "inwardness," "subjectivity," artistic "estrangement" from the real, and the championing of the private individual against the public "dimension" of coercion and mass domination. Marcuse recognizes his essential distance from orthodox Marxist esthetics (as represented, say, by Georg Lukács and Ernst Fischer), a distance evident in the writings on art and culture of all the Frankfurt theorists. Marcuse's quest for liberation leads to an affirmation of esthetic "modernism" and "estrangement," which is also an affirmation of the utopia expressed by the elitist avant-garde of the present and by the high culture of the past. In contrast to most versions of Marxist esthetics, Marcuse argues that "the radical qualities of art, that is to say, its indictment of the established reality and its invocation of the beautiful image (*schöner Schein*) of liberation are grounded precisely in the dimensions where art *transcends* its social determination and emancipates itself from the given universe of discourse and behavior while preserving its overwhelming presence. Thereby art creates the realm in which the subversion of experience proper to art becomes possible" (*AD* 6).

The Frankfurt Institute theorists are not concerned to distinguish among kinds or even degrees of mass society and culture, but tend rather to attack the category of socialization itself, in any of its manifestations. Liberation and the utopian promise of happiness retreat into the imaginary realm of the work of art, which is also the modern repository of religious transcendence, come part way down from the clouds. The genuine work of art—defiant, inscrutable, inaccessible to the masses with their reified false consciousness—takes on an enormous historical importance from the standpoint of Critical Theory as the expression of dialectical negativity. It holds up a mirror to society opposite in kind from the simple reflectionist mirror of the realistic novelists, of Stendhal and Balzac, which was only the fallacious meta-phor of positivism translated into fiction. Rather than showing the world as it is, the true work of art shows it as it is by also showing it what it is not, shadowing forth the liberation it has failed to achieve. But to identify the true work of art from a dialectical perspective proves harder than to define it abstractly. The category of genuine art comes to include everything from Greek myths and fairy tales to Kafka, Schönberg, and Samuel Beckett's theater of the absurd. The imagination of freedom finds an infinite number of refuges in the fantasies and creations of the artists. Critical Theory thus offers a definition of art that runs counter to Georg Lukács's idea of "critical realism" as represented by the novels of Stendhal and Balzac and to the various kinds of official socialist realism, as well as to industrialized mass culture.

Marcuse's theories end in a classicism whose chief aim is to defend radical consciousness in art against the pressures of a "one-dimension-al" world that seems to deny all avenues to radical political practice. The hope is that the nurturing of genuine art will lead to a gradual increase in the "new sensibility" needed to demolish one-dimension-ality and to estheticize experience. Much the same classicist formula-tion is evident in the other Frankfurt theorists, for whom the mass media or "the culture industry" also represent a primary threat to mankind's ultimate liberation. The very devices that seem to promise the diffusion of culture to the masses—cheap books and newspapers, public schools, film, radio, television—and hence also to be among those productive forces most promising of utopia, the instruments for a possible estheticization of experience, are instead blocking libera-tion, cutting off communication, either co-opting or obliterating cul-ture, and liquidating subjectivity and privacy. As Horkheimer writes in his essay "Art and Mass Culture":

> Europe has reached the point where all the highly developed means of communication serve constantly to strengthen the barriers "that divide human beings"; in this, radio and cinema in no way yield the palm to airplane and gun. . . . To the extent that the last works of art still communicate, they denounce the prevailing forms of commu-nication as instruments of destruction, and harmony as a delusion of decay. [CT 279]

Mass communication is noncommunication, the destruction both of community and of privacy. About the latter, Horkheimer says: "The gradual dissolution of the family, the transformation of personal life into leisure and of leisure into routines supervised to the last detail, into the pleasures of the ball park and the movie, the best seller and the radio, has brought about the disappearance of the inner life" (*CT* 277). Much the same conclusion about the destructive effects of "the culture industry" is reached by the other Frankfurt theorists. Reviewing the mass culture theories of the Frankfurt Institute, Adorno writes:

> The total effect of the culture industry is one of anti-enlightenment, in which . . . enlightenment, that is the progressive technical domination of nature, becomes mass deception and is turned into a means for fettering consciousness. It impedes the development of autonomous, independent individuals who judge and decide consciously for themselves. . . . If the masses have been unjustly reviled from above as masses, the culture industry is not among the least responsible for making them into masses and then despising them, while obstructing the emancipation for which human beings are as ripe as the productive forces of the epoch permit. ["Culture Industry Reconsidered" 18–19]

Adorno's remarks about "enlightenment" here echo the title of the seminal work of the Frankfurt Institute, *The Dialectic of Enlightenment*, which he and Horkheimer wrote during World War II. The title summarizes the paradoxical thesis to which all of the Frankfurt theorists return in all of their works, the progressive decay of Enlightenment reason into the irrationality and barbarism of modern mass society. "Progress becomes regression."[14] Reason itself, the main item in the heritage of positive classicism, is in decline or eclipse, but it is also the source of the eclipse. The application of reason to society through science, democratization, and industrialization, involving the progressive domination of nature through technological and commercial expansion, tragically entails the progressive domination of people as well. Social rationalization—that is, modernization—means also social

---

14. Max Horkheimer and Theodor W. Adorno, *Dialectic of Enlightenment*, tr. John Cumming (New York: Seabury, 1972 [1944]), p. xv. Abbreviated in the text as *DE*.

irrationalization. In these fatal processes, the "culture industry" plays
a key role, transforming the critical negativity inherent in genuine art
into shallow affirmation, "enlightenment" into "mass deception."
"The whole world is made to pass through the filter of the culture
industry" (*DE* 126), and it is deadened, along with its consumers, as a
result. Among the most rational of modern scientific techniques, the
mass media have produced only "the retreat from enlightenment into
mythology"—in the terrors of Nazism and World War II we witness
"the self-destruction of the Enlightenment" (*DE* xiii).

The ultimate paradox is that, aiming for freedom, "Enlightenment
is totalitarian" (*DE* 6). It stops at nothing. Like Jacques Ellul's great
Juggernaut of "technological society," "Enlightenment" for Adorno
and Horkheimer aspires to nothing less than the domination of the
entire world and the reduction of all society to a "universal concentration camp." But what is there to hold up against this suicidal process
except Enlightenment itself? Here is where Critical Theory comes to
the fore: reason itself must answer to the irrationality of reason. This
view suggests again a version of classicism, the need for a higher
culture to respond to the failures of culture. Adorno and Horkheimer
recognize this dilemma from the start of their analysis: "The issue is
not that of culture as a value, which is what the critics of [mass]
civilization, Huxley, Jaspers, Ortega y Gasset and others have in
mind. The point is rather that the Enlightenment *must consider itself*,
if men are not to be wholly betrayed" (*DE* xv).

Negative classicism is likely to emerge from any analysis of progress
that sees it as also regression: civilization losing its grip, reverting to
Caesarism and barbarism, falling to ruins. As Horkheimer says, "The
fundamental concepts of civilization are in a process of rapid decay."[15]
In the works of both the Critical Theorists and the conservative defenders of culture, the classical models against which the modern world
measures its rise and fall—whether tragedy or beauty or the Socratic
dialectic—become instead shadowy goals, limits we cannot pass. And
to both groups, the very instruments that promise to universalize
culture—the mass media—appear to be among the primary causes of
the regression of civilization into barbarism. "The curse of irresistible

15. Max Horkheimer, "The End of Reason," *Studies in Philosophy and Social
Science*, 9 (1941), 366.

progress is irresistible regression" (*DE* 36). "Dialectic of Enlightenment" is almost another name for "negative classicism," or at least for the "eclipse of reason" through empire, mass culture, and totalitarianism, the historic processes whereby reason and civilization turn into their opposites. As Horkheimer suggests, the ideal of reason first shone forth clearly in "the golden age of Plato and Aristotle"; we have been moving farther and farther away from it ever since.

The basic pattern of Frankfurt Institute thinking is oxymoronic, as is always true of dialectical thought: thesis into antithesis. Virtually everything that liberalism perceives as symptomatic of progress, Critical Theory perceives as symptomatic of social regression. With Hegel and Marx, the dialectic was positive, progressive, each term in the series working its way up through negation of its contrary and of itself, even through bloodshed and oppression, into higher forms. With Adorno and Horkheimer, the procedure is reversed: negative now replaces positive in a series of "negative dialectics." Adorno's title, in fact, means something quite different from "the negation of the negation" in Hegel. As Marx stood Hegel on his head, so now Adorno turns both Marx and Hegel upside down by suggesting that the dialectical process of history may as a whole be negative, destructive. "*Negative Dialectics* is a phrase that flouts tradition. As early as Plato, dialectics meant to achieve something positive by means of negation; the thought figure of a 'negation of negation' later became the succinct term." Adorno seeks "to free dialectics from such affirmative traits" (*ND* xix). His position of course corresponds to the negative, destructive turn that he believes history itself to have taken in his own time.

For all the Frankfurt theorists, the supposedly progressive forces of social change have cheated mankind. This historic reversal (and reversal of history) is beautifully expressed in Walter Benjamin's ninth "Thesis on the Philosophy of History." Describing Paul Klee's painting *Angelus Novus*, in which an angel appears to be "about to move away from something he is fixedly contemplating," Benjamin continues:

> This is how one pictures the angel of history. His face is turned toward the past. Where we perceive a chain of events, he sees one single catastrophe which keeps piling wreckage upon wreckage and hurls it in front of his feet. The angel would like to stay, awaken the dead, and make whole what has been smashed. But a storm is blow-

ing from Paradise; it has got caught in his wings with such violence that the angel can no longer close them. This storm irresistibly propels him into the future to which his back is turned, while the pile of debris before him grows skyward. This storm is what we call progress.   [IL 257–58]

Here one senses the depth and intricacy of Benjamin's pessimism as well as the Messianic quality of his thought. Perhaps less than any of his Frankfurt associates was Benjamin convinced that history would work its way out of violence and oppression into liberation. For that very reason, he tends to express himself in terms of "Messianic time," miraculous reversals of what appear to be the inevitable tendencies of history. The angel cannot see what lies ahead, only the ruins piling up behind (the perfect image of the negative classicist), a quality the angel shares with the Jews who, Benjamin says, "were prohibited from investigating the future." Therefore the Jews revered the past, culture, tradition, as all that they were permitted to see. "This does not imply, however, that for the Jews the future turned into homogeneous, empty time. For every second of time was the strait gate through which the Messiah might enter" (IL 264). This quality of apocalyptic expectation, too, is shared by negative classicism.

Messianic hope blossoms from the very despair that Benjamin expresses. Nowhere is this more evident than in his attitude toward the mass media. Whereas the other Frankfurt theorists treat the mass media or "the culture industry" in uniformly negative terms, as the cement of the status quo and the destroyers of genuine culture, Benjamin entertains the prospect of liberation coming about partly through the mass media. In his seminal essay "The Work of Art in the Age of Mechanical Reproduction" (1936), Benjamin starts by describing the destructive effects of industrial techniques on traditional art forms. Such techniques of reproduction as lithography disrupt the concept of authenticity, the "aura" of the work of art, which is dependent on its uniqueness, the fact of its nonreproducibility. The multiplication of new techniques through the nineteenth and into the twentieth century, including most obviously photography and cinema, has involved nothing less than "the liquidation of the traditional value of the cultural heritage" (IL 221). So far, Benjamin's thinking about mass culture parallels that of Marcuse, Adorno, and Horkheimer. But at the same time that he recognizes the conquest of "mechanical reproduction" over traditional art as destructive, he also thinks of it as emancipatory. The new techniques have been nothing less than revolutionary.

> For the first time in world history, mechanical reproduction emancipates the work of art from its parasitical dependence on ritual. To an ever greater degree the work of art reproduced becomes the work of art designed for reproducibility. From a photographic negative, for example, one can make any number of prints; to ask for the "authentic" print makes no sense. But the instant the criterion of authenticity ceases to be applicable to artistic production, the total function of art is reversed. Instead of being based on ritual, it begins to be based on another practice—politics. [*IL* 224]

The emancipation of art from ritual and also from the aristocratic monopoly of its ownership has politicized it in several ways. In one direction, art has become a commodity, merchandise, its reified forms identical to the mass culture that Adorno and Marcuse anathematize. In another direction, it has become democratized, increasingly available to everyone, and this second direction points ahead to just that utopia of "the aesthetic dimension"—life itself as a work of art—about which Marcuse speculates.

The politicization of art has involved the increasing demand for its pleasures and for happiness itself on the part of the masses, even including the appearance of what Benjamin calls "modern man's legitimate claim to being reproduced" (*IL* 232). As these demands by the masses for the estheticization of experience grow, two paths open up into the future. So long as the radical implications of these demands are blunted by being met only by reified, commercialized mass culture, and so long as the mechanization of art proceeds without a transformation of property relations, the result will be fascism, which, Benjamin argues, involves "the introduction of aesthetics into political life" (*IL* 241). This in turn suggests how bourgeois mass culture leads to the self-destruction of civilization: "All efforts to render politics aesthetic culminate in one thing: war." The other path, necessarily entailing the transformation of property relations, is communism, which opposes fascism on the cultural front by demystifying art, insisting that art is always political. This direction would mean recognizing and carrying through to their logical conclusion the radical implications of the mass media, creating a wholly emancipatory mass culture partly by making esthetic experience as universal as possible. Benjamin closes his essay with a quotation from Nero and an allusion to F. T. Marinetti's fascistic Futurist credo:

> "*Fiat ars—pereat mundus*," says Fascism, and, as Marinetti admits, expects war to supply the artistic gratification of a sense perception that has been changed by technology. This is evidently the consummation of "*l'art pour l'art*." Mankind, which in Homer's time was an object of contemplation for the Olympian gods, now is one for itself. Its self-alienation has reached such a degree that it can experience its own destruction as an aesthetic pleasure of the first order. This is the situation of politics which Fascism is rendering aesthetic. Communism responds by politicizing art.   [*IL* 242]

In contrast to Benjamin, the other Frankfurt theorists continued to see no liberating potential in that mass media. As Martin Jay puts it, "What they . . . feared was that mass art had a . . . political function diametrically opposed to [genuine art's] traditionally 'negative' one; art in the age of mechanical reproduction served to reconcile the mass audience to the status quo." But Benjamin, "while mourning the loss of the aura, . . . paradoxically held out hope for the progressive potential of politicized, collectivized art."[16] Lenin, Trotsky, and Sergei Eisenstein, after all, had seen much the same potential in film, a new epic medium. It has remained for younger Marxists to rescue the hopeful side of Benjamin's analysis and to hold it up critically against the culture theories of the other Frankfurt intellectuals. In his essay "Constituents of a Theory of the Media," Hans Magnus Enzensberger writes that "with a single great exception, that of Walter Benjamin [he also mentions Brecht], Marxists have not understood the consciousness industry and have been aware only of its bourgeois-capitalist dark side and not of its socialist possibilities."[17] Lukács, Horkheimer, and Adorno have all failed in this respect. Even the New Left, Enzensberger thinks, has been guilty of overlooking "the revolutionary potential" of the mass media. "It often seems as if it were precisely because of their progressive potential that the media are felt to be an immense threatening power; because for the first time they present a

    16. Jay, *The Dialectical Imagination*, p. 211.
    17. Hans Magnus Enzensberger, *The Consciousness Industry: On Literature, Politics and the Media* (New York: Seabury, 1974), p. 116.

basic challenge to bourgeois culture and thereby to the privileges of the bourgeois intelligentsia"—including the Marxist bourgeois intelligentsia. In similar terms, Todd Gitlin accuses Marcuse of failing to think dialectically in the development of his "one-dimensional thesis," which "did not show how one-dimensional forms could generate at least the seeds of their negations. For one thing, he missed the ambiguity of television's effects."[18]

For their part, Marcuse, Adorno, and Horkheimer all recognize from time to time the emancipatory potential of industrial technology, if not more specifically of the mass media. Horkheimer, for example, says explicitly and on several occasions that modern social regression cannot be blamed on technology: "The fault is not in machines."[19] Properly used, technology should increase productive capacity, eliminate scarcity, and make liberation possible, as Marx said it could. But this kind of statement, almost in the nature of an aside, comes in the midst of Horkheimer's general "critique of instrumental reason," another name for which is "technological rationality." And when Horkheimer turns from machinery in general to the mass media in particular, although he rejects romantic Luddism as unrealistic, he expresses nothing more hopeful than resignation in face of the inevitable technicization of the world:

> The stereotyped rejection of television . . . which was still customary a few years ago in German families which considered themselves educated highlights with special clarity the impossibility of turning the clock back. It may indeed be true that when a child acquires its first knowledge of the world not through interaction with his father but through the [TV] screen and its images, not through spontaneous stimuli but through immediate reaction to signs, the end result is intellectual passivity. Yet the absence of a set from his parents' home only leads to the child being looked down on by his companions in school, to feelings of inferiority and worse. The flight into the past is no help to the freedom that is being threatened. [*CIR* 140]

Adorno's later pronouncements on mass culture are more negative

18. Todd Gitlin, "Sixteen Notes on Television and the Movement," in *Literature in Revolution*, ed. George Abbott and Charles Newman (New York: Holt, Rinehart and Winston, 1972), p. 351.

19. Max Horkheimer, *Critique of Instrumental Reason* (New York: Seabury 1974), p. 28. Abbreviated in the text as *CIR*.

even than Horkheimer's and Marcuse's, partly because he develops definitions of genuine and mass culture which are completely irreconcilable, and partly because of a European parochialism that resulted, for example, in his inability to see any emancipatory value in jazz. When Adorno writes that authentic culture "is the perennial protestation of the particular against the general," he has left himself no way to approve of any techniques of standardization and reproduction in the arts. Culture is always singular, unique, and protective of the singular and the unique; to use Benjamin's term, it is always "auratic." Mass culture, therefore, can only be a travesty of the genuine article. From such a perspective, a deadly, totalitarian uniformity settles over everything that tumbles into the gaping category of mass culture. "What parades as progress in the culture industry, as the incessantly new which it offers up, remains the disguise of an eternal sameness: everywhere the changes mask a skeleton which has changed just as little as the profit motive itself since the time it first gained its predominance over culture" ("Culture Industry Reconsidered," p. 14). Whenever Adorno, Horkheimer, and Marcuse link the mass media up to politics, the tie is always to fascism. When Adorno writes about television, for example, it is to confirm "the suspicion widely shared, though hard to corroborate by exact data, that the majority of television shows today aim at producing, or at least reproducing, the very smugness, intellectual passivity, and gullibility that seem to fit in with totalitarian creeds even if the explicit surface message of the shows may be anti-totalitarian."[20]

The positions of all the Frankfurt theorists on the issue of technology are at best vague. Apart from distinguishing "the culture industry" from the rest of technology as a separate and apparently more negative category, they do not confront the question of the possible destructive and totalitarian effects of machinery as such, nor do they distinguish between certain kinds of clearly destructive machinery (weapons, for instance) and other, constructive kinds (the printing press, for example). They try to adhere to Marx's technological optimism, but do so only in retreat. Their major lines of argument all point the other way, to the destructive effects of the development of

20. Theodor W. Adorno, "Television and the Patterns of Mass Culture," in Bernard Rosenberg and David Manning White, eds. *Mass Culture: The Popular Arts in America* (Glencoe, Ill.: The Free Press, 1957), p. 479.

"instrumental" or "technological reason" itself. This is the central theme of *The Dialectic of Enlightenment* which, just as much as *The Decline of the West*, expresses both positive and negative classicism.

Like Freud in *Totem and Taboo* and Nietzsche in *The Genealogy of Morals* (they are following Nietzsche's lead in particular), Adorno and Horkheimer turn to the remote past to perform anthropological spadework on modern mass society. They attempt to explain the origin of civilization itself, or how "the dialectic of enlightenment" has worked its way forward from the beginning, only, seemingly, to destroy itself in the present. To do so, they turn to *The Odyssey*, much as Freud turns to *Oedipus Rex*, both for the authority of positive classicism and for traces of primitive psychic and social organization. According to their analysis, Odysseus turns out to be the first bourgeois and the embodiment of "enlightenment" extricating itself from "mythology." *The Odyssey* portrays "the adventures through which subjectivity . . . escapes from the prehistoric world" (*DE* 78). At the same time, the emergence of "subjectivity"—Odysseus himself, the rational, calculating ego—entails the substitution of self-sacrifice for the practice of human sacrifice to the gods. And in sacrifice itself Adorno and Horkheimer perceive the first vestige of economic exchange. In language that approximates both Freud's and Nietzsche's, they proclaim that "the history of civilization is the history of the introversion of sacrifice. In other words: the history of renunciation" (*DE* 54–55).

As for Freud and Nietzsche, "renunciation" is a constructive process only up to a point, after which it becomes destructive. The progress of civilization is thus once again seen to be cyclic, working its way forward only until that limit is reached beyond which what is renounced erupts in the present with explosive force—"the return of the repressed," which Marcuse in *Eros and Civilization* construes more hopefully, as both destructive and liberating. For Adorno and Horkheimer, fate itself is cyclic, at least according to the repetitive fixations of mythology. The self—Odysseus as ego—seeks to break out of the cycle. "In myth each moment of the cycle discharges the previous one, and thereby helps to install the context of guilt as law. Odysseus opposes this situation. The self represents rational universality against the inevitability of fate" (*DE* 58). But rational universality—"enlightenment"—puts from itself the very nature that it must

reassimilate in order to break the fatal wheel. Escape from the cycle of
fate will also be cyclic, a return to what has been objectified and
distanced from man in the construction of the mythic pantheon. Man
struggles to free himself from nature only to find that nature in one
way or another always takes its revenge.

To put Adorno and Horkheimer's argument in slightly different
terms, from the beginning of society mythology and enlightenment
have been dialectically entwined. The attempt to put mythology completely to one side and follow enlightenment alone seems to be the
path of culture and progress, but is ultimately self-destructive. What
was rejected with mythology—"nature" both external and internal—
returns with a vengeance. What we are witnessing in the twentieth
century is, as it were, Odysseus going mad, falling to pieces, committing suicide, because of the rejection of nature which enlightenment
entails. In fascism and the growth of "the culture industry," we see
the end of the line for the Odyssean project and "the retreat from
enlightenment into mythology" (*DE* xiii). This is "the myth of the
twentieth century," fascism or "ideology" in general, the destructive
fraud practiced by those rational instruments of ultimate irrationality,
the mass media, controlled "by the wholly enlightened as they steer
society toward barbarism" (*DE* 20). Francis Bacon's vision of scientific
knowledge leading to "the dissolution of domination" has been a noble
one. "But in the face of such a possibility, and in the service of the
present age, enlightenment becomes wholesale deception of the
masses" (*DE* 42). Thus, as they look out upon the terror and chaos of
World War II, Adorno and Horkheimer seek to explain the paradox
that "the fully enlightened earth radiates disaster triumphant" (*DE* 3).

Unlike traditional dialectical thinking, their argument does not lead
to any vision of the next stage of history that will surpass through
synthesis the defeats and terrors of the present. *The Dialectic of
Enlightenment* ends with a fragment on "the genesis of stupidity," and
with other fragments in which the authors turn to the writings of "the
conservatives" to express their own deep pessimism about the future
of the human enterprise. Having begun by invoking Nietzsche's researches into classical literature, and having developed their theme
through three brilliant essays on *The Odyssey*, on the Marquis de
Sade's *Juliette*, and on "the culture industry: enlightenment as mass
deception," Adorno and Horkheimer arrive at the "well-founded

conclusion "terror and civilization are inseparable" (*DE* 217). Despite their nominal Marxism, they are prepared even to turn to the writings of that most reactionary and pessimistic theorist, Joseph de Maistre, who at the time of the French Revolution already understood how the most progressive and "enlightened" theories can have the most disastrous results. In his *Soirées de Saint Pétersbourg*, Adorno and Horkheimer find corroboration for their earlier assertion that "the fallen nature of modern man cannot be separated from social progress" (*DE* xiv):

> Culture has developed with the protection of the executioner. Here the book of Genesis, which tells of the fall from Paradise, coincides with the *Soirées de Petersbourg*. All work and pleasure are protected by the hangman. To contradict this fact is to deny all science and logic. It is impossible to abolish the terror and retain civilization. Even a lessening of terror implies a beginning of the process of dissolution. Various conclusions can be drawn from this—from the groveling respect for Fascist barbarity to refuge in the circles of Hell. But there is another conclusion: to laugh at logic if it runs counter to the interests of men.   [*DE* 217–18]

Laughter, however, is not the solution that Adorno and Horkheimer are looking for, nor is *The Dialectic of Enlightenment* a book that will ever prompt its readers to smile. After such a paragraph, it is difficult to think of its authors as holding forth any hope about the future liberation of humanity from the cycles of fate, which might as well be "the circles of Hell." Apart from the idea that "the enlightenment must consider itself," the only possibility of liberation in *The Dialectic of Enlightenment* is associated with the remote past, at the back of civilization itself, beyond the division of labor, beyond even those primitive societies which do not yet know the practice of human sacrifice. This possibility is implicit in the song of the Sirens to which Odysseus listens lashed to the mast, while his men, ears plugged, row for home. Odysseus the master can hear their music; his "proletarian" oarsmen cannot. "Thus the enjoyment of art and manual labor break apart as the world of prehistory is left behind" (*DE* 34). But in the Sirens' song itself Adorno and Horkheimer seem to hear the music of "the aesthetic dimension," or the lure of a time and place where labor and the struggle for civilization end in a utopian wholeness and peace beyond the madness of history. Of course they know that this road back into the past is closed. They are lashed, we all are lashed, to the mast of civilization.

Given our predicament, we have no choice but to use for our libera-tion the very principle that seems to be leading us to inevitable ship-wreck. "Enlightenment" itself is the only thing that can steer us away from the disasters spawned by "enlightenment."

> We are wholly convinced—and therein lies our *petitio principii*—
> that social freedom is inseparable from enlightened thought. Nev-
> ertheless, we believe that we have just as clearly recognized that the
> notion of this very way of thinking, no less than the actual historic
> forms—the social institutions—with which it is interwoven, already
> contains the seed of the reversal universally apparent today. If en-
> lightenment does not accommodate reflection on this recidivist ele-
> ment, then it seals its own fate.   [*DE* xiii]

This is hardly a hopeful prospect, since their entire essay—like many of the other productions of the Frankfurt School—shows the "rever-sal" of enlightenment but not how to undo that reversal.

Though jumping over Rome into the prehistory of classical civiliza-tion, *The Dialectic of Enlightenment* follows the pattern of negative classicism clearly enough. Unless "enlightenment" can "consider it-self" in some powerful and final way, history will continue to move in cycles, and the Spenglerian morphology will prove to be inescapable. The Roman experience in any case hovers just in the background of Adorno and Horkheimer's analysis. "Roman reason" is equivalent to "instrumental reason," or the rationalization of mass society (*DE* 115). "Stoicism"—the philosophy of private resignation against public dis-order and tragedy—"is the bourgeois philosophy" (*DE* 96). And throughout their essay, "barbarism" is "the other face of culture" (*DE* 111–12).

In several of his later writings Horkheimer in particular dwells upon the fate of the Roman Empire. At an early stage in his career, well before World War II, he had written optimistically about the end of the Middle Ages that "the enemies of the Inquisition turned that dusk into the dawning of a new day. Nor does the dusk of capitalism have to usher in the night of mankind although today it certainly seems to be threatening it."[21] Some thirty years later, after the disasters of Nazism

---

21. Max Horkheimer, *Dawn and Decline: Notes 1926–1931 and 1950–1969*, tr. Michael Shau (New York: Seabury, 1978), p. 17. Abbreviated in the text as *DD*.

and the war and near the end of his career, he was no longer so hopeful—if the passage just quoted can be called hopeful. In a fragment entitled "Mass Media," Horkheimer, sounding very much like a Spengler or an Ortega, writes:

> In this doomed civilization which attempts in precipitous haste to counter the threat of a new, even more overpowering migration than those from the third to the sixth century by producing the means to annihilate life and by patterning itself on dictatorships that bristle with armaments, there is no purpose other than money and power, and so madness erupts. If one wants to hear its daily voice simply turn the radio [on] at any time whatever, one is flooded by a carnival of unleashed hucksters and a sprinkling of outmoded jazz and boogy-woogy in between. That is in America, the progressive country. The expectation that things might be better in parochial Europe is disappointed at the first sound. It is worse. The lilting melodies, the lying good cheer, the folklore of the backward nations betray by their gesture of innocence and harmony that they are the masks of envy and malice. The more profound someone's thirst for revenge, the more sensitively he reacts to pain and dissonance in kitsch and art. The daily voice of the nations proclaims that they no longer see a task ahead, that spirit has abandoned them. The time of a new migration is dawning.   [*DD* 186]

In 1930, "the dawning of a new day" expressed for Horkheimer his apocalyptic hope for a revolutionary liberation in the near future. In 1960, the only dawning that he can see is that of a new barbarism, and the mass media—so often according to liberal theory the sources of an at least potential enlightenment—are the open gates through which the first hordes of invaders are streaming.

The richness and appeal of the culture-industry theories of the Frankfurt Institute philosophers stem partly from their ability to combine conservative and Freudian strains of pessimism with Marxism. They emphasize both the difficulties and the desirability of a liberation from forms of oppression that liberals ordinarily do not acknowledge, including the nearly universal false consciousness which, they argue, is the main product of the mass media. Like Camus, they are positive classicists who insist on the values of freedom, reason, and culture, but without any of Camus's sometimes easy, optimistic rhetoric in face of the "absurd," which in their works takes the always political form of human oppression. Like Nietzsche and Freud, they recognize that oppression has its roots in human nature, even while, following Freud and Marx, they insist that freedom from the chains of illusion—ultimately the only source of oppression—is possible. Often their pessimism, in the guise of negative classicism, seems completely to overshadow their Marxist hopes for the future; then ideas of liberation, though continuing to reverberate through their writings, themselves appear to be mirages, the illusions of an impossibly remote utopia. But in the theme of freedom as the estheticization of experience, and in Benjamin's insight into the liberating potential of the mass media, they adumbrate a future universal enlightenment that shall no longer dissolve into its opposite.

CHAPTER 8

Television: Spectacularity
vs. McLuhanism

In a society dominated by the production and consumption of
images, no part of life can long remain immune from the inva-
sion of spectacle.

—CHRISTOPHER LASCH

i

THE Frankfurt Institute's analysis of the totalitarian tendencies of the "culture industry" seems especially relevant to television, partly because it is the mass medium that takes the abolition of the "aura" of older cultural forms to its farthest limits. Television like radio has also invaded that sanctuary of the potentially free individual, the home, monopolizing the communication channels even of privacy. And television has flooded its own channels with propaganda for consumerism, imperializing new psychic markets for the products of "late capitalism." Summarizing these concerns, Oskar Negt writes that the "bourgeois public sphere," which is "in an irretrievable process of decay" as evidenced through its invasion by the mass media, "has . . . turned the *citoyen*, on whom it once relied, into a consumer, who sees the path to the television knob as the way to freedom and autonomy."[1] This is of course the same pattern that Juvenal saw of past rights and responsibilities abandoned in favor of present appetites.

According to all the Frankfurt Institute theorists, television, "even

1. Oskar Negt, "Mass Media: Tools of Domination or Instruments of Liberation? Aspects of the Frankfurt School's Communications Analysis," *New German Critique*, 14 (Spring 1978), p. 65.

if the explicit surface message of the shows may be antitotalitarian," tends toward fascism. In similar language, Todd Gitlin, former president of Students for a Democratic Society, writes: "TV programs aim to narrow and flatten consciousness—to tailor everyman's world view to the consumer mentality, to placate discontent, to manage what cannot be placated, to render social pathologies personal, to level class-consciousness."[2] From the Marxist perspective, all the mass media reinforce bourgeois hegemony and blunt the development of radicalism. In *False Promises: American Working Class Consciousness* (1973), for example, Stanley Aronowitz denounces "mass art" as "a one-way communication [which] takes on the character of domination." Modern history has been characterized by a trend "toward the replacement of all the traditional forms of proletarian culture and everyday life . . . with a new, manipulated consumer culture. . . . The institutions of mass culture . . . have become central to the process of reproducing the labor force in proportion to the weaknesses of family, church, and school."[3]

From a conservative perspective, television is again likely to be treated as undermining true values, consciousness, society. The attacks made on television and the other news media by the Nixon administration were aimed chiefly at journalists, whom Spiro T. Agnew alliteratively stigmatized as "the nattering nabobs of negativism." Implicit in these attacks, however, is an indictment of the networks themselves as undemocratic, un-American, decadent. In a Des Moines speech on 13 November 1969, Agnew asked:

> What is the end value [of the networks' endless pursuit of controversy]—to enlighten or to profit? What is the end result—to inform or to confuse? How does the ongoing exploration for more action, more excitement, more drama serve our national search for internal peace and stability?

2. Todd Gitlin, "Sixteen Notes on Television and the Movement," in George Abbott White and Charles Newman, eds., *Literature in Revolution* (New York: Holt, Rinehart and Winston, 1972), p. 345.

3. Stanley Aronowitz, *False Promises: The Shaping of American Working Class Consciousness* (New York: McGraw-Hill, 1973), pp. 100 and 95. Perhaps the most interesting development in recent Marxist media theory is Jürgen Habermas's concept of "distorted communication," which draws on both Freud and the Frankfurt Institute analysis. See Habermas, *Knowledge and Human Interests* (Boston: Beacon, 1971), pp. 214–45, *Communication and the Evolution of Society* (Boston: Beacon, 1979), and *Legitimation Crisis* (Boston: Beacon, 1973).

> . . . What has this passionate pursuit of "controversy" done to the
> politics of progress through local compromise essential to the func-
> tioning of a democratic society?[4]

The "nattering nabobs" themselves are not always quick to defend
their medium. Shortly after the demise of his CBS "See It Now"
program in 1958, Edward R. Murrow told the Radio-Television News
Director Association: "If there are any historians . . . a hundred years
from now and there should be preserved the kinescopes for one week
of all three networks, they will find recorded, in black-and-white or
color, evidence of decadence, escapism and insulation from the realities of the world. . . . If we go on as we are, then history will take its
revenge, and retribution will [catch] up with us." This remark is
quoted by Murrow's colleague on the original CBS news team, Fred
Friendly, who in *Due to Circumstances Beyond Our Control* indicts
the television industry for its "inexorable flight from quality" in pursuit of profits. "I think of commercial television like Times Square,"
says Friendly elsewhere. "In trying to make more money, the lowest
common denominator was catered to. And now TV entertainment,
like Times Square, is nothing more than a slum."[5]

From its commercial beginnings in the late 1940s, television has
been accused more often—and from more ideological perspectives—
of causing cultural and political decadence than has any earlier communications medium. Whatever it broadcasts is apt to be interpreted
as antithetical to high culture. It appears to be a sort of anticlassical
apparatus for automatic barbarization; its characteristics of passive
mass spectacle readily lend themselves to Roman analogizing. Re-
counting Richard Nixon's 1952 "Checkers" speech, Milton Shulman
says that having viewers write to the Republican National Committee
stating whether or not they wanted Nixon to remain on the Republican ticket "was, in its way, the electronic equivalent of the mobs
in the Roman Colosseum being asked to give a thumbs up or a thumbs
down sign about the fate of an intended victim."[6] Similarly, in his *New*

4. Spiro T. Agnew, "The Des Moines Speech," in Michael C. Emery and Ted
Curtis Smythe, eds., *Readings in Mass Communication: Concepts and Issues in the
Mass Media* (Dubuque, Iowa: William C. Brown, 1974), p. 504.

5. Edward R. Murrow quoted by Fred W. Friendly, *Due to Circumstances Beyond Our Control* (New York: Vintage, 1968), p. 99. And Friendly quoted in "Why Is
TV So Bad?" *Newsweek*, 16 February 1976, p. 72.

6. Milton Shulman, *The Ravenous Eye* (London: Collins, 1973), p. 54.

Republic account of the influence of television on the 1965 Watts rebellion, John Gregory Dunne writes: "With its insatiable appetite for live drama, television turned the riots into some kind of Roman spectacle, with the police playing the lions, the Negroes the Christians."[7] In both of these examples, television as a purveyor of news and not just of entertainment is likened to bread and circuses, and in the first one, it appears to be acting to enhance a democratic electoral process—the opposite of what Juvenal meant. Defending television and other forms of mass culture against such criticisms, David Manning White says: "The mass culture critic always insinuates that in some previous era the bulk of men were rational, pacific, and learned. The good old days—like the Roman Empire under Nero? Admittedly, the Romans didn't have a television set to watch the lions massacre the various unwilling guests during the Coliseum half-time shows."[8] For many of its critics television is the machinery of a universal narcissism, a fake magic mirror on the wall forever distracting, infantilizing, and consequently barbarizing its viewers. The ultimate televiewer may be the zombified housewives who sit narcotized before their wallscreens in Ray Bradbury's *Fahrenheit* 451, which portrays a book-burning society of the near future. Television, despite occasional religious programming, and despite functioning as an ersatz religion by producing a new mythology based on commodity fetishism, is secular, dominated by profiteering, basely and blatantly ideological. "All levels of mass-media 'realism,' whether barracks in *Stalag 17* or staterooms on the *Loveboat*," writes John Phelan, "are dead ends of contemporary nihilism."[9] Television, the most modern and apparently progressive piece of cultural equipment, seems also to be the most decadent.

Any survey of criticisms of the medium will contain many that have to do with content, or with the ideas, values, and prejudices expressed on television programs. Such criticisms often conclude with proposals for reform, such as cutting back on violence in shows consumed by

7. John Gregory Dunne, "A Riot on TV," *New Republic*, 11 September 1965, p. 27.

8. David Manning White, in Bernard Rosenberg and David Manning White, eds., *Mass Culture Revisited* (New York: Van Nostrand Reinhold, 1971), pp. 13–14.

9. John M. Phelan, *Disenchantment: Meaning and Morality in the Media* (New York: Hastings House, 1980), p. 42.

children. Content can at least theoretically be upgraded, although the economic obstacles to improvement may be overwhelming. Only the most sanguine observers expect the commercial television networks to reform themselves. "Because television can make so much money doing its worst," says Friendly, "it often cannot afford to do its best." Even "efforts to improve [technical] quality in television films must be made at financial risk."[10] Given this dismal picture of commercial television, proposals for reforming its content invariably sound naive. Whether the blame falls on the cynicism and irresponsibility of the network managers or on the degraded cultural standards of the masses depends, of course, on the critic's ideological perspective. Another type of media criticism bypasses program content, however, to focus on the general psychological effects of televiewing and on the intrinsic structure of the medium. When the stress is on psychological effects, the results often declare television to be addicting, a "narcotic," a new "opium of the people," as in Marie Winn's *The Plug-in Drug* (1977). According to the maverick Federal Communications Commissioner, Nicholas Johnson: "Television leaves its addicts waterlogged. Only rarely does it communicate anything meaningful to their lives. No wonder so many Americans express . . . a deep-seated hostility toward television. Too many realize, perhaps unconsciously but certainly with utter disgust, that television is itself a drug."[11] When the stress is on intrinsic structure, the results involve some version of Marshall McLuhan's thesis that "the medium is the message." Program content is beside the point. The critic is drawn either toward McLuhan's sort of technological determinism, though often without his optimism, or toward neo-Luddite demands for the abolition of television itself, as in Jerry Mander's *Four Arguments for the Elimination of Television* (1978).

Three out of four of Mander's arguments seem to stress content rather than structure. These three are entitled: "the mediation of experience," "the colonization of experience," and "the inherent biases of television." The word "inherent" in the last title, however, suggests the structural nature of that argument, and as Mander ex-

10. Friendly, *Due to Circumstances Beyond Our Control*, p. xii.

11. Nicholas Johnson, "What Can We Do About Television?" in Emery and Smythe, *Readings in Mass Communication*, p. 22. See also Nicholas Johnson, *How to Talk Back to Your Television Set* (New York: Bantam, 1970).

plains it "mediation" applies largely to the physiological effects of the machinery of television. The first two arguments and much of the fourth are in any case redundant; much of Mander's ingenuity goes into the third, clearly structural argument, entitled: "effects of television on the human being." Here it becomes evident that Mander is less concerned about television as a political institution than as a pollutant. He worries about its hypnotic and narcotic effects; about "image emulation" ("are we all taped replays?"); and about "the ingestion of artificial light." Perhaps his most striking section concerns the experiments in the effects of artificial light conducted by the photobiologist John Ott. "Pink fluorescent light produced the highest rate of cancer in rats; natural daylight the lowest."[12] Other sorts of artificial light produce other nefarious results. Mander concludes that the artificial light of color television (or black and white) must do the same. Radioactivity aside, Mander thinks, television acts as one more environmental poison. Mander's presentation of all four arguments might be characterized as expressing a sort of reasonable paranoia, according to which almost anything may be poisonous until proved safe.

Though he emphasizes the hypothetical effects of television, Mander does not neglect politics. He interprets nearly every antidemocratic tendency in modern society as a result of television, at times sounding like Horkheimer and Adorno: "There is considerable evidence that the science fiction vision of arbitrary reality inevitably leading to autocracy has already begun to materialize. We can see it in action in the quasi-religious philosophies that are now sweeping the country, gathering in millions of devotees" (99). Thus we are given to understand that the new Dark Age is the product of television. In any case, under the rubric of "the mediation of experience," Mander lists "eight ideal conditions for the flowering of autocracy," among which the third involves the "separation" of people "from each other" (or massification). To effect this "autocratic" goal, Mander says, "spectator sports are excellent, so are circuses, elections, and any spectacles in which focus is outward and interpersonal exchange is subordinated to mass experience" (98). Bread and circuses here merges with its

12. Jerry Mander, *Four Arguments for the Elimination of Television* (New York: Morrow Quill, 1978), p. 174.

opposite, political responsibility and participation; any notion that television can convey intelligent and useful information is cancelled by the identification of elections with entertainments.

When he emphasizes politics, Mander agrees with the critique from the left, according to which true political consciousness is drowned out by mass media distraction, ideology, compensatory vicarious experience. Among other authorities, Mander cites the mass culture theories of the French "situationist" Guy DeBord, who in *Society of the Spectacle* (1967) writes: "The spectacle is the existing order's uninterrupted discourse about itself, its laudatory monologue. It is the self-portrait of power in the epoch of its totalitarian management of the conditions of existence."[13] "Spectacle" and "spectacular relations" are DeBord's versions of such concepts as false consciousness and ideology. His stress is on the production of an all-absorbing imagery that, like Caesar Augustus's *Res gestae*, reflects only its own glory. "Spectacle" is the ultimate result of commodity fetishism, a narcissistic self-reflection that is the social form of the equally narcissistic psychic privatization of the individual in mass-capitalist society. "This society which eliminates geographical distance reproduces distance internally as spectacular separation" (sec. 167). Watching replaces living, as in spectator sports and televiewing. Reality retreats behind the façade of an imagery shaped by the mass media and the ad industry, which is "the material reconstruction of the religious illusion" (sec. 20). Bread and circuses reappears on the scene of history as the ultimate production and self-defense of the empire of capital. "The spectacle *is* capital to such a degree of accumulation that it becomes an image" (sec. 34, my emphasis).

DeBord's elaboration of the concept of "spectacle," with its evocation of Roman imperial *spectaculi*, is similar in several ways to the numerous recent American analyses of "image making" and the impact of television on electoral politics. DeBord himself cites Daniel Boorstin's *The Image* (1961), which, he says, "describes the commercial consumption of the American spectacle but never reaches the concept of spectacle because he thinks he can exempt private life, or the notion of 'the honest commodity,' from this disastrous exaggera-

13. Guy DeBord, *Society of the Spectacle* (Detroit: Red and Black, 1977), section 24. First published as *La société du spectacle* (Paris: Buchet-Chastel, 1967).

tion" of the power of mass culture imagery. But despite his liberalism, Boorstin's concept of the "pseudo-event" is close to DeBord's "spectacle," perhaps especially because of its pervasiveness, deluging all aspects of social life. "The making of the illusions which flood our experience has become the business of America," writes Boorstin.[14] Though he defends much of this mass production of imagery as necessary, respectable, and democratic, Boorstin also associates it with ideas of decadence, and particularly with the notion that the mass media substitute the phony for the real, untruths for truth: "What ails us most is not what we have done with America, but what we have substituted for America. We suffer primarily not from our vices or our weaknesses, but from our illusions. We are haunted, not by reality, but by those images we have put in place of reality" (6). Boorstin's argument leads to a call for self-reform ("each of us must disenchant himself") which DeBord finds unrealistic, but the critical aspects of their analyses almost coincide. And both "spectacle" and "image" have special theoretical resonance in an age of television, in which information so often threatens to degenerate into an uninterrupted and unanalyzed flow of pictures so realistic that they seem almost as good as "being there."

Boorstin's essay bears comparison to such recent general works of social criticism as Richard Sennett's *The Fall of Public Man* (1977) and Christopher Lasch's *The Culture of Narcissism* (1978). Narcissism as Lasch defines it is an all-encompassing category like DeBord's "spectacle," which is one reason why Lasch's criticism of *The Image* approximates DeBord's. "Even Boorstin," Lasch writes, "minimizes the degree to which appearances—'images'—dominate American society. Backing away from the more disturbing implications of his study, he draws a false distinction between advertising and propaganda, which

14. Daniel Boorstin, *The Image: A Guide to Pseudo-Events in America* (New York: Atheneum, 1971 [1961]), p. 5. In a later essay, Boorstin writes: "Television has conquered the nation with blitzkrieg speed and has received unconditional surrender. A bewildered America still hasn't found its bearings. For television has brought us Too Much Too Soon. Without anybody having planned it so, we feel our heads swimming with instant experience. We get our news before anybody (including the commentator) has had a chance to reflect on what it means or whether it's worth being called news. If our TV myopia is not to become an incurable history-blindness, an inability to see beyond this evening's screen, we must find antidotes for Too Much Too Soon" (*Democracy and Its Discontents: Reflections on Everyday America* [New York: Vintage, 1975], p. 22).

allows him to posit a sphere of technological rationality—one that includes the operations of the state and much of the routine of modern industry—into which the irrationality of image making cannot penetrate."[15] In contrast to Boorstin's "pseudo-event" and "image," which do not account for all contemporary cultural phenomena, Lasch's "narcissism" is an all-pervading psycho-social equivalent of DeBord's "spectacle" and of other Marxist versions of false consciousness.

Lasch offers one of the most complete—and repetitious—catalogues of social decadence made by any recent social critic. A sampling of his table of contents yields such dismal items as "the void within," "the spread of stupefaction," "the atrophy of competence," "the eclipse of achievement," "the collapse of authority," "the abdication of authority," "the degradation of sport," "the trivialization of athletics," "the flight from feeling," and "the trivialization of personal relations." Whether explicitly or only as background, the mass media—the machinery of narcissism—are ubiquitous in his analysis. Boorstin's idea that we live in a world of pseudo-events and quasi-information reappears in Lasch's belief that the media are undermining such traditional gauges of meaning as truth and falsehood.

> The role of the mass media in the manipulation of public opinion has received a great deal of anguished but misguided attention. Much of this commentary assumes that the problem is to prevent the circulation of obvious untruths; whereas it is evident, as the more penetrating critics of mass culture have pointed out, that the rise of mass media makes the categories of truth and falsehood irrelevant to an evaluation of their influence. Truth has given way to credibility, facts to statements that sound authoritative without conveying any authoritative information. [74]

Propaganda for consumerism—that is, advertising—is the main product that the media are structured to convey. And consumerism is nothing more than the economic reflection of narcissism. "The media give substance to and thus intensify narcissistic dreams of fame and glory, encourage the common man to identify himself with the stars and to hate the 'herd,' and make it more and more difficult for him to accept the banality of everyday existence" (21). The apparently public

---

15. Christopher Lasch, *The Culture of Narcissism: American Life in an Age of Diminishing Expectations* (New York: Norton, 1978), p. 75.

culture of the mass media vampirizes private life and the family, but it also vampirizes public life, substituting image making for politics, the cult of personalities and stars for issues. Citing DeBord, Lasch writes, "The attempt to civilize the masses has now given rise to a society dominated by appearances—the society of the spectacle. In the period of primitive accumulation, capitalism subordinated being to having, the use value of commodities to their exchange value. Now it subordinates possession itself to appearance and measures exchange value as a commodity's capacity to confer prestige—the illusion of prosperity and well-being" (72). Spectacular mass culture is commodity fetishism carried to such an extreme that the illusion of value derived from wanting and possessing a thing replaces both the exchange and the use values of the thing itself. Only the machinery of illusion, the mass media, could effect this ultimate hollowing out of value.

Lasch's concept of narcissism and DeBord's of spectacle are categories for other recent social critics as well. Richard Sennett's thesis of the gradual disintegration of the public realm in industrial society, for example, leads him to both narcissism and the mass media as interrelated causes of contemporary decadence. What fills the emptied public realm is a false privatization of self-absorption intensified by the psychologizing and consumerism of mass culture. Sennett traces "the erosion of public life" to factors well prior to the development of the electronic media, but television, movies, and radio exacerbate the trend. "Electronic communication is one means by which the very idea of public life has been put to an end."[16] Television gives the illusion of involvement in public affairs, but televiewing is a "passive" and "intimate" activity that instead diminishes involvement. "The mass media infinitely heighten the knowledge people have of what transpires in the society, and they infinitely inhibit the capacity of people to convert that knowledge into political action" (283).

Sennett rejects as silly the idea that "just as moral rottenness is supposed to have sapped Rome's power to rule the West, it is said to have sapped the modern West's power to rule the globe." He nevertheless offers his own version of Juvenal's tenth satire: "As in Roman times, participation in the *res publica* today is most often a matter of

16. Richard Sennett, *The Fall of Public Man: On the Social Psychology of Capitalism* (New York: Vintage, 1978 [1977]), p. 282.

going along, and the forums for this public life, like the city, are in a state of decay" (4). Sennett suggests that the decadent Romans may have been better off than we are; they were able to turn to religion, whereas we have only the narcissistic hollowness of our secularized mass culture to substitute for public life.

> The difference between the Roman past and the modern present lies in the alternative, in what privacy means. The Roman in private sought another principle to set against the public, a principle based on religious transcendence of the world. In private we seek out not a principle but a reflection, that of what our psyches are, what is authentic in our feelings. We have tried to make the fact of being in private, alone with ourselves and with family and intimate friends, an end in itself. [4].

This is another way of saying, of course, that the modern republic has been transformed into the psychological society. As Sennett puts this theme: "Masses of people are concerned with their single life-histories and particular emotions as never before; this concern has proved to be a trap rather than a liberation" (5).

In all of these studies—Lasch, Sennett, Mander, DeBord, Boorstin, the Frankfurt theorists, as well as the critiques of psychological society mentioned in Chapter 5—a central paradox is that the highly public mass media erode the public sphere by subjectivizing or privatizing it.[17] But as the public sphere is hollowed out, so is the individual, the meaning of whose existence depends upon participation in a public community. The isolated, narcissistic ego becomes the hero or heroine of every mass-mediated experience, the source and aim of the grandest, most glamorous daydreams and wish fulfillments, in an infinite hall of mirrors. The ideas of image, spectacle, and narcissism share a regressive visual element, moreover, which itself helps to explain how the most progressive cultural techniques can lead to results that point to decadence and barbarism. In his analysis of the concept of reification, Joseph Gabel argues that false consciousness emphasizes space at the expense of time. So, he adds, does schizophrenia, which he treats as the psychological form of the social catego-

---

17. Compare Jürgen Habermas, *Toward a Rational Society: Student Protest, Science, and Politics*, tr. Jeremy J. Shapiro (Boston: Beacon, 1970), pp. 42–43, quoted in Chapter 1, pp. 41–42.

ry of false consciousness.[18] So, too, I would add, does television, at least as it is most often employed, for immediate sensation and immediate commercial gain. Even television journalism—the "news" (the antithesis of "history")—tends to reduce everything to immediate visual experience, time into space and words into pictures (the quantity of words in a television news story as compared to a newspaper account of the same event will ordinarily be quite small). In the electronic mass media, seeing becomes believing. The domination of visual imagery in any cultural medium will perhaps always evoke questions about what is not shown, about the reality behind the apparitions on the surface. On a philosophical level, these questions echo Platonic doubts about physical appearances and about all the arts as third-hand reflections of the ideal. On a less abstract level, they may merely express a loss of depth or of temporality. The visible is only surface and present, never so vast as the invisible or as the past and future, which are infinite.

Dependence on the visible thus entails a paradoxical blindness, which in turn subverts the power of the visual mass media. Here is one way, I believe, in which "the medium is the message." Quite apart from the brutality and degradation of human life involved in the Roman games, the fact of their spectacularity was often held against them, especially by their early Christian critics. Salvianus condemns "the amphitheaters, the concert halls, games, parades, athletes, rope dancers, pantomimes and other monstrosities" as offering "pictures of vice" through which "the whole people commits fornication mentally." For Salvianus, to see is also to participate in what is seen, and to lose track of what is unseen. On similar grounds, Tertullian writes that the public shows, including all theatrical performances, are "idolatry"; they "belong to the devil, his pomp and his angels."[19] Tertullian condemns the mobs of spectators at arenas, abosrbed in "spectacle," both for their cruelty and for their "blindness" to everything of true worth (271–73), and says: "Ears and eyes are the servants of the spirit, nor can the spirit be clean whose servants are dirty" (277). And

18. Joseph Gabel, *False Consciousness: An Essay on Reification*, tr. Margaret A. Thompson (New York: Harper and Row, 1975 [1962]).

19. Salvianus, *On the Government of God*, tr. Eva M. Sanford (New York: Columbia University Press, 1930), pp. 162–63. Tertullian, *Apology and De Spectaculis*, tr. T. R. Glover (New York: The Loeb Classical Library, 1931), p. 243.

at the end of *De Spectaculis*, citing 1 Corinthians (2:9), he asks: "But what are those things which eye hath not seen nor ear heard, nor ever entered into the heart of man? I believe, things of greater joy than circus, theatre or amphitheatre, or any stadium" (301). Because the invisible surrounds and in some sense transcends the visible, the reduction of experience to visual imagery by any cultural medium will seem to liquidate essence, leaving only the hollow forms of an idolatrous liturgy or of a narcissistic self-worship behind.

Spectacularity, at least partly intrinsic to the machinery of television itself, seems also to be the essence of most mass culture. According to Daniel Bell:

> Mass entertainments (circuses, spectacles, theaters) have always been visual, but there are two distinct aspects of contemporary life that necessarily emphasize the visual element. First, the modern world is an urban world. Life in the great city and the way stimuli and sociability are defined provide a preponderance of occasions for people to *see*, and *want* to see (rather than read and hear) things. Second is the nature of the contemporary temper, with its hunger for action (as against contemplation), its search for novelty, and its lust for sensation.[20]

"Temper" begs the question of what shapes it, so that Bell's second explanation must be referred to the first one, or to other sources of the contemporary emphasis on the visual, such as television. In any case, the tendency toward the visual and consequently toward the superficial and immediately apprehensible is strong in many cultural formations that come to be widely shared, from plays and circuses to cinema and television. Commercial television, in fact, aims just at this quality of superficiality: anything deeper or more difficult will fail to hold the attention of large audiences for long periods of time. This tendency has nothing to do with the intelligence or sophistication of the audience (despite Bell's assertion about the weaknesses of the "contemporary temper," which are not very different from Ortega's strictures against the mindlessness of the masses). Superficiality (a near synonym for spectacularity) is rather the result of deliberate commercial attempts to produce cultural forms that are consumable through mini-

20. Daniel Bell, *The Cultural Contradictions of Capitalism* (New York: Basic, 1976), pp. 105–6.

mum effort by the maximum number of people—just the opposite, of course, of what is valued by those classicist theories that stress difficulty, profundity, and "aura" as elements of cultural worth.

Jerzy Kosinski's fable about an illiterate gardener who soars to media and political stardom can be read as a study of spectacularity. At the start of *Being There*, Chance has never ventured beyond the confines of the Old Man's house and garden; his only source of information about the outside world has been television. He is like those cases of "wild children" so fascinating to psychologists, only instead of having been lost in the wilderness and reared by animals, he has been lost in the city and reared by television. Educated electronically, he cannot read and write; he is a complete "videot"; and he himself has no more reality than the TV image that he mimicks. But it is as an image that he functions and succeeds in the real world, after he has been evicted from the Old Man's house. The perfect student of the mass media, Chance soars to stardom once the media discover him, and by the end of the tale he is being touted as the perfect candidate for the vice-presidency (in the movie, the presidency). Throughout most of the story, however, Chance's only ambition is to become even more thoroughly an image and a media creature than he already is. It is his way of belonging, because he can relate to other people only through television. "Chance . . . wanted to see himself reduced to the size of the screen; he wanted to become an image, to dwell inside the set." And yet: "Television reflected only people's surfaces; it also kept peeling their images from their bodies until they were sucked into the caverns of their viewers' eyes, forever beyond retrieval, to disappear. Facing the cameras with their unsensing triple lenses pointed at him like snouts, Chance became only an image for millions of real people. They would never know how real he was."[21] The fear of the mass reproduction of images, reducing people themselves to the unreal status of phantoms, is here brought to a paranoid extreme; the tube sucks the life's blood from individuals and leaves them with even less authenticity than images on glass. Kosinski sums up those theo-

21. Jerzy Kosinski, *Being There* (New York: Bantam, 1972 [1971]), pp. 50 and 54. For a vivid expression of many of Kosinski's fears about television, see Gunther Anders. "The Phantom World of TV," *Dissent*, 3 (1956), 14–24, reprinted in Bernard Rosenberg and David Manning White, eds., *Mass Culture: The Popular Arts in America* (Glencoe, Ill.: The Free Press, 1957), pp. 358–67.

ries, running from Lasch, DeBord, and Mander back to Ortega, Eliot, Jaspers, and beyond, that see all manifestations of mass culture in terms of psychological vampirism. Chance's videocy is the hollowness of all previous "mass men" writ large. And his unwitting political triumph reflects the connection made in both conservative and radical theories between the mass media and the demise of democratic institutions. "For me," writes Kosinski, "imagining groups of solitary individuals watching their private, remote-controlled TV sets is the ultimate future terror: a nation of videots."[22] In *Being There*, Kosinski offers an updated version of *1984*, with television playing the role of Big Brother.

ii

Kosinski's novel can also be read as a negative version of the theories of Marshall McLuhan. Different though they seem, Kosinski and McLuhan share several assumptions about the impact of the mass media on present culture and future society. First, they both attribute enormous influence to the media, giving them primacy or near primacy among causal factors in contemporary social change. Second, they both tend to assume that "the medium is the message," or at least that form in communications is more important than content. Third, they both believe that the electronic media are causing a decline of verbal literacy. And fourth, they both assume that the mass media are capable of reshuffling the cards of identity, or that television can erase the personal characteristics of individuals and replace them with others—"mass" characteristics in Kosinski and "tribal" ones in McLuhan. On the same set of assumptions it is clearly possible to construct visions of the future that are either bleak or utopian. Viewed in this light, Kosinskism is a pessimistic version of McLuhanism, in which the mechanical optimist's future global village is replaced by a global Buchenwald.

To put it the other way around, the mass culture theories of both Kosinski and McLuhan can be understood as versions of negative classicism. Though McLuhan is a technological optimist, he often

22. Jerzy Kosinski, "A Nation of Videots: An Interview with David Sohn," *Media and Methods*, 11 (April 1975), 24–31, 52–57.

seems merely to be putting a cheerful face on the apocalyptic fears of writers like Kosinski and the Frankfurt theorists, who perceive mass-mediated culture as involving the destruction of enlightenment (or enlightenment committing suicide, as in Adorno and Horkheimer), the decline and fall of past high culture, and the death of freedom. The communications machinery that McLuhan places at the center of history seems to run on its own momentum, without human agency. The machines talk to us, concoct our dreams, flood our minds with images, and we do their bidding. Such a reified treatment of technology sounds dystopian, but McLuhan's gospel of communications is full of utopian anticipations.

In *Understanding Media* (1964), McLuhan observes that "each new technology creates an environment that is itself regarded as corrupt and degrading."[23] Perhaps this is the law governing all classicisms: the difficulty of accepting the new casts a utopian glow over the old. McLuhan adds: "When writing was new, Plato transformed the old oral dialogue into an art form. When printing was new the Middle Ages became an art form. . . . And the industrial age turned the Renaissance into an art form." (*UM* viii) McLuhan's argument should serve as a warning against any easy condemnation of a new technology, communications medium, or art form as decadent. Socrates, he reminds us, was opposed to writing because he thought it would erode memory. Similarly, many contemporary culture critics are opposed to television, radio, and cinema because they think they will erode literacy. Not that they are wrong: McLuhan himself announces the death of verbal literacy in terms nearly as dramatic as Nietzsche's announcement of the death of God in *The Gay Science*. Perhaps McLuhan's is the more disturbing declaration, at least for intellectuals who turn to books rather than to the supernatural for both social and personal salvation. McLuhan appears almost to be announcing the death of culture.

Like Kosinski, most writers look upon the alleged decline and fall of literacy with dismay. This is John Simon's reaction, for example, in *Paradigms Lost: Reflections on Literacy and Its Decline* (1980). Similarly, in *Strictly Speaking: Will America Be the Death of English?*

---

23. Marshall McLuhan, *Understanding Media: The Extensions of Man* (New York: McGraw-Hill, 1965 [1964]), p. viii. Abbreviated as *UM* in the text.

(1974), Edwin Newman (of all people! one of television's "talking heads") tells us everything we ever wanted to know about "the decline in language"—especially other people's language—blaming it at least partly on television. If there are more linguistic Cassandras now than ever before in history (and they have always existed), that is in part a result of the influence of McLuhan, a reformed English teacher. But the facts showing a decline in literacy are either slim or nonexistent. College entrance exam scores and similar evidence may show declines in levels of reading and writing skills among some groups compared to previous generations, but they also show increases among some other groups. And they do not show an increase in actual illiteracy. Moreover, figures showing how little the average person reads as compared with how much television the same statistical abstraction watches have no bearing on the idea of a decline in literacy: the same average person today may be reading more—as well as watching 100 percent more television—than the average person five or ten decades ago. And as Walter J. Ong has noted, McLuhan is simply mistaken in arguing as though each new communications medium pushes aside all previous ones. Print did not eliminate writing, and television is not abolishing the book. Each new medium alters the ways in which earlier ones are needed and used, but without obliterating them. Thus, the idea that television is causing the death of verbal literacy is illogical from several angles.[24]

But illogical ideas often have great influence, especially when they achieve the status of myth. This is true of negative classicism in most of its forms, and it is also true of the idea of a decline of literacy—one of the many minor variations of negative classicism. Though aware that most intellectuals will view the idea of the demise of verbal literacy with horror, McLuhan himself is sanguine about the future. He reverses most of the judgments about mass culture made by the Frankfurt theorists. Far from a classicist in any ordinary sense, McLuhan is, with some reservations, a cheerfully apocalyptic modernist. For one thing, the old verbal literacy will be replaced by a new visual literacy, based on the electronic mass media. For another, McLuhan views the dying book-based culture as something less than

24. Walter J. Ong, *Interfaces of the Word: Studies in the Evolution of Consciousness and Culture* (Ithaca: Cornell University Press, 1977), p. 82.

worthy of preservation. The "Gutenberg galaxy"—book-oriented, linear, alphabetic—blinded its creators and participants to much and also isolated them from each other, leading to nationalism, imperialism, and modern global warfare. In contrast, the new visual culture (which, McLuhan thinks, is even more "tactile" than visual, at least in the case of television) will put us back in touch with each other, restoring lost community and uniting us harmoniously in one "global village." Print "detribalizes"; television "retribalizes." By "retribalize," McLuhan does not exactly mean "barbarize," but neither does he dodge the primitivistic implications of his theories. As he says in *Take Today: The Executive as Dropout* (1972), "The new *avant-garde* is the primitive."[25] By avant-garde, McLuhan appears to mean not experimental artists, but the new generation of media addicts about whom Nicholas Johnson, Jerry Mander, and others are concerned. This latest generation is even classicist in a crazy way, because it retreats into the past to find the form of the future: "The mystery of retrieval of ancient forms amidst innovation has been universally manifested in the recovery of the Middle Ages in many of its forms by the young TV generation" (*TT* 167). In his book on careers in television, Bob Shanks remarks that cave dwellers made gathering around the fire a ritual that has lasted through the ages: we repeat it today by gathering around the "cool fire" of television. Shanks adopts this image from McLuhan, "a kind of media messiah" who has prophesied that "all the tribes of the world will one day gather around the cool fire in a common 'global village.'"[26]

McLuhan's retribalization theory may not offer an exact parallel to conservative and Marxist ideas of regenerative barbarism, but there is another reason for comparing McLuhanism at least with Marxism. Marx asserts the causal primacy in history of economic modes of production, which have a formative influence (although not, for Marx, a completely determining one) over all other manifestations of social life, including culture. The economic "base" supports and in some large, vague way shapes the cultural "superstructure." Though com-

25. Marshall McLuhan and Barrington Nevitt, *Take Today: The Executive as Dropout* (New York: Harcourt Brace Jovanovich, 1972), p. 263. Abbreviated as *TT* in the text.
26. Bob Shanks, *The Cool Fire: How to Make It in Television* (New York: Norton, 1976), pp. ix–x.

munications technology replaces economic base in his essays, McLuhan offers much the same kind of argument. Communications technology itself may be viewed as part of the economic base (though it may also be seen as an ambiguously mixed category, somewhere between base and superstructure). Given the centrality of "the culture industry" for the Frankfurt Institute Marxists, McLuhan's stress on the mass media as causal factors in history might almost be mistaken for a Canadian version of Horkheimer and Adorno. But the differences are obvious. Even the most deterministic variety of Marxism still leads to an insistence on the need for political action to achieve social change. McLuhan, however, suggests that the program of history is fixed from the beginning, that political action is pointless because the real causes of social change are beyond human control, and anyway that the goal of history is a utopian (albeit "tribal") harmony, so that there is no reason to seek change. Despite the fact that his theme is violent social and cultural upheaval, McLuhan is an apologist for the mass media and for the ever-changing status quo.

McLuhan's philosophy of history is based on the neo-Darwinian theology of Pierre Teilhard de Chardin and on the ideas of Harold Innis, who in *Empire and Communications* (1950) and *The Bias of Communications* (1951) argues that large-scale social changes are "facilitated" if not exactly "caused" by innovations in communications technology. Tracing the effects on social structure of stone, papyrus, parchment, and paper, Innis concludes that light, portable media (papyrus, paper) facilitate extension in space, whereas heavy, less portable or less reproducible media (stone, parchment) facilitate extension in time. The "space-binding" media lead to imperial expansion and secularization; the "time-binding" media, to decentralization and the development of social institutions focused on religion. Applied to television, Innis's idea of "space-binding" media might approximate Joseph Gabel's analysis of the substitution of space for time in false consciousness and schizophrenia. At any rate, a combination of two media—papyrus and parchment, for example—also favors the rise of empires. According to Innis:

> Concentration on a medium of communication implies a bias in the cultural development of the civilization concerned either towards an emphasis on space and political organization or towards an emphasis on time and religious organization. Introduction of a second medium

tends to check the bias of the first and to create conditions suited to the growth of empire. The Byzantine empire emerged from a fusion of a bias incidental to papyrus in relation to political organization and of parchment in relation to ecclesiastical organization.[27]

All of Innis's arguments have an after-the-fact quality: because both papyrus and parchment were used in Byzantium, he suggests that they facilitated its rise; because mainly papyrus was used in Rome, he suggests that it facilitated its rise. Innis also explains the decline of Rome as a result partly of the loss of the Egyptian papyrus industry. Despite his use of vague terms like "facilitated" rather than unequivocal ones like "caused" and his attempt to adduce evidence in a responsible, scholarly manner, Innis offers a monocausal theory of the rise and fall of empires hardly distinguishable from explanations of Rome's fall by lead poisoning, or by climactic change, or by the neurotic foibles of this or that emperor.

Innis's theories undergo both an expansion and a loss of scholarly rectitude in McLuhan. Perhaps it would be fair to say that McLuhan plays Engels to Innis's Marx. Just as Engels's popularizations rendered Marx's theories more deterministic than they in fact are, so McLuhan transforms Innis's soft technological determinism into something much harder. Innis likes the vague term "bias," suggesting that a particular communications medium gives a society a tendency or direction toward a certain kind of organization. McLuhan foregoes vagueness for the capricious certitude of headline rhetoric: "HEIDEGGER SURF-BOARDS ALONG ON THE ELECTRONIC WAVE AS TRIUMPHANTLY AS DESCARTES RODE THE MECHANICAL WAVE," reads one of the headlines (for that is what McLuhan is mimicking) in *The Gutenberg Galaxy*.[28] Another one reads: "PRINT, IN TURNING THE VERNACULARS INTO MASS MEDIA, OR CLOSED SYSTEMS, CREATED THE UNIFORM, CENTRALIZING FORCES OF MODERN NATIONALISM" (*GG* 199). The strident quality of this assertion contrasts sharply with its original in Innis, who writes: "With printing, paper facilitated an effective development of the vernaculars and gave expression to their

27. Harold A. Innis, *Empire and Communications* (Oxford: Clarendon, 1950), p. 216.

28. Marshall McLuhan, *The Gutenberg Galaxy: The Making of Typographic Man* (Toronto: University of Toronto Press, 1965 [1962]), p. 248. Abbreviated as *GG* in the text.

vitality in the growth of nationalism."[29] McLuhan asserts far too much. Innis, despite contrary appearances, asserts very little.

McLuhan's headline translations of Innis's vague hypotheses involve both a hardening of their deterministic implications and an emphasis upon their apocalyptic features. Innis is an economic historian, more concerned with the past than with present or future. It has been left to his disciple to apply his theories to modern communications media such as television. Despite numerous historical pronouncements, McLuhan is essentially a prophet, riding the waves of "future shock" on the same surfboard as his version of Martin Heidegger—or, more appropriately, as his version of Teilhard de Chardin. For it is from Teilhard that McLuhan draws the idea that, beyond turning the world into a "global village," the mass media are evolving into an immense "overmind" or "noösphere." Extensions of people as are all tools and technologies, the electronic media are forming a world brain or collective consciousness that will translate us into ultimate evolutionary perfection. But some of McLuhan's language describing Teilhard's theory falls short of utopian optimism, sounding instead like negative classicism:

> This externalization of our senses creates what [Teilhard] de Chardin calls the "noösphere" or a technological brain for the world. Instead of tending towards a vast Alexandrian library the world has become a computer, an electronic brain, exactly as in an infantile piece of science fiction. And as our senses have gone outside us, Big Brother goes inside. So, unless aware of this dynamic, we shall at once move into a phase of panic terrors, exactly befitting a small world of tribal drums, total interdependence, and superimposed co-existence. [GG 32]

Perhaps the present trends toward negative classicism and apocalyptic dread correspond to the "phase of panic terrors" McLuhan warns of. But it is difficult to distinguish McLuhanism itself from negative classicism, except that the former cheerfully embraces the mass media and mass culture despite occasional ominous language about the internalization of Big Brother.

McLuhan shares with negative classicism a sense of the violent disruption of past culture and society by the mass media. His rosy

29. Innis, *Empire and Communications*, p. 216.

vision of the future beams through a rhetoric of "bomb culture" violence and imagined endings, alphas and omegas, a version of history
that "explodes" and "implodes" in response to technological innovation:

> We know from our own past the kind of energy that is released, as by
> fission, when literacy explodes the tribal family unit. What do we
> know about the social and psychic energies that develop by electric
> fusion or implosion when literate individuals are suddenly gripped
> by an electromagnetic field such as occurs in the new Common
> Market pressure in Europe? Make no mistake, the fusion of people
> who have known individualism and nationalism is not the same pro-
> cess as the fission of "backward" and oral cultures that are just
> coming to individualism and nationalism. It is the difference be-
> tween the "A" bomb and the "H" bomb. The latter is more violent,
> by far.   [*UM* 50]

History is not clearly cyclic for McLuhan (despite "retribalization"), as
it is for most negative classicists; rather, it is both progressive and
catastrophic, as it tends to be in Marx. Each new communications
medium "explodes" or "implodes" society into a new phase. Because
there are many media (clocks, clothes, bicycles, movies, etc., down to
television and computers), history goes by jolts and leaps. But the
cosmic collision between the Gutenberg galaxy and the onrushing
media galaxy is especially violent, transforming all the terms of social
life even as it offers the prospect of peace and harmony in the global
tribal village of the future. McLuhanism involves a sort of big bang
theory of history and the mass media. And the main electronic medium involved in the smash-up with print and past culture is television.

Perhaps nothing has contributed more to McLuhan's success than
the fact that he offers a cheerful version of negative classicism, a
prophetic and total reading of past and future according to which all
will be well because all will be well. His vision offers hope to anyone
who would like to believe that technology will rescue the world from
the traps and disasters that technology has helped produce. "There is
a deep faith to be found in this new attitude," McLuhan writes of his
old Panglossism, "a faith that concerns the ultimate harmony of all
beings" (*UM* 5–6). McLuhan offers descriptions and indictments of
decadence, but these are associated with the past rather than with the
future. Innocence was lost when Gutenberg fell: with the printing

press, mankind was thrust out of its tribal garden into the harsh world of typographical literacy, and things have been in an unhealthy state ever after. "Since nearly all our technologies and entertainment since Gutenberg have been not cool, but hot; and not deep, but fragmentary; not producer-oriented, but consumer-oriented, there is scarcely a single area of established relationships, from home and church to school and market, that has not been profoundly disturbed in its pattern and texture" (*UM* 312). Thus McLuhan reverses the diagnosis of most mass culture critics, who see decadence in our falling away from the book and who discover "videocy" and losses of political freedom in the cultural domination of the electronic media. McLuhan's version of Roman decadence also attributes an unhealthy influence to verbal literacy in the evolution of the "bread and circuses" syndrome. Arguing that the separation of producer and consumer caused by the division of labor leads to decay, an idea that again approximates Marxism, McLuhan says:

> Before Roman literate bureaucracy, nothing comparable to the Roman consumer specialists had been seen in the world. This fact was institutionalized in the individual known as "parasite," and in the social institution of the gladiatorial games. (*Panem et circenses.*) The private sponge and the collective sponge, both reaching out for their rations of sensation, achieved a horrible distinctness and clarity that matched the raw power of the army machine. [*UM* 100–101]

McLuhan here obviously parts company from Harold Innis, who attributes the rise of the Roman Empire largely to the development of a literate and efficient bureaucracy and its fall largely to the harm done to that bureaucracy by the demise of the papyrus industry.

McLuhan's version of the Roman experience leads him to deny rather than to assert parallels with the modern experience. Mankind was traveling a Roman road before the advent of the mass media, but the global village that McLuhan foresees will be the antithesis of imperialism. There is an obvious way, of course, in which the world is shrinking through new communications and transport technologies (as well as through overpopulation, which McLuhan ignores). Many studies of the international impact of television and the communications industries, however, do not present happy pictures of a global village in which lion shall lie down with lamb, but dismal pictures of what Alan Wells has called "picture tube imperialism." No doubt print did provide a spur to the growth of national consciousness in and around the sixteenth century in parts of Europe, but nationalism and imperialism both reached their ugly apogee in the twentieth century, unhampered—in fact, abetted—by radio, telegraph, telephone, airplane, steamship, and efficient postal service. Television as a mechanism does not add anything to the peace- and village-making powers of these other world-spanning technologies. As Herbert Schiller says in *Mass Communications and American Empire*:

> Unavailable to expansionists of earlier times, modern mass communications perform a double service for their present-day controllers. At home, they help to overcome, by diversion in part, the lack of popular enthusiasm for the global role of imperial stewardship. Abroad, the antagonism to a renewed though perhaps less apparent colonial servitude has been quite successfully . . . deflected and confused by the images and messages which originate in the United States but which flow continuously over and through local information media.[30]

If Schiller's analysis of the international impact of American mass media is added to Lasch's or Mander's vision of the psychological and social vampirism of television, any notion of a utopia throbbing euphorically to the rhythms of electronic tom-toms must be condemned as naive or as a new version of fascism.

At the same time, more clearly than any other recent cultural theorist, McLuhan recognizes the utopian potentiality of the mass media. He too readily assumes that the mere existence of television and computers is breaking down nationalism and other blindnesses that, he believes, print-based culture has caused. But he provides an important counter to the mythology of negative classicism which dominates recent culture theory and which obscures certain liberating forces, at least some of which are—as McLuhan insists—inherent in the technology of mass communications. The electronic "noösphere" or international culture now evolving continues to reflect nationalism and to be controlled by commercial, ideological, imperialistic interests, but in his dramatic way McLuhan points to possible uses of

---

30. Herbert I. Schiller, *Mass Communications and American Empire* (Boston: Beacon, 1971), p. 2. See also Alan Wells, *Picture Tube Imperialism?* (Maryknoll, N.Y.: Orbis, 1972).

the mass media that lie beyond and would subvert those interests. These uses will remain mere potentialities, however, so long as the present institutional structures of the mass media remain unchanged.

From the heady, apocalyptic patterns of thought that television inspires, it seems anticlimactic to turn to practical questions of the improvement of program content and the reform of cultural institutions. But most theoretical perspectives—whether Marxist, conservative, McLuhanist, or something else—seem to lead to one form or another of historical determinism and therefore to short-circuit practice. Because television cannot be isolated from its institutional contexts and uses, it is illogical to argue that the medium by itself is leading us down either a rosy path to a utopian global village or a rocky path to a totalitarian videocracy. Government-dominated television in the Soviet Union is already totalitarian, but not because of the medium. But what about the business-dominated television of the United States? There are two main obstacles in the way of feeling optimistic about television as it has evolved in this country. One is that the commercialization of culture co-opts, blurs, or just drowns out criticism of the status quo. To use the language of Adorno and Horkheimer, what the three commercial networks produce is "ideology" and "hegemony," not "enlightenment." The second obstacle is that the television industry operates as a virtual monopoly subject at best only to "imperfect competition." The enormous power that both its critics and its defenders attribute to television rests in America in large part with the three commercial networks, which decide what viewers see, hear, and to some indefinable but obviously very large extent think. In the case of totalitarian socialism, the problem for democracy is clear enough. In the case of capitalist society, the problem may be shadowed by various illusions of freedom, but is just as clear: to break down monopolistic patterns of ownership and decision making and to make communications systems as flexible and responsive to local, democratic, and individual needs as possible. The history of cable television in the United States offers a good example of how a democratic potential, inherent in a new technology, can be deflected by existing institutions. Cable promises diversification and local control. While it has meant more channels to watch, however, local cable companies have been bought up or controlled by the networks and program content follows the old patterns.

The entrenched power of the television networks and the other mass media causes reform efforts to look quixotic and deflects theory into deterministic paths. In this context, negative classicism often seems truer than cautiously hopeful pronouncements about increased "accessibility" and the application of mass communications to community uses. The historian of American broadcasting, Erik Barnouw, might therefore be pronouncing the last word on television when he writes: "In this sense the overwhelming absorption of tens of millions of mid-twentieth century Americans in football games and struggles against cattle rustlers was a political achievement. Along with welfare legislation, it seemed an American equivalent of the Roman 'bread and circuses.'"31

Barnouw is aware, however, that for all their similarity to Roman spectacles, the modern mass media are historically without precedents. Television provides free "spectacle" for the masses, and it clearly also acts to reinforce hegemony. But it acts in other ways, too, and suggests still more uses that could involve worldwide increases in understanding, knowledge, political accommodation, and cultural growth of the kind McLuhan foresees. These improved uses will not come about automatically, as a result of some inherent tendency to enlightenment in the machinery of television itself. On the contrary, partly because of its visual-spatial nature, the machinery seems to have an opposite tendency. It must be used with great care if it is to enhance enlightenment. How far short television now falls of its potential for enlightenment can be seen in the large number of pessimistic and deterministic theories it spawns, or in other words in its present obvious affinity for negative classicism.

The spectacular qualities of television seem to cry out for Roman analogies. According to Umberto Eco in his essay, "Are We Going Towards a Visual Civilization?": "A democratic civilization will save itself only if it will make the language of the image into a stimulus to critical reflection, not an invitation to hyponosis." Eco's remark points to a possible program of reform through semiological analysis—a program perhaps like Roland Barthes's critique of mass culture "mythologies," coupled with some institutional manner of making such a

---

31. Erik Barnouw, *Tube of Plenty: The Evolution of American Television* (London: Oxford University Press, 1977 [1975]), p. 367.

critique effective, perhaps through the schools. But for those who believe that imagery is inevitably linked to myth, false consciousness, schizophrenia, and the substitute dreamwork of artful propagandists, Eco's observation can offer no hope. Elèmire Zolla, who sees mass-mediated imagery as the cause of "the eclipse of the intellectual" and consequently of the downfall of civilization, declares that Eco's remark is like saying: "If we can find alcohol that makes us sober and temperate, we will be saved from alcoholism."[32] Given a world of hollow mass men and "somnambulists" whose heads have been stuffed with the industrialized dreamwork of Hollywood and Madison Avenue, Zolla thinks there is little for it but a retreat into stoicism. Intellectuals should not "collaborate in our own ruin by making ourselves into what the barbarians have not yet succeeded in making of us," says Zolla. "We can break the spell of the movie house, just as Marcus Aurelius escaped the mimes and the gladiators" (202). But meanwhile the world at large—the masses, and possibly "we" intellectuals as members of the masses—surrender to the latest products of industrialized romanticism:

> So we are flung into a world of dreams produced by industry, no longer fabricated individually by the addicts. We are obliged to make a distinction not only between dream and authentic reality but also between contaminated and uncontaminated reality, and if we ever manage to free ourselves from this clinging mud, we are seized by horror before the mob of somnambulists who hem us in on every side. But just as only peoples weakened by decay are overcome by the barbarians, so only a humanity that has renounced reality in favor of the dream could succumb to the industry of the dream. [219]

In his remarks on industrialized dreamwork and somnambulism, Zolla offers a modern version on a mass scale of Augustine's story about the seduction of Alypius by the games, with a moral for intellectuals close to Seneca's belief that "Nothing is so ruinous to good character as to spend time at any spectacle."[33] For the masses, Zolla thinks, there is

---

32. Elèmire Zolla, *The Eclipse of the Intellectual*, tr. Raymond Rosenthal (New York: Funk & Wagnalls, 1968), p. 222.

33. Seneca, *Ad Lucilium Epistulae Morales*, ed. L. D. Reynolds (Oxford: Clarendon, 1965), letter vii: 2, vol. I, p. 12.

no question of "good character." But for the intellectuals, their very existence is at stake—the seductions of the modern circuses, the mass media, are powerful and pervasive—and if the intellectuals fall, who then will defend true culture from the barbarians? This fear underlies Zolla's account of the corrosive effect of bread and circuses on ancient civilization, which is being repeated and intensified by the mass media today:

> Ancient tragedy began to decline from the times of Andronicus and Lucius Accius because of the circuses, but disgust was always vivid among liberal men. Cicero expressed it to Atticus, and Pliny approved of Mauricius, who hoped for the abolition of the games, while the pedagogues taught Marcus Aurelius not to degrade himself by siding with the circus factions. The Spartans forbade the helots and perioeci to sing the lyrics of Ademan and Terpander, leaving them only vulgar dances and ridiculous songs: an inhuman and horrifying standard of conduct which, however, contained the distinction between human and vulgar recreation. Today this distinction is being destroyed, and to the circuses that corrupted the Roman nation are added the willfully vulgar spectacles of the radio, television, and movies. So the pressure is greatly increased. What is even worse, this industry that fixes the mass in its subhuman characteristics is no longer isolated by a reaction of horror. [161]

If television is making the world a smaller place, it is doing so through the production of spectacularity in the form of mediocre (or worse) programs that stimulate narcissism rather than true self-reflection and public involvement. It undermines a possible enlightenment by exchanging its brilliant, insistent imagery and its brazen consumer ideology for our vague ideas. Joseph Conrad, who knew something about civilization and savagery—who knew especially how easily civilization can revert to savagery—might have been describing the social effects of television when he wrote about the "civilizing zeal" of Mr. Kurtz—or, better, when he wrote about the mercenary zeal of the Eldorado Exploring Expedition: "Their talk . . . was the talk of sordid buccaneers: it was reckless without hardihood, greedy without audacity, and cruel without courage; there was not an atom of foresight or of serious intention in the whole batch of them, and they did not seem aware these things are wanted for the work of the world. To tear treasure out of the bowels of the land was their desire, with no more moral purpose at the back of it than there is in burglars breaking into a safe." Light comes from the boxes in our living rooms and there seems to be no distinction just now between it and the light of Western civilization. But this is only another way of saying that this also is "one of the dark places on the earth." Marlow adds: "I was thinking of very old times, when the Romans first came here, nineteen hundred years ago"—but he is also thinking, of course, about the modern world.

CHAPTER 9

Conclusion: Toward
Post-Industrial Society

We see now that the abyss of history is deep enough to hold us all.

—PAUL VALÉRY

TOO often responses to cultural innovations are similar to William Wordsworth's reaction to *The Illustrated London News*. Upon seeing one of the first issues of the new journal in 1846, Wordsworth was appalled by what he took to be its wholesale substitution of pictures for words. On the verge of the age of mass literacy, here seemed to be an obvious symptom of cultural decline. He saw in its pages not just a barbarization of culture but a return to caveman days, at least if we are to take literally his sonnet "Illustrated Books and Newspapers," which is a kind of McLuhanesque elegy upon the disappearance of "discourse," the "written word," and "printing." The sestet reads:

> A backward movement surely have we here,
> From manhood—back to childhood; for the age—
> Back towards caverned life's first rude career.
> Avaunt this vile abuse of pictured page!
> Must eyes be all in all, the tongue and ear
> Nothing? Heaven keep us from a lower stage.[1]

Perhaps Wordsworth sensed the treacherous superficiality of the visual. But rather than interpreting *The Illustrated London News* as a symptom of cultural decay it seems better to regard it as a symptom of

1. William Wordsworth, "Illustrated Books and Newspapers," *Complete Poems* (Oxford: Oxford University Press, 1965), p. 383.

the spread of literacy and information to the newly formed bourgeois public and urban-industrial masses. Wordsworth overlooked the fact that the new journal was full of words as well as pictures. Like Socrates' fears of writing, his sonnet may stand as an example of negative classicism at its most irrational, condemning as regressive or decadent any innovation whose cultural potential it fails to appreciate.

At the same time, negative classicism as it has developed from the nineteenth century forward has consistently pointed to weaknesses in the emergent mass culture and to contradictions in industrialized society which are far from imaginary. The Roman circuses may be a good analogy for television, for example, for a number of reasons: they both substitute immediate, visual experience for anything deeper or less immediate; they both impinge from above or outside on mass audiences of nonparticipatory spectators; they both seem to substitute false experiences of community or "destructive *Gemeinschaft*" for something more genuine; and the "sex and violence" content of commercial television appeals, like the Roman games, to sadomasochistic instincts.

In dwelling upon these and other similarities between "bread and circuses" and modern mass culture, however, negative classicism often ignores the considerable differences between them. The similarities are taken to mean that we are locked in a cyclic pattern of decline and fall: after the circuses come the barbarians and a new Dark Age. To some hard-to-define extent, the structure of a mass medium like television clearly does shape history, but to suggest that it is the main or even the only shaper is to succumb to historical fatalism. To believe that the present institutional arrangements of the media are so monolithic and entrenched as to be inaccessible to change is likewise fatalistic. Avoiding these theoretical impasses, Raymond Williams has insisted upon the idea—or ideal—of a common culture as something to be achieved, rather than as something that either just happens or fails to happen as a by-product of technologies and modes of production. In *Television: Technology and Cultural Form* (1974), Williams argues that all communications media—all machinery, in fact—are the results of conscious intention. Rather than the deterministic formulation: "technology alters our world," Williams insists on another, radical formulation: "we alter our world through technology."[2] Like all

2. Raymond Williams, *Television: Technology and Cultural Form* (New York: Schocken, 1975 [1974]), p. 128.

technological determinisms, the first formulation reifies technology, even though technology is obviously man-made. The second formulation may exaggerate the chances for change (although Williams recognizes the great complexity and intractability of many social patterns), but it also seeks to reverse reification, to return the tools to their makers.

Such an approach leads Williams to a condemnation of McLuhanism as an ideology "welcomed by the 'media-men' of the existing institutions. It gives the gloss of avant-garde theory to the crudest versions of their existing interests and practices, and assigns all their critics to pre-electronic irrelevance" (128). In McLuhan's work, Williams adds, "as in the whole formalist tradition, the media were never really seen as practices" but merely as "psychic adjustments." The result is that, for McLuhan, "intention . . . is irrelevant, and with intention goes content." This means in turn that "all media operations are in effect desocialized," even though, Williams notes, "it is then interesting that from this wholly unhistorical and asocial base McLuhan projects certain images of society: 'retribalisation' by the 'electronic age'; the 'global village'. [But] as descriptions of any observable social state or tendency, in the period in which electronic media have been dominant, these are . . . ludicrous" (127–28).

Williams avoids any version of negative classicism that equates television with inevitable decadence and barbarization. By his logic, any theory or any cultural medium that does not work to expand democratic choice might well be considered decadent. But the techniques of mass communications themselves are "at worst neutral." They are more "impersonal" than earlier techniques, but they also add to the precious human stock of cultural forms and alternatives, the machinery of our potential collective intelligence and esthetic fulfillment. Difficulties arise when these techniques are put to exploitative uses— as Williams says, when the idea of "masses" is added to the idea of "communications." In this manner, the whole theory of mass communications comes to depend "on a minority in some way exploiting a majority."[3] And as Williams's *Modern Tragedy* makes plain, he sees no incompatibility between the machinery of television and cultural excellence or tragic vision. Television offers a range of alternative uses

3. Raymond Williams, *Culture and Society, 1780–1950* (New York: Harper and Row, 1966 [1958]), pp. 301, 314.

which, under capitalism, have narrowed to commercial exploitation. Under totalitarian socialism, they have narrowed to political exploitation. But television technology still offers the prospect of a "new universal accessibility."

"The medium is the message," however, to the extent that mass culture has inherent, structural tendencies that render it simultaneously liberating and totalitarian. Williams believes that it is totalitarian to the extent that it imposes a uniform product on its consumers, without real variation or choice, or to the extent that it is monologic instead of dialogic. But Williams downplays such structural features as its dependence on visual, immediate, and easily consumable images that contribute to its totalitarian monologic institutional structure. At the same time, the creation of a mass audience, increasingly on a global scale, who are both literate and knowledgeable about society at least to the extent that mass mediated news allows them to be, is an unprecedented historical achievement. "Bread and circuses" may be an apt metaphor for the sports and entertainment shows on commercial television; it does not fit the news, news documentaries, or much of what is now broadcast on educational stations around the world.

The problem to which Williams points is one partly of reducing the totalitarian and maximizing the liberating tendencies in all the mass media. The primary solution lies in the democratic control of the media. In both capitalist and communist countries, Williams believes, such democratic control would entail a radical restructuring of the institutions of mass culture. In the United States and Western Europe, it would entail the breakdown of corporate monopoly ownership and the socialization of the media at local, community, and national levels—at the very least, I would add, the treatment of the media as public utilities, with missions similar to publicly funded schools and universities. In the Soviet Union and Eastern Europe, I believe that it would entail abolishing centralized bureaucratic control and turning the machinery of mass culture over to democratic collectives like Solidarity in Poland. Because such restructurings are not now occurring and do not seem likely to occur in the near future, I also believe that some version of negative classicism is justified, although it can not be one that locates the cause of social breakdown in mass culture itself.

By itself, however, negative classicism is unlikely to offer directions for effecting the institutional changes just suggested. In neither capitalist nor communist countries, moreover, is there now a clear-cut historical agent—such as the proletariat, the public, or the intelligentsia—from whom such directions for change are emanating. But there remains the utopian promise of liberation inherent in the mass media themselves. This is the most positive, unpredictable feature in a social landscape that looks increasingly dismal and that in great measure merits the doomsaying of negative classicism. The bread and circuses analogy seems to be largely accurate insofar as it detects widespread social, cultural, and environmental decay behind the façades of technological progress; it seems to be most inaccurate when it finds in mass culture or the mass media a primary cause—in some versions, *the* primary cause—of that decay.

What, then, can be done—technologically, politically, educationally—to bring the liberating features of the mass media to the fore and to blunt or eliminate their totalitarian tendencies? Technological innovations that make for fuller, more varied, more democratic communications—two-way electronic hookups, satellite broadcasting, videodiscs, "communications webs," and so on—should be encouraged. Political reform movements that attempt to break down the monopolistic or totalitarian control of the institutions of mass culture should be encouraged. And educational attempts to improve or upgrade the intellectual quality of mass culture should be encouraged. The maximization of the liberating potential of the mass media may be a long way off; but they are the only machinery through which a genuine, global, "common culture" can be achieved. Technology cannot be the cure for the ailments caused by technology; the situation that led Thoreau to proclaim that "men have become the tools of their tools" must be reversed before the promise of liberation inherent in the mass media can be realized. But it is only through the opening doors of communications systems that "the masses" enter the field of history as something more than exploitable objects—as the possible agents of social change and the potential masters of their situation. If, as Marx held, the factories first called the masses into being, then the mass media first created the possibility of their solidarity, enlightenment, and ultimate freedom.

What shapes would a liberated, global, common culture take? Be-

sides Williams and McLuhan, a number of social theorists have specu-
lated about such a culture. As a variety of technological optimism,
McLuhan's "electronic theodicy" can be traced back to the early
stages of the Industrial Revolution, just as I have sought to trace
negative classicism back to the same period. According to James
Carey and John Quirk, McLuhanism is only one version of "an increasingly prevalent and popular brand of the futurist ethos that identifies electricity and electrical power, electronics and cybernetics,
with a new birth of community, decentralization, ecological balance
and social harmony. This set of notions is most readily associated
with . . . McLuhan, but his status as a celebrity merely obscures his
position in a school of thought that has been articulated . . . over
many decades and that has many spokesmen in our time."[4]

What Carey and Quirk call "the mythos of the electronic revolution" was expressed in the early 1970s by several writers who prophesied the emergence of a "knowledge society," based on the mass
media, computerization, and an expansion of the service sector of the
economy. According to Daniel Bell in *The Coming of Post-Industrial
Society* (1973), large-scale heavy industry and its economy are evolving into a society in which the "service" and "knowledge" industries
will be dominant. Automatization and computerization will transform
much blue-collar work, freeing people for other sorts of culturally
more advanced and rewarding jobs, and for greatly increased periods
of leisure. Instead of a new Dark Age, Bell thinks, we are headed
toward an age of potential enrichment for all. Bell's influential "venture in social forecasting" expresses several reservations about the
present social order, including the mass media, but his 1973 vision of
the future is not shadowed by the threats of decadence and barbarism.
The trouble with the media, Bell believes, is not that they are manufacturing one sort of darkness or another, but rather that they are
eroding privacy and adding up to a "communications overload," a glut
of knowledge.[5] Both effects are distressing, but both have their positive sides as well. If "psychic distance" or privacy is being eclipsed, so
is "social distance," including the breakdown of prejudice, racial and

4. James W. Carey and John J. Quirk, "The Mythos of the Electronic Revolution,"
Part 1, *The American Scholar*, 39 (Spring 1970), p. 220.
5. Daniel Bell, *The Coming of Post-Industrial Society: A Venture in Social Forecasting* (New York: Basic, 1976 [1973]), p. 316.

class divisions, and national and international conflicts. Although the "communications overload" produces bewilderment and anomie, another name for it might be cultural diversity.

> Whatever else may be said about the twentieth century, it has produced the greatest bombardment of aural and visual materials that man has ever experienced in his history. To the linotype, camera, typewriter, telephone, and telegraph, the twentieth century has added radio (and radio telephone), teletype, television, microwaves, communication satellites, computers, xerography, and the like. Transistors and miniaturization not only facilitate an incredible packaging of communication senders, receivers, and recorders in the confines of a space ship, they also allow automobile telephony, walkie-talkies, portable radio and television sets, and finally, on the agenda, person-to-person communication by "wrist-watch" radio anywhere in the country (and soon the world?).   [316]

Such a description suggests at least one fallacy in much writing about contemporary mass culture: although mass culture is monologic or one-way communication, the machinery of the mass media themselves is characterized by an increasing diversification. For Bell, the problem is not the narrowing of consciousness through massification and manipulation, but a kind of stupefaction by surfeit. He expresses other more familiar reservations about the effects of the mass media when he writes: "One may applaud the fact that the nature of the mass media increases the likelihood of a spectacular rise in 'participatory democracy,' but . . . instances [of democratic involvement] are also more likely to arise out of emotional issues . . . so that the loss of insulating space may itself permit the setting off of chain reactions which may be disruptive of civil politics and reasoned debate" (316). Thus Bell suggests that the masses, or those responding to the mass media, are likely to be irrational and possibly dangerous, just as Ortega, Freud, and Le Bon said they were.

Overall, however, *The Coming of Post-Industrial Society* offers a moderately optimistic account of how present economic, technological, and political trends are likely to be extended in the near future. Bell sees the future in terms of more of the same, only multiplied and improved. If "post-industrial society" will not be utopia, neither will it involve the collapse of civilization. But in his next book, published three years later, Bell's thinking turns in the direction of negative classicism. *The Cultural Contradictions of Capitalism* (1976) describes problems and crises—"the disjunction of realms"—that may prevent the evolution of a beneficent post-industrial order, leading instead to the emergence of new forms of repression and social disintegration. In his earlier book, Bell worries about how "contemporary culture, with the victory of modernism, has become anti-institutional and antinomian" (478). The values of the decadent and Bohemian artists of the nineteenth century, inimical to industrialism and the bourgeoisie, were then marginal. But the radical counterculture of the 1960s, Bell believes, shows that these same values have become dominant, so that there is a sharp "contradiction" between contemporary culture and the economic and political order. In particular, "the lack of a rooted moral belief system is the cultural contradiction of the society, the deepest challenge to its survival" (480).

In the earlier work, this problem sounds like a minor note in the context of the array of data and authorities Bell cites to flesh out the image of "post-industrial society." In the later book, the threat to society posed by "modern culture" is at the center of Bell's vision, which becomes correspondingly eschatological. Whereas in the earlier study "communications overload," though problematic, could be construed as the side effect of a healthy diversification, in the later one it is symptomatic of social breakdown. Contemporary culture is in "a shambles" both because of the mass media and because of what Bell calls "modernism," which he suggests is "demonic" and defines as "the disruption of *mimesis*."[6] There is "a lack of a center" in cultural affairs, and in the other "realms"—the economy and "polity"—as well. In the arts, confusion reigns partly because of a breakdown of the boundaries between high and mass culture. "High art itself is in disarray, if not 'decadent' (though that term has never been adequately defined); the 'public' is now so culturally voracious that the avant-garde, far from needing defenders among the critics, is in the public domain" (136). If high art degrades itself by entering the public domain, mass culture is already degraded, well down the road toward

---

6. Daniel Bell, *The Cultural Contradictions of Capitalism* (New York: Basic, 1976), pp. 169, 19, and 110.

social disintegration. Bell offers a pessimistic version of McLuhanism, according to which contemporary culture is picture- rather than print-based:

> The visual media—I mean here film and television—impose their pace on the viewer and, in emphasizing images rather than words, invite not conceptualization but dramatization. In the emphasis television news places on disasters and human tragedies, it invites not purgation or understanding but sentimentality and pity, emotions that are quickly exhausted, and a pseudo-ritual of a pseudo-participation in the events. And, as the mode is inevitably one of over-dramatization, the responses soon become either stilted or bored. [108]

Bell finds McLuhan's thesis of the unification of the world through the mass media "to be without much meaning, except on a trivial level." He adds: "If anything, the spread of wider communication nets tends to bring about the disintegration of larger societies into fragmentary ethnic and primordial units," and by "primordial" he seems to mean something like regressive (108).

According to Bell, both "modernism," in the sense of avant-garde or high art, and mass culture are expressing themselves in increasingly irrational and dangerous ways. The result is a conflict between the disruptive "hedonistic" culture and the rational, technological-economic sphere, with the democratic polity as a third sphere whose dissolution the conflict threatens. Almost all the disruption comes from the culture, from modernism and the mass media together; Bell does not squarely confront the question of the possible irrationality of the supposedly rational technological order. The economic sphere "emphasizes functional rationality, technocratic decision making, and meritocratic rewards"; the culture emphasizes "apocalyptic moods and anti-rational modes of behavior," no doubt including much negative classicism. Bell identifies this disjunction with nothing less than "the historic cultural crisis of all Western bourgeois society. This cultural contradition is . . . the most fateful division in the society" (84).

In contrast to his earlier post-industrial prophecy, the crisis Bell now predicts is similar to others in the past which were resolved only "over long historical time-frames." "It took almost 300 years for Christianity to become established in the Roman Empire, and as Gibbon remarked of the conversion of Constantine, Rome then passed into an intolerable phase of its history, a phase that lasted for 250 years" (175). Bell hopes that the liberal reforms of "the public household" which he recommends will forestall the decline and fall of the modern world, but part of the cure he prescribes again smacks of negative classicism. In the cultural realm, "there has been a double process of decay. On the institutional level there has been *secularization,* or the shrinking of the institutional authority and role of religion as a mode of community. On the cultural level there has been *profanation,* the attenuation of a theodicy as providing a set of meanings to explain man's relation to the beyond" (167). Bell seeks to reverse these decadent trends by a "great instauration," or revival of the sacred. He sees religious irrationality sprouting up everywhere, but these manifestations of the sacred he identifies with "cults," and hence with another aspect of the destructive chaos of modern culture. "Where religions fail, cults appear. This situation is the reverse of early Christian history, when the new coherent religion competed with the multiple cults and drove them out because it had the superior strength of a theology and an organization. But when theology erodes and organization crumbles, when the institutional framework of religion begins to break up, the search for a direct experience which people can feel to be religious facilitates the rise of cults" (168). What Bell is looking for is some analogue to the rise of Christianity—the "religious answer" to "the shambles of modern culture" (168).

From the cautious optimism of *The Coming of Post-Industrial Society,* Bell has shifted toward negative classicism, but apparently only with reluctance. Other "post-industrial" theorists have been less hesitant about aligning their theories with the mythology of decline and fall. McLuhan shows how the terms of a post-industrial eschatology can be rendered optimistically. Behind its doomsaying, negative classicism often looks forward to a barbarian renaissance or a new age of faith. In a chapter entitled "Meditation on the Dark Age, Past and Present," William Irwin Thompson, who agrees with many of McLuhan's ideas, argues enthusiastically that "industrial society is strangling in its own contradictions" and that "we are no longer living in civilization."[7] In common with Daniel Bell, Roberto Vacca, L. S. Stavrianos, Nicholas Berdyaev, William Morris, and many other writers back at least to Thomas Carlyle, Thompson has rediscovered "the promise of the coming Dark Age."[8]

For many artists and intellectuals, the nightmare is represented not by Rome's fall, but by its continued domination. Negative classicism becomes a hopeful, even utopian mythology to the extent that the downfall of capitalist or mass or technological society is longed for. On the one hand, a popular writer like Alvin Toffler offers an eschatological version of technological optimism that is mainly hopeful, and that therefore bears few traces of negative classicism. In "the book that makes sense of the exploding eighties," *The Third Wave*, Toffler echoes many of McLuhan's apocalyptic ideas, including his tidal imagery; his account of present and future social transformation shows that "the human story, far from ending, has only just begun."[9] On the other hand, another popular writer like Theodore Roszak, expressing more doubts about the future than Toffler, is more drawn to negative classicism. But Roszak also sees a utopian promise in the downfall of the present industrial world order, even though that promise is hard to discern behind such apocalyptic rhetoric as this:

> For those of us who feel the inherited mass and class identities of our age crumbling away, it is indeed as if a desert gathered about us. We ask who we are, what we are, where we are to turn . . . and there is no one who can answer for us. We must make our own path. We must, and we do. In an era that has sent astronauts to scale the mountains of the moon, it is tempting to entertain Promethean images of ourselves, to see ourselves as space pioneers and star voyagers. But . . . another image . . . may be better suited to our condition—something humbler, more somber, yet no less heroic: that of the first desert fathers making their way beyond the walls of a failing empire, searching for their salvation in the trackless waste.[10]

7. William Irwin Thompson, *Evil and World Order* (New York: Harper and Row, 1976), pp. 13 and 10.

8. L. S. Stavrianos, *The Promise of the Coming Dark Age* (San Francisco: Freeman, 1976); Roberto Vacca, *The Coming Dark Age* (Garden City, N. Y.: Doubleday, 1973 [1971]); Nicholas Berdyaev, *The End of Our Time* (New York: Sheed and Ward, 1933).

9. Alvin Toffler, *The Third Wave* (New York: Bantam, 1980), p. 1.

10. Theodore Roszak, *Person/Planet: The Creative Disintegration of Industrial Society* (Garden City, N. Y.: Doubleday, 1978), p. 286.

Roszak believes that salvation can be found in the acknowledgment of "the rights of the person" and "the rights of the planet," but these will entail a complete restructuring of industrial society.

Those post-industrial theorists like Roszak who advocate decentralization, a return to grass-roots democracy, and the scaling down of technology envisage a culture based on leisure, community, and equality, in harmony with the natural environment. They also conceive of that culture as universal, shared on a worldwide basis, outgrowing the violent nationalisms of the last two centuries, but without liquidating ethnic and communal diversity. Those who propound this vision—Ivan Illich and E. F. Schumacher, for instance—might be described as utopian negative classicists. According to Schumacher's "Buddhist economics," based on the prospect of an "intermediate" "technology with a human face," mass production "is inherently violent, ecologically damaging, self-defeating in terms of non-renewable resources, and stultifying for the human person."[11] Buddhist economics instead holds forth the prospect of a decentralized, democratic, ecologically safe technology of "production by the masses" (154). In comparable terms, Illich calls for the building of a "deschooled," decentralized society of "convivial tools." By "conviviality," Illich means "the opposite of industrial productivity," entailing "autonomous and creative intercourse among persons, and the intercourse of persons with their environment."[12] For Illich, dialogue is the measure of the presence or absence of genuine communication: mass culture by definition is a category of tools and artifacts that shut off dialogue, that are essentially monologic, that create "masses" of technicized, passive consumers divorced from authority over the means of production. The machines that we now have must be converted to convivial uses or thrown onto the junkpile of unplanned obsolescence. "Not even television must be ruled out" from the category of potentially convivial tools, however, though Illich is hesitant about making any positive claims for its dialogical possibilities—it has proved too

11. E. F. Schumacher, *Small is Beautiful: Economics as if People Mattered* (New York: Harper and Row, Perennial Library, 1975 [1973]), p. 154.

12. Ivan Illich, *Tools for Conviviality* (New York: Harper and Row, Perennial Library, 1973), p. 11. See also Illich's *Toward a History of Needs* (New York: Bantam, 1980).

easy for television to work for "the degradation of everyone into a compulsory voyeur" (26).

Illich finds it impossible, however, to abandon the mass media in his scheme of conviviality. In *Deschooling Society*, he argues that "the choice is between two radically opposed institutional types," one of which he calls "manipulative" and the other, "convivial."[13] As society is presently constituted, manipulative institutions—those which make up bureaucratic, rationalized, "mass society"—dominate, though there are also examples of convivial institutions. Schools are Illich's primary example of manipulation. To the world programmed for ever-increasing industrial productivity and consumption through one-way, massifying, "scholastic funnels," Illich contrasts "a world made transparent by true communication webs" (150). Such a phrase is reminiscent of McLuhan's electronic theodicy, but Illich does not share McLuhan's sanguine media determinism. Only through radical political consciousness and practice can convivial institutions come to outnumber manipulative ones. Like McLuhan's, however, Illich's vision presupposes a high level of technological finesse; the idea of a world made democratic and communitarian by "reticular structures for mutual access" (110) or "learning webs" is obviously dependent upon electronics, which are in turn obviously dependent upon mass production and heavy industry.

The same difficulty is evident in E. F. Schumacher, who in *Good Work* speaks approvingly of "the explosive growth of electronic media and computers that have put the world inside everyone's living room" at the same time that he finds "the worst features of capitalist irresponsibility" in "the field of the communication media—in sections of the press, the entertainment industries, book publishing, and so forth." The optimistic side of these statements again sounds like McLuhan, though there is no equivalent in *Understanding Media*, given the assumption that "the medium is the message," for Schumacher's belief that "the worst exploitation practiced today is 'cultural exploitation,' namely, the exploitation by unscrupulous moneymakers of the deep longing for culture on the part of the less privileged and undereducated groups in our society."[14] Clearly, nei-

13. Ivan Illich, *Deschooling Society* (New York: Harper and Row, 1972), p. 76.
14. E. F. Schumacher, *Good Work* (New York: Harper and Row, 1980), pp. 158, 30.

ther Illich nor Schumacher is quarreling with machinery so much as with the uses to which machinery is put. They both share McLuhan's sense of the utopian promise of the mass media, though without McLuhan's belief that the media by themselves constitute a historical force making for utopia. Their questions are close in kind to McLuhan's, however, especially insofar as they point to relatively optimistic versions of "the end of our time."

Something like a post-industrial utopian vision also emerges from the Critical Theory of the Frankfurt Institute, particularly in the work of Herbert Marcuse and Erich Fromm. Fromm should perhaps be viewed as a popularizer, not as an immediate peer of Adorno, Horkheimer, and Marcuse. In any case, in *The Sane Society* (1955), Fromm presents a blueprint for a "healthy" polity, based on meaningful work, participatory culture, and "communitarian socialism." The degradation of present mass culture, Fromm believes, is a far cry from the "collective art" that he envisages as ideal. Where are we, he asks, in comparison with this ideal? "Religious rituals have little importance any more . . . [and] secular rituals hardly exist." There is little in contemporary culture that answers to "the needs of the total personality." Fromm believes that "the movies, the crime reports, the liquor, the fun" are no adequate substitutes for "meaningful, shared artistic activities."

> What help is it to have almost no illiteracy, and the most widespread higher education which has existed at any time—if we have no collective expression of our total personalities, no common art and ritual? Undoubtedly a relatively primitive village in which there are still real feasts, common artistic shared expressions, and no literacy at all—is more advanced culturally and more healthy mentally than our educated, newspaper-reading, radio-listening culture.[15]

The change to "humanistic communitarianism" (361), Fromm says, must not occur violently, but through a cultural transformation brought about by education. According to his scheme, the "automatization of work" and other technological capabilities, including the mass media, are not to be cast aside, but will have their "communitarian" uses.

15. Erich Fromm, *The Sane Society* (New York: Holt, Rinehart and Winston, 1976 [1955]), p. 348.

From a more abstract theoretical perspective, Marcuse is less willing than Fromm to try to specify the shapes of the future liberated
society which, in *Eros and Civilization,* he contends is possible
through the abolition of "surplus repression." Reversing Freud, who
believed that society was inevitably based on repression of the instincts, Marcuse speculates about the achievement of a "non-repressive civilization." Such a utopian condition, he acknowledges, would
entail "regression," an "instinctual liberation" that, in terms of existing institutions, would be a "relapse into barbarism."[16]

> However, occurring at the height of civilization, as a consequence
> not of defeat but of victory in the struggle for existence, and sup-
> ported by a free society, such liberation might have very different
> results. It would still be a reversal of the process of civilization, a
> subversion of culture—but *after* culture had done its work and cre-
> ated the mankind and the world that could be free. It would still be
> "regression"—but in the light of mature consciousness and guided
> by a new rationality. Under these conditions, the possibility of a
> non-repressive civilization is predicated not upon the arrest, but
> upon the liberation, of progress. [181]

A non-repressive order is to be achieved by the fulfillment rather than
by the defeat of progress—in other words, by the realization of the
utopian promise inherent in technology, including the mass media.
This fulfillment is summed up in Marcuse's conception of the "aesthetic dimension," which in its social development will involve "the
transformation of toil (labor) into play, and of repressive productivity
into 'display'—a transformation that must be preceded by the conquest of want (scarcity) as the determining factor of civilization" (176).

Both Marcuse's "non-repressive civilization" and Fromm's "sane
society" are utopias based on the concepts of abundance and of shared
art or culture. On at least these grounds, they are similar to the post-
industrial visions of Schumacher, Illich, and a number of other theorists who look forward, in Illich's words, to "the advent of an Age of
Leisure (*scholē*) as opposed to an economy dominated by service industries."[17] Ironic as it may seem in the context of negative classicism,

16. Herbert Marcuse, *Eros and Civilization* (New York: Vintage, 1962 [1955]), p.
181.
17. Illich, *Deschooling Society,* p. vi.

the concept of leisure on a mass or global basis dominates contemporary social theory as a longed-for-goal, one rendered at least distantly
possible by present levels of scientific and technological achievement.
But the idea of leisure itself, as the Greek term *scholē* suggests, is
rooted in classicist definitions of culture and "the good life." In the
most radical, utopian versions of post-industrial theory, the past once
again serves as a model for the future.

According to Sebastian de Grazia in *Of Time, Work, and Leisure*
(1962), "leisure" does not mean "free time" or "time off from work."
The "ideal of leisure" is in fact the opposite of "an ideal of free time,"
which Grazia believes has "taken the field" in industrialized America.
"There is no doubt that Americans have reached a new level of life.
Whether it is a good life is another matter. This much is clear: it is a
life without leisure. . . . Leisure is a state of being free of everyday
necessity, and the activities of leisure are those one would engage in
for their own sake. As fact or ideal it is rarely approached in the
industrial world."[18] For Grazia, the place where the ideal of leisure
was first and most fully realized was Periclean Athens. In contrast,
modern America, with its pseudo-leisure of mass-mediated entertainments and distractions, is parallel to Rome: "Easy Street might be
something like ancient Rome at the time of the rise of the *plebs
urbana*. The workers were a dedicated and skilled few—administrators, lawyers, artisans, merchants, inventors, and military officers.
The *plebs* were those who had free time and the vote to insure their
bread and circuses. The circuses, like TV, went on at all times of the
day. We are the Romans of the modern world (330)."

As Grazia recognizes, the Greek ideal of leisure or *scholē*, of a life of
contemplation and cultural enrichment, is rooted in the sacred, free
from the trammels of secular, economic motivation. Similarly, according to the Catholic theologian Joseph Pieper, "Culture depends for its
very existence on leisure, and leisure, in its turn, is not possible
unless it has a durable and consequently living link with the *cultus*,
with divine worship."[19] Besides linking it to the sacred, Pieper like
Grazia connects leisure to "the Christian and Western conception of

18. Sebastian de Grazia, *Of Time, Work, and Leisure* (Garden City, N. Y.: Doubleday Anchor Books, 1964 [1962]), p. 312.
19. Joseph Pieper, *Leisure, the Basis of Culture* (New York: Pantheon, 1964
[1952]), p. 5.

the contemplative life," which is "the source of the distinction between the *artes liberales* and the *artes serviles*, the liberal arts and
servile work." Modern secularization has eroded the sacred basis of
leisure and consequently of genuine culture, while democratization
has eroded the distinction between "liberal arts" and "servile work."
Leisure and culture alike have been swallowed up by the category of
work, Pieper thinks, which in turn loses its significance as a means to
transcendent ends. "There is in fact no *room* in the world of 'total
labour' either for divine worship, or for a [sacred] feast. . . . There can
of course be games, *circenses*, circuses—but who would think of describing that kind of mass entertainment as festal?" (47).

The preservation of genuine culture as a realm of values superior to
bread and circuses thus appears to be identical to the search for
transcendence, which can be carried out in one of two ways: either
through a restoration of religious belief (Pieper, Eliot, Kierkegaard) or
through a completely individualistic "transcendence" of "the world"
(Nietzsche, Jaspers, Kierkegaard again). From either perspective, as
we have seen, it is impossible to conceive of culture on a mass, secular
basis. The ideal of a common culture or a leisure society which is
shared by everyone vanishes behind religious reaction or various
brands of elitist politics. (Pieper's religious affiliation is clear; Grazia
divides people into "two classes," a minority capable of true leisure
and a majority whom he imagines as forever mired in killing time at
the circuses.) But Raymond Williams, Ivan Illich, and Herbert Marcuse in their very different ways suggest another possibility, the construction of a shared culture of the highest humanistic and creative
value on a mass, even global scale.

If such a utopian goal is accepted as possible, we can no longer view
the mass media as inevitably making for decadence or barbarism. Indeed, Williams, Illich, and Marcuse show that it is difficult to imagine
how a common culture on a global scale can be established without the
mass media. At the same time, however, all three wish to transform
the institutions that control the media, for they believe that such a
culture will not develop through the media as they are now constituted in either capitalist or communist societies. We cannot have
Athens again without some form of electronic communications and
without a world in which all men and women are citizens rather than
slaves, barbarians, or masses. As the main instruments by which the

masses—that is, all of us—communicate, the mass media today carry the theoretical burden for the failure of society to become the new Athens. They now produce ideology instead of enlightenment, circuses instead of communal festivities, distraction instead of contemplation, narcissism instead of wisdom. The media thus play the roles of both leading villain and hero in theories of both impending doom and utopian fruition. While they narcotize, delude, and distract, they also radiate a utopian promise—one which they may never fulfill—of potential leisure and prosperity for all. As Hans Magnus Enzensberger puts it, even "consumption as spectacle is—in parody form—the anticipation of a utopian situation."[20]

Although McLuhan has no solid basis for his belief that the mass media will automatically lead us to the "noösphere," negative classicism tends to underestimate the extent to which a kind of utopian anticipation pervades contemporary mass culture. The diffusion of negative classicism through the mass media themselves, as in those science fiction stories and films that foreshadow the advent of a new Dark Age, may seem more dystopian than utopian. Apocalyptic suggestions of "the last days" in television and Hollywood disaster films may be no more than the latest fad in entertainment; then again, such films may exercise an important, albeit subliminal, influence that will help to prevent the cultural, social, and ecological catastrophes they depict. In *The Pursuit of Loneliness: American Culture at the Breaking Point* (1970), Philip Slater observes: "Popular songs and film comedies for fifty years have been engaged in a sentimental rejection of our dominant mores, maintaining that the best things in life are free, that love is more important than success, that keeping up with the Joneses is futile, that personal integrity should take precedence over winning, and so on. But these protestations must be understood for what they are: a safety valve."[21] Negative classicism today, however, as represented by Slater's bestselling essay itself, involves a far more thorough and serious "rejection of our dominant mores," and it is not yet possible to tell where its dissemination will lead. Perhaps like the educated nihilism to which Karl Löwith attributes World War I, it will

20. Hans Magnus Enzensberger, *The Consciousness Industry: On Literature, Politics and the Media* (New York: Seabury, 1974), p. 112.

21. Philip Slater, *The Pursuit of Loneliness: American Culture at the Breaking Point* (Boston: Beacon 1976 [1970]), p. 10.

only add to the mounting ruins it decries. Perhaps it is the contemporary equivalent of the "failure of nerve" that is often cited as a cause of the downfall of previous civilizations. Perhaps also, however, the citizens of Treves, though reveling in the coliseum, are at last beginning to hear the barbarians hammering at the gates.

But who are the barbarians? The most obvious and frequent answer today is: all those millions of poor in Asia, Africa, and Latin America whom the "progress" of industrialism either has not touched or has ruthlessly exploited. They are the hordes outside the walls of technological civilization, slowly besieging it. One day they will break down the gates and put an end to the circuses, along with much else. But there are also internal barbarians—the masses within industrial society. Insofar as technological "progress" has failed to transform alienated masses into enlightened publics, it has failed to be progress. Insofar as it has failed to bring prosperity, justice, and freedom to the Third World, it has also failed to be progress.[22] Of course by this reasoning the new Vandals and Huns include everyone, humanity at large. Perhaps there is a hopeful note in the universality of our predicament, similar to Walter J. Ong's observation that "barbarians turn out rather regularly to be the custodians—often the only custodians—of the culture on which they prey."[23]

Partly because they are historically unprecedented and partly because of their immense power the mass media generate the feeling that they must be leading us toward either a utopian global village or a new Dark Age. The promise of the media seems incongruous beside the mythology of negative classicism that they also increasingly project. Acocalyptic hope and despair, utopia and dystopia, seem to be built into their circuitry, like a set of transistors tuning in prophecy. But our historical situation itself is torn by contradictions, on the razor's edge between the potential "humanization" of man and "planetization" of the earth on the one hand and the complete destruction of life or at least of civilization by war and totalitarianism on the other. It is no wonder that every book of social criticism written today, if it is at all interesting, reads like a new Book of the Apoc-

22. For an analysis of who the next barbarians may be, see Anthony Hartley, "The Barbarian Connection: On the 'Destructive Element' in Civilised History," *Encounter*, May 1980, pp. 20–27.
23. Walter J. Ong, *The Barbarian Within* (New York: Macmillan, 1962), p. 275.

alypse. It is also no wonder that so much comes to depend on how the mass media are used in the near future: as many versions of negative classicism declare, humanity must educate itself quickly, or perish.

Some versions of negative classicism encourage the view that the downfall of modern civilization is something to be looked forward to, something even to work toward. Too often they do not ask how to prevent decadence and barbarism from running their course. Problems of democratic reform and rational social planning are submerged by apocalyptic political theories or by an equally apocalyptic religious reaction. In the same manner, versions of negative classicism that treat decline and fall as inevitable, part of the cycles of historical destiny, encourage stoic resignation in confronting a future that looks unavoidably bleak and ruinous. Though for many recent theorists like Theodore Roszak and William Irwin Thompson, negative classicism holds out a utopian prospect, it is far from offering the transcendent, positive kind of faith envisaged by Daniel Bell and the other prophets of a new age of religion. We are, it seems, going through a period of defeat and stoic resignation before the dawn of the new faith. Thompson argues that "cultural transformations do not proceed in easy transitions; they move in quantum leaps, and only a conversion experience or a revelation can give one the energy to leap across the abyss that separates one world view from another. A Roman Senator cannot become a Frankish Christian without first dying and being reborn."[24] We only have faith that we are declining and falling; we do not yet have faith in our ability to build a new civilization or to revitalize the old one. Only if it can instill in people something more than apocalyptic dread—only if it can create on a mass basis the desire, wisdom, and courage to alter the world for the better—will negative classicism succeed in doing more than contributing to the decadence and barbarism that it seems to deplore.

We, the newest barbarians, in the midst of this declining civilization, must learn to preserve what we are ravaging. To do so, we must also learn to change it and ourselves in ways that are radical, even utopian, and that, to many, will at first look decadent, or barbaric, or both. The mass media must help to teach us that these changes can and should be made.

24. Thompson, *Evil and World Order*, pp. 54–55.

Index

BREAD AND CIRCUSES

Designed by G. T. Whipple, Jr.
Composed by The Composing Room of Michigan, Inc.
in 10-1/2 point Caledonia (Linotron 202), 2-1/2 points leaded,
with display lines in Caledonia Bold.
Printed offset by Thomson-Shore, Inc.
on Warren's Number 66 text, 50 pound basis.
Bound by John H. Dekker & Sons, Inc.
in Holliston book cloth
and stamped in Kurz-Hastings foil.

Library of Congress Cataloging in Publication Data

BRANTLINGER, PATRICK, 1941–
    Bread and circuses.

    Includes bibliographical references and index.
        1. Mass media—Social aspects—History. 2. Mass
society—History. 3. Culture. 4. Popular culture.
5. Classicism. I. Title.
HM258.B735 1984   302.2'34   83-45134
ISBN 0-8014-1598-5